The Marriage and Family Workbook
An Interactive Reader, Text and Workbook

Robert Manis
Community College of Southern Nevada

Allyn and Bacon
Boston London Toronto Sydney Tokyo Singapore

Copyright © 2001 by Allyn & Bacon
A Pearson Education Company
160 Gould Street
Needham Heights, Massachusetts 02494-2130

Internet: www.abacon.com

ISBN 0-205-30931-3

Printed in the United States of America

10 9 8 7 6 5 4 3 2   03 02 01

Table of Contents

Part Four -- Marriage Adjustments: Children and Work

Part Five -- Communication and Conflict

Part Six -- Changes

Preface

Everyone knows that there have been many changes in marriages, families and relationships over the last forty years.

Society is on a learning curve about all three. All persons, as members of their respective marriages, families and relationships are part of that. Their trial and error collective wisdom is part of it, too. That is why I believe Marriage and Family is especially suitable for a discussion-oriented course. I have taught this course for more than seven years, with students ranging from sixteen to seventy, and with everyone from born-again Christians to radical lesbians. So long as everyone agrees simply to listen to each other's experience and opinion, all generally works out well. Often discussions are cut short by the end of class time.

This book differs from a text by being arranged into modules. Modules include a chapter with introductory material and an article or two. Following the reading are several pages of exercises, including Defining Terms, What Do You Think (discussion questions) and the Media Watcher and Video Viewer activities. I recommend considering the module as a whole and fully utilizing the various features. The pages are perforated for easy tear-out.

Unlike most texts, this workbook has discussion questions that are real, and have been tested in classrooms. There are many ways to use them, but the way that has worked best for me is to assign the questions to be filled out as homework, then to split into small groups, one question per group. Each group discusses the question separately, then reports the results to the class as a whole, and allows comments and further discussion. The instructor simply acts as a facilitator, mediator, and corrector of any factual errors. At the end of discussion students may tear out their filled-in responses and turn them in for credit.

Another activity I use is a reaction paper based on the articles. The format for this is given in the Appendix. These short papers can be assigned weekly or fortnightly.

The Media Watcher and Video Viewer features are other activities that tie in-class reading with outside class. Students can be assigned to rent videos, watch TV or recollect their viewing and relate it to each week's readings.

I would like to acknowledge Edith Blas for her patience and support throughout the writing and revision of this book; my parents Jerry and Laura Manis who have put much theory into practice over 50 years of marriage; Sarah Kelbaugh and Karen Hanson at Allyn & Bacon who had faith in this project; reviewers Allan Bramson (Wayne County Community College), Nils Hovik (Lehigh Carbon Community College) and Irwin Kantor (Middlesex County College); my former student Jesko who gave me the idea; and Carl Merrifield and my sister Lisa Manis for ideas and support at various times and places.

Robert Manis, June 1999

Part One
Family Systems

Module One

Cross-Cultural Family Patterns

---

*A*s we survey cultures around the world, perhaps nowhere but in the family do we find similarities in function to be so strong, but the diversity in form so striking. Though the family exists in all cultures, its form varies considerably from place to place and from one period to another. Quite often when we look at another culture's practices we may be shocked or even disgusted, and feel it quite impossible that they could behave in such a way. Of course, such feelings can occur even within a society, as when a young unmarried couple decide to cohabit and are refused an apartment by an older or more religious landlord. The young couple may feel discriminated against, and the landlord may feel like he or she is being asked to condone a sin. It is important to suspend judgement of the practices of other cultures a bit. To blindly judge other cultures by our own standards is called ethnocentrism, and when we realize that everybody thinks that their way of doing things is right or natural, we can appreciate that others may also think our practices are a bit strange.

Functions of the family

*F*amilies exist in all societies because they perform functions that are necessary for the society's success or survival. In fact, the activities that the family performs are so important that families are often called the "backbone of society." In some societies, families are the only form of social organization. Sociologists have identified several critical functions provided by the family that occur in virtually all societies:

[1] **Socialization.** Socialization is the process by which knowledge, beliefs, and values are taught to members of society.In all societies, the family is the first and most influential source of socialization. Parents teach their children many of the skills and attitudes which will help them fit into society. Of course, the socialization process continues in other ways throughout life, but the socialization received in the family setting is a powerful and basic influence that may be felt for the rest of one's life.

Chapter Preview:

Functions of the Family

Diversity of Family Patterns

Focus: Polygamy
   Polygyny in Saudi Arabia
   Polyandry in Tibet

Article: "Arranging a Marriage in India"

[2] **Sexual regulation.** Every society regulates sexual activity in order to reduce conflict: first, because sexual activity may kindle powerful feelings, and second, because reproduction is central to kinship or relatedness which forms the basis of our identity and social roles. Sexual regulation includes norms about marital, pre-marital, and extra-marital sex as well as the incest taboo, a universal regulation against marriage and sexual relations with certain kin. Although the incest taboo occurs in all societies, who and what it specifically prohibits varies between societies, as we will see.

[3] **Security.** Because human beings require a long period of growth before maturity, there is a need for a stable environment to provide for the physical care of children. Humans also have emotional needs, too, and the family provides a setting for emotional nurturance and support. Kinship provides a sense of mutual obligation that allows these needs to be filled.

[4] **Social placement.** Because kinship is a basis of identity and mutual obligation, the family is a powerful force in determining social standing. The family is used to pass property from generation to generation through inheritance, and often determines social position through prestige. Clear-cut traditions about family status may serve to reduce conflict in many societies, although they can sometimes stifle opportunity and change as well.

Diversity in Family Patterns

Despite the commonalities of basic family functions throughout the world, there is quite a diversity in how these functions are actually performed. This is because humans, as thinking beings, are free to develop their own solutions in response to different historical and environmental situations. Societies differ about such topics as who gets to choose a partner, the age of marriage, sexual positions and practices, birth-control, the incest taboo, and even the numbers of husbands and wives. According to a study reported by Robertson [1989], polygamy (multiple spouses) may well be the traditional "family value," in that the vast majority of "pre-industrial" societies (194 of 219) studied by anthropologists permit it. We will discuss forms of polygamy in the Focus section shortly.

Many societies have traditionally practiced arranged marriages. This is because the family is primarily an economic institution (see the "security" function, above). Indeed, the term "economics" comes from the Greek word *oikos*, meaning "household." The choice of a child's spouse is one of the most important decisions for both the child and, in societies without old-age insurance, the parents as well. Arranged marriages persist to this day, and in some nations like India and Japan, co-exist with "choice" marriages. Although "love" marriages are desired in modern Japan, Japanese shyness inhibits the success of this Western import and nearly one-half of all marriages end up being arranged by parents and others. Arranged marriage in India is the topic of the featured article in this section.

The age of marriage also varies, from birth or early childhood in some cultures, to, most commonly, the onset of puberty in most traditional societies, to the early thirties in some strata of Victorian society. Perhaps the strangest to our eyes is the Pacific island culture which arranges marriages of boys at birth to teen-aged wives. The boy is soon taken from his mother and raised by his wife until he becomes old enough to assume husbandly duties.

Sexual positions are by no means universal. The common western position of the man lying on top, has come to be known as the "missionary" position, allegedly because missionaries attempted to convert Polynesians to their sexual practices as well as their religion. Other cultures favor side-by-side, female superior, sitting or other positions. The incest taboo itself varies. In some cultures marrying the wife of a deceased brother is favored, while in others it is outlawed. Brother and sister marriages were common in the royal families of Ancient Egypt. In parts of India and the Arab world, pacifying of baby boys by masturbation is practiced by their mothers; here it would be considered sexual abuse.

Attitudes about homosexuality also vary. In Judaeo-Christian cultures, homosexuals are heavily stigmatized. Although there have been no cultures that preferred homosexuality to heterosexuality, some other cultures have been much more accepting. Ancient Greece was known for such a different attitude. "Platonic" or an elevated, non-sexual love was really between an older man and a younger to whom he taught philosophy, art and other matters. The fact that it had a special name signifies that sexual love between the two was all too common. Sappho wrote poetry about the love between women. Open homosexuality was seen as a bit scandalous, but nothing to merit hatred or discrimination.

In most Native American tribes, homosexuals and transvestites were quite tolerated, even in some cases seen as a bit special or "two-spirited," having both male and female qualities. If a boy wanted to stay with the women and do feminine things, that was alright, too (Lame Deer, 1972).

□ Focus: Polygamy

Although its practice is declining somewhat nowadays, polygamy or at least the permitting of polygamy has been a significant practice throughout history. 19th Century Mormons justified their practice of polygamy on the Christian Bible's admonition to "Be fruitful and multiply" and the practice of taking multiple wives by Hebrew kings. In the modern world, monogamy is the norm throughout Europe, the Americas and northern Asia. Polygamy is allowed in southern Asia, the Middle East and Africa. In most cases this is due to the influence of Islam, which permits marrying four wives.

There are two types of polygamy: **polygyny** and **polyandry**. Polygyny is marrying more than one woman, Polyandry is marrying more than one man. Polygyny is by far the most common of the two practices, probably reflecting the superior power of males in most societies. In this section, we will explore the practice of each type of polygamy, polygyny in Saudi Arabia and polyandry in Tibet.

Polygyny in Saudi Arabia

Saudi Arabia is a land of oil, sheiks, harems, and the veil. It is also a rapidly modernizing country where jets and computers mix sometimes uncomfortably with camels and the traditional religion of the Koran. The Koran permits Moslem men to wed up to four wives. They may also keep other women as **concubines**, or mistresses. Moslem society demands women be secluded and protected from men, hence the development of the harem or "hiding place" and the *abbayah* (*chador* in Iran) and veil, garments that cover women from head to toe.

According to Sandra Mackey, author of *The Saudis*, Saudi Arabians believe that seduction is likely when men and women consort, so every effort is made to keep them apart except for their relatives and legal mates. This custom is known as *hijab,* or curtain and refers both to the customs of veiling and seclusion. In practice, this means that separate institutions have evolved to allow women to bank, work and shop to some extent apart from men. Where that is impossible, men are required to escort their wives through their daily rounds. When women are at home they spend most of their time in the company of other women, relatives, and other wives. There is both tension and camaraderie between the different wives. The first wife, usually the oldest, has a form of seniority, but often a younger wife can gain power by her attractiveness or by being the first to provide a male heir. Polygyny is primarily practiced by the upper classes, for the simple reason that it is expensive, not only to provide for the additional wives, but for the additional children each will bear as well. For that reason the decision to take on another wife is usually not done lightly. Men choose to take other wives for a several reasons: sexual variety, to produce a son, or for social status. In the last case, a man might marry another wife, in the same way a rich American might buy a Mercedes Benz, to show that he is a man of wealth or because it is expected of a man in his position. For the woman it is a decision whether to become one of several wives of the prominent man, or the sole wife of someone less well-off. Often there are strong family pressures to unite with the wealthy family.

Power in polygynous marriages is largely held by the male. This is mainly because polygynous marriages tend to occur within extremely male dominated societies. This power is reinforced by the ability of the male to dissolve the marriage at will, by saying "I divorce you" three times. The veil and abbayah can be seen in a similar fashion. Ostensibly to protect a woman's modesty and honor, hijab is also an attempt to protect a man's "property" from seduction or insult by other men, according to the Ferneas (1979). While modern women have sought to throw off the shackles of hijab for several decades, in recent years it has made a comeback with the resurgence of Islam and the rejection of Western values throughout the Middle East.

Polyandry in Tibet

Quite rare compared to polygyny, a particular form of polyandry called fraternal polyandry is practiced in the harsh altitudes of high Tibet. Fraternal polyandry, where several brothers marry the same woman, is actually one of the world's rarest forms of marriage, but is not uncommon in Tibet. ˙ Practiced since ancient times, it is still a popular and respected form of marriage. Mentioned several times in Heinrich Harrer's classic *Seven Years in Tibet*, fraternal polyandry has been most studied by anthropologist Melvyn Goldstein, who has become the subject's leading expert. Goldstein studied this and other forms of marriage in Tibet since he was a graduate student visiting the area in the 1960s.

According to Goldstein, the mechanics of such a marriage are simple. Parents arrange a marriage between two, three, or more brothers and a single girl. Marriage ceremonies may take place with all the brothers acting as grooms, or the eldest brother representing the rest. If one brother is too young, he may stay in his birth family until he is old enough to join the marriage in his mid-teens. Goldstein documented the case of Dorje, Pema, and Sonam, three brothers who were about to jointly marry a girl from the next village. Dorje was fifteen, and his brothers twenty-two and twenty-five. Once married, the eldest brother is the dominant authority, but all the brothers share the work and participate as sexual partners with the wife. Neither males nor females in Tibet find this arrangement repulsive or scandalous, and the norm is for the wife to treat them all the same. Heinrich Harrer came across several cases of this during his travels ranging from the lowest classes to the highest.

Children are treated similarly, according to Goldstein, with no attempt to link the children with their particular biological father. Even if a brother knows if a child is his, he shows no favoritism, and the children, in turn, consider all the brothers equally their father. In terms of actual sleeping arrangements, the bride will sleep with the eldest brother most of the time, but the two of them will have the responsibility to see that the other brothers have opportunities for sexual access as well. Since the harshness of the Tibetan climate requires males to travel a lot, temporary absences facilitate that process. There is also a strong cultural norm calling for the wife not to show favoritism.

Tibetan society allows a variety of different types of marriage. Fraternal polyandry and monogamy are the most common, and polygyny also occurs, usually when a wife is infertile. Occasionally, unmarried cohabitation also occurs usually in case of Buddhist monks or nuns who choose to have a child without leaving their order. Divorce is relatively simple in polyandrous marriages; if a brother becomes dissatisfied, he may leave the marriage and start up a new household, but any children he has must be left behind. In one case witnessed by Harrer, a woman married to three brothers left all of them when she fell in love with a traveling stranger.

According to both Harrer and Goldstein, the reason for choosing polyandry is essentially materialistic. When Goldstein asked Dorje why he preferred joining his two older brothers rather than take his own wife, Dorje replied that it prevented the division of the family land and animals, which allowed them a higher standard of living than could be obtained separately. Dorje's new wife answered similarly. She said

she expected to be better off economically with three husbands to support her and her children. According to Goldstein, fraternal polyandry seems to function in a similar way to the eighteenth century English practice of primogeniture. In the English landed classes, only the eldest son could inherit the family estate, while the rest had to seek employment in the military, clergy or elsewhere. This practice prevented the estate from being broken up into increasingly smaller fragments as the number of descendants multiplied over generations. Similarly, fraternal polyandry limits the property to a single set of heirs per generation who, by sharing a wife, pass the property on to another single set of heirs in the next generation.

Like all marriages, fraternal polyandry is not without its potential pitfalls. Tibetans Goldstein talked to mentioned several. Younger brothers may chafe under a lifetime of subordination to an older brother. If there is a substantial age difference between brothers, the wife may find the youngest immature. When the youngest grows older, he may consider the wife too "ancient." Favoritism can occur despite cultural ideals, and as in all families, individual likes and dislikes can cause friction. Another disadvantage occurs with regard to the left-over women. Since males and females are relatively equal in numbers, having multiple husbands means some women remain unmarried. According to Goldstein, this occurs to nearly a third of all women. These unmarrieds either continued to live at home, worked as servants or became Buddhist nuns. Being single did not preclude child-bearing. Tibetans tolerate discreet extramarital affairs, and in the village Goldstein studied nearly half of the unmarried women had children, though usually much fewer than did married women.

Facilitated by the harsh climate and a feudal-type economy, fraternal polyandry has flourished in Tibet for hundreds of years. But it may not last long. Discouraged by the Chinese who conquered Tibet in the 1950s and their economic and political coercion, Tibetans are being forced off the land in increasing numbers to participate in the new hybrid communist-market economy. Within a generation, Goldstein felt, the end of traditional land-holding patterns would cause Tibet to end of one of the world's most unusual family arrangements. □

References

Fernea, Elizabeth & Robert Fernea. 1979. "A look behind the veil." *Human Nature*. January.

Goldstein, Melvyn. 1987. "When brothers share a wife." *Natural History*. March.

Harrer, Heinrich. 1996 [1953]. *Seven Years in Tibet*. New York: Jeremy Tarcher.

Lame Deer, J.F. & R. Erdoes. 1972. *Lame Deer, Seeker of Visions*. New York: Simon & Shuster.

Mackey, Sandra. 1981. *The Saudis*. New York: Ballantine.

Robertson, Ian. 1989. *Sociology*. New York: Harper & Row.

☐ Arranging a Marriage in India

Serena Nanda

From the book, The Naked Anthropologist, *1992. edited by Phillip Devita.*

> Sister and doctor brother-in-law invite correspondence from North Indian professionals only, for a beautiful, talented, sophisticated, intelligent sister, 5' 3", slim, M.A. in textile design, father a senior civil officer. Would prefer immigrant doctors, between 26-29 years. Reply with full details and returnable photo. A well-settled uncle invites matrimonial correspondence from slim, fair, educated South Indian girl, for his nephew, 25 years, smart, M.B.A., green card holder, 5' 6". Full particulars with returnable photo appreciated. --Matrimonial Advertisements, "India Abroad"

In India, almost all marriages are arranged. Even among the educated middle classes in modern, urban India, marriage is as much a concern of the families as it is of the individuals. So customary is the practice of arranged marriage that there is a special name for a marriage which is not arranged: It is called a "love match."

On my first field trip to India, I met many young men and women whose parents were in the process of "getting them married." In many cases, the bride and groom would not meet each other before the marriage. At most they might meet for a brief conversation, and this meeting would take place only after their parents had decided that the match was suitable. Parents do not compel their children to marry a person who either marriage partner finds objectionable. But only after one match is refused will another be sought.

As a young American woman in India for the first time, I found this custom of arranged marriage oppressive. How could any intelligent young person agree to such a marriage without great reluctance? It was contrary to everything I believed about the importance of romantic love as the only basis of a happy marriage. It also clashed with my strongly held notions that the choice of such an intimate and permanent relationship could be made only by the individuals involved. Had anyone tried to arrange my marriage, I would have been defiant and rebellious!

At the first opportunity, I began, with more curiosity than tact, to question the young people I met on how they felt about this practice. Sita, one of my young informants, was a college graduate with a degree in political science. She had been waiting for over a year while her parents were arranging a match for her. I found it difficult to accept the docile manner in which this well-educated young woman awaited the outcome of a process that would result in her spending the rest of her life with a man she hardly knew, a virtual stranger, picked out by her parents.

"How can you go along with this?" I asked her, in frustration and distress. "Don't you care who you marry?"

"Of course I care," she answered. "This is why I must let my parents choose a boy for me. My marriage is too important to be arranged by such an inexperienced person as myself. In such matters, it is better to have my parents' guidance."

I had learned that young men and women in India do not date and have very little social life involving members of the opposite sex. Although I could not disagree with Sita's reasoning, I continued to pursue the subject.

"But how can you marry the first man you have ever met? Not only have you missed the fun of meeting a lot of different people, but you have not given yourself the chance to know who is the right man for you."

"Meeting with a lot of different people doesn't sound like fun at all," Sita answered. "One hears that in America the girls are spending all their time worrying about whether they will meet a man and get married. Here we have the chance to enjoy our life and let our parents do this work and worrying for us."

She had me there. The high anxiety of the competition to "be popular" with the opposite sex certainly was the most prominent feature of life as an American teenager in the late fifties. The endless worrying about the rules that governed our behavior and about our popularity ratings sapped both our self-esteem and our enjoyment of adolescence. I reflected that absence of this competition in India most certainly may have contributed to the self-confidence and natural charm of so many of the young women I met.

And yet, the idea of marrying a perfect stranger, whom one did not know and did not "love," so offended my American ideas of individualism and romanticism, that I persisted with my objections.

"I still can't imagine it," I said. "How can you agree to marry a man you hardly know?"

"But of course he will be known. My parents would never arrange a marriage for me without knowing all about the boy's family background. Naturally we will not rely only on what the family tells us. We will check the particulars out ourselves. No one will want their daughter to marry into a family that is not good. All these things we will know beforehand."

Impatiently, I responded, "Sita, I don't mean know the family, I mean, know the man. How can you marry someone you don't know personally and don't love? How can you think of spending your life with someone you may not even like?"

"If he is a good man, why should I not like him?" she said. "With you people, you know the boy so well before you marry, where will be the fun to get married? There will be no mystery and no romance. Here we have the whole of our married life to get to know and love our husband. This way is better, is it not?"

Her response made further sense, and I began to have second thoughts on the matter. Indeed, during months of meeting many intelligent young Indian people, both male and female, who had the same ideas as Sita, I saw arranged marriages in a different light. I also saw the importance of the family in Indian life and realized that a couple who took their marriage into their own hands was taking a big risk, particularly if their families were irreconcilably opposed to the match. In a country where every important resource in life: a job, a house, a social circle is gained through family connections, it seemed foolhardy to cut oneself off from a supportive social network and depend solely on one person for happiness and success.

Six years later I returned to India to again do fieldwork, this time among the middle class in Bombay, a modern, sophisticated city. From the experience of my earlier visit, I decided to include a study of arranged marriages in my project. By this time I had met many Indian couples whose marriages had been arranged and who seemed very happy. Particularly in contrast to the fate of many of my married friends in the United States who were already in the process of divorce, the positive aspects of arranged marriages appeared to me to outweigh the negatives. In fact, I thought I might even participate in arranging a marriage myself. I had been fairly successful in the United States in "fixing up" many of my friends, and I was confident that my matchmaking skills could be easily applied to this new situation, once I learned the basic rules. "After all," I thought, "how complicated can it be? People want pretty much the same things in a marriage whether it is in India or America."

An opportunity presented itself almost immediately. A friend from my previous Indian trip was in the process of arranging for the marriage of her eldest son. In India there is a perceived shortage of "good boys," and since my friend's family was eminently respectable and the boy himself personable, well educated, and nice looking, I was sure that by the end of my year's fieldwork, we would have found a match.

The basic rule seems to be that a family's reputation is most important. It is understood that matches would be arranged only within the same caste and general social class, although some crossing of subcastes is permissible if the class positions of the bride's and groom's families are similar. Although dowry is now prohibited by law in India, extensive gift exchanges took place with every marriage. Even when the boy's family do not "make demands," every girl's family nevertheless feels the obligation to give the traditional gifts, to the girl, to the boy, and to the boy's family. Particularly when the couple would be living in the joint family, that is, with the boy's parents and his married brothers and their families, as well as with unmarried siblings which is still very common even among the urban, upper-middle class in India, the girl's parents are anxious to establish smooth relations between their family and that of the boy. Offering the proper gifts, even when not called "dowry," is often an important factor in influencing the relationship between the bride's and groom's families and perhaps, also, the treatment of the bride in her new home.

In a society where divorce is still a scandal and where, in fact, the divorce rate is exceedingly low, an arranged marriage is the beginning of a lifetime relationship, not just between the bride and groom but between their families as well. Thus, while a girl's looks are important, her character is even more so, for she is being judged as a prospective daughter-in-law as much as a prospective bride. Where she would be living in a joint family, as was the case with my friend, the girl's ability to get along harmoniously in a family is perhaps the single most important quality in assessing her suitability.

My friend is a highly esteemed wife, mother, and daughter-in-law. She is religious, soft-spoken, modest, and deferential. She rarely gossips and never quarrels, two qualities highly desirable in a woman. A family that has the reputation for gossip and conflict among its womenfolk will not find it easy to get good wives for their sons. Parents will not want to send their daughter to a house in which there is conflict.

My friend's family were originally from North India. They had lived in Bombay, where her husband owned a business, for forty years. The family had delayed in seeking a match for their eldest son because he had been an Air Force pilot for several years, stationed in such remote places that it had seemed fruitless to try to find a girl who would be willing to accompany him. In their social class, a military career, despite its economic security, has little prestige and is considered a drawback in finding a suitable bride. Many families would not allow their daughters to marry a man in an occupation so potentially dangerous and which requires so much moving around.

The son had recently left the military and joined his father's business. Since he was a college graduate, modern and well traveled, from such a good family, and, I thought, quite handsome, it seemed to me that he, or rather his family, was in a position to pick and choose. I said as much to my friend.

While she agreed that there were many advantages on their side, she also said, "We must keep in mind that my son is both short and dark; these are drawbacks in finding the right match." While the boy's height had not escaped

my notice, "dark" seemed to me inaccurate; I would have called him "wheat" colored perhaps, and in any case, I did not realize that color would be a consideration. I discovered, however, that while a boy's skin color is a less important consideration than a girl's, it is still a factor.

An important source of contacts in trying to arrange her son's marriage was my friend's social club in Bombay. Many of the women had daughters of the right age, and some had already expressed an interest in my friend's son. I was most enthusiastic about the possibilities of one particular family who had five daughters, all of whom were pretty, demure, and well educated. Their mother had told my friend, "You can have your pick for your son, whichever one of my daughters appeals to you most."

I saw a match in sight. "Surely," I said to my friend, "we will find one there. Let's go visit and make our choice." But my friend held back; she did not seem to share my enthusiasm, for reasons I could not then fathom.

When I kept pressing for an explanation of her reluctance, she admitted, "See, Serena, here is the problem. The family has so many daughters, how will they be able to provide nicely for any of them? We are not making any demands, but still, with so many daughters to marry off, one wonders whether she will even be able to make a proper wedding. Since this is our eldest son, it's best if we marry him to a girl who is the only daughter, then the wedding will truly be a gala affair." I argued that surely the quality of the girls themselves made up for any deficiency in the elaborateness of the wedding. My friend admitted this point but still seemed reluctant to proceed.

"Is there something else," I asked her, "some factor I have missed?" "Well," she finally said, "there is one other thing. They have one daughter already married and living in Bombay. The mother is always complaining to me that the girl's in-laws don't let her visit her own family often enough. So it makes me wonder, will she be that kind of mother who always wants her daughter at her own home? This will prevent the girl from adjusting to our house. It is not a good thing." And so, this family of five daughters was dropped as a possibility.

Somewhat disappointed, I nevertheless respected my friend's reasoning and geared up for the next prospect. This was also the daughter of a woman in my friend's social club. There was clear interest in this family and I could see why. The family's reputation was excellent; in fact, they came from a subcaste slightly higher than my friend's own. The girl, who was an only daughter, was pretty and well educated and had a brother studying in the United States. Yet, after expressing an interest to me in this family, all talk of them suddenly died down and the search began elsewhere.

"What happened to that girl as a prospect?" I asked one day. "You never mention her any more. She is so pretty and so educated, what did you find wrong?"

"She is too educated. We've decided against it. My husband's father saw the girl on the bus the other day and thought her forward. A girl who 'roams about' the city by herself is not the girl for our family." My disappointment this time was even greater, as I thought the son would have liked the girl very much. But then I thought, my friend is right, a girl who is going to live in a joint family cannot be too independent or she will make life miserable for everyone. I also learned that if the family of the girl has even a slightly higher social status than the family of the boy, the bride may think herself too good for them, and this too will cause problems. Later my friend admitted to me that this had been an important factor in her decision not to pursue the match.

The next candidate was the daughter of a client of my friend's husband. When the client learned that the family was looking for a match for their son, he said, "Look no further, we have a daughter." This man then invited my friends to dinner to see the girl. He had already seen their son at the office and decided that "he liked the boy." We all went together for tea, rather than dinner (it was less of a commitment) and while we were there, the girl's mother showed us around the house. The girl was studying for her exams and was briefly introduced to us.

After we left, I was anxious to hear my friend's opinion. While her husband liked the family very much and was impressed with his client's business accomplishments and reputation, the wife didn't like the girl's looks. "She is short, no doubt, which is an important plus point, but she is also fat and wears glasses." My friend obviously thought she could do better for her son and asked her husband to make his excuses to his client by saying that they had decided to postpone the boy's marriage indefinitely.

By this time almost six months had passed and I was becoming impatient. What I had thought would be an easy matter to arrange was turning out to be quite complicated. I began to believe that between my friend's desire for a girl who was modest enough to fit into her joint family, yet attractive and educated enough to be an acceptable partner for her son, she would not find anyone suitable. My friend laughed at my impatience: "Don't be so much in a hurry," she said. "You Americans want everything done so quickly. You get married quickly and then just as quickly get divorced. Here we take marriage more seriously. We must take all the factors into account. It is not enough for us to learn by our mistakes. This is too serious a business. If a mistake is made we have not only ruined the life of our son or daughter, but we have spoiled the reputation of our family as well. And that will make it much harder for their brothers and sisters to get married. So we must be very careful."

What she said was true and I promised myself to be more patient, though it was not easy. I had really hoped and expected that the match would be made before my year in India was up. But it was not to be. When I left India my friend seemed no further along in finding a suitable match for her son than when I had arrived.

Two years later, I returned to India and still my friend had not found a girl for her son. By this time, he was close to thirty, and I think she was a little worried. Since she knew I had friends all over India, and I was going to be there for a year, she asked me to "help her in this work" and keep an eye out for someone suitable. I was flattered that my judgment was respected, but knowing now how complicated the process was, I had lost my earlier confidence as a matchmaker. Nevertheless, I promised that I would try.

It was almost at the end of my year's stay in India that I met a family with a marriageable daughter whom I felt might be a good possibility for my friend's son. The girl's father was related to a good friend of mine and by coincidence came from the same village as my friend's husband. This new family had a successful business in a medium-sized city in central India and were from the same subcaste as my friend. The daughter was pretty and chic; in fact, she had studied fashion design in college. Her parents would not allow her to go off by herself to any of the major cities in India where she could make a career, but they had compromised with her wish to work by allowing her to run a small dressmaking boutique from their home. In spite of her desire to have a career, the daughter was both modest and home-loving and had had a traditional, sheltered upbringing. She had only

one other sister, already married, and a brother who was in his father's business.

I mentioned the possibility of a match with my friend's son. The girl's parents were most interested. Although their daughter was not eager to marry just yet, the idea of living in Bombay, a sophisticated, extremely fashion-conscious city where she could continue her education in clothing design was a great inducement. I gave the girl's father my friend's address and suggested that when they went to Bombay on some business or whatever, they look up the boy's family.

Returning to Bombay on my way to New York, I told my friend of this newly discovered possibility. She seemed to feel there was potential but, in spite of my urging, would not make any moves herself. She rather preferred to wait for the girl's family to call upon them. I hoped something would come of this introduction, though by now I had learned to rein in my optimism.

A year later I received a letter from my friend. The family had indeed come to visit Bombay, and their daughter and my friend's daughter, who were near in age, had become very good friends. During that year, the two girls had frequently visited each other. I thought things looked promising.

Last week I received an invitation to a wedding: My friend's son and the girl were getting married. Since I had found the match, my presence was particularly requested at the wedding. I was thrilled. Success at last! As I prepared to leave for India, I began thinking, "Now, my friend's younger son, who do I know who has a nice girl for him . . . ? " □

❏ Postscript: Further Reflections on Arranged Marriage

This essay was written from the point of view of a family seeking a daughter-in-law. Arranged marriage looks somewhat different from the point of view of the bride and her family. Arranged marriage continues to be preferred, even among the more educated, Westernized sections of the Indian population. Many young women from these families still go along, more or less willingly, with the practice, and also with the specific choices of their families. Young women do get excited about the prospects of their marriage, but there is also ambivalence and increasing uncertainty, as the bride contemplates leaving the comfort and familiarity of her own home, where as a "temporary guest" she had often been indulged, to live among strangers.

Even in the best situation she will now come under the close scrutiny of her husband's family. How she dresses, how she behaves, how she gets along with others, where she goes, how she spends her time, her domestic abilities--all of this and much more--will be observed and commented on by a whole new set of relations. Her interaction with her family of birth will be monitored and curtailed considerably. Not only will she leave their home, but with increasing geographic mobility, she may also live very far from them, perhaps even on another continent. Too much expression of her fondness for her own family, or her desire to visit them, may be interpreted as an inability to adjust to her new family, and may become a source of conflict. In an arranged marriage the burden of adjustment is clearly heavier for a woman than for a man. And that is in the best of situations.

In less happy circumstances, the bride may be a target of resentment and hostility from her husband's family, particularly her mother-in-law or her husband's unmarried sisters, for whom she is now a source of competition for the affection, loyalty, and economic resources of their son or brother. If she is psychologically, or even physically abused, her options are limited, as returning to her parents' home, or divorce, are still very stigmatized. For most Indians, marriage and motherhood are still considered the only suitable roles for a woman, even for those who have careers, and few women can comfortably contemplate remaining unmarried. Most families still consider "marrying off" their daughters as a compelling religious duty and social necessity. This increases a bride's sense of obligation to make the marriage a success, at whatever cost to her own personal happiness.

The vulnerability of a new bride may also be intensified by the issue of dowry which, although illegal, has become a more pressing issue in the consumer conscious society of contemporary urban India. In many cases, where a groom's family is not satisfied with the amount of dowry a bride brings to her marriage, the young bride will be constantly harassed to get her parents to give more. In extreme cases, the bride may even be murdered, and the murder disguised as an accident or suicide. This also offers the husband's family an opportunity to arrange another match for him, thus bringing in another dowry. This phenomena, called dowry death, calls attention not just to the "evils of dowry" but also to larger issues of the powerlessness of women as well. ☐

—Serena Nanda. Used with Permission

DEFINING TERMS

Socialization

Incest Taboo

Polygamy

Polyandry

Harem

Arranged Marriage

WHAT DO YOU THINK?

1. What are the advantages and disadvantages of polyandry in Tibet?

2. How does polyandry and polygyny affect or reflect the different power of the sexes in Tibet and Saudi Arabia?

3. What are the advantages and disadvantages of arranged marriages?

4. Who benefits more from arranged marriages, parents or children? Why?

 **MEDIA WATCHER:**

Give examples of families from other countries you have seen on the news, on TV or in the movies. How do they differ from American families?

5. What functions of the family are most important in modern society?

 VIDEO VIEWER:

Rent the movie "Joy Luck Club." Contrast the arranged marriage in the film with the article in this chapter. What other differences are there between traditional Chinese families and American ones?

Module Two

Contemporary American Families

"Happiness is having a large, loving, caring, close-knit family that lives in another city."
-George Burns

*W*hat is happening to the American family? Every place we look we see: dysfunctional families, divorce, single parents, teen-age mothers . . . Where is it all leading? Every day we are bombarded--by politicians, experts, talk show hosts--with images that the family is changing, threatened or even dying. Perhaps the best way to find out is by surveying the landscape of the modern American family, finding out what is "out there," and finding out what is not.

There has a been a dramatic change in family life is many parts of American society in the last forty years. And there has been a dramatic change in the way we think about the family as well. In the 1950s, as now, most people hoped to marry and have children and stay together until "death do us part." But those who didn't were seen as strange and different and perhaps even a little dangerous. Single women were often described as "spinsters" or "old maids," divorcees were seen as seductresses out to steal other men's wives, and many firms preferred to hire only "family men" who were more "wholesome" and responsible than bachelors. And worst, children born out of wedlock were seen as "bastards," as if it were some fault of their own.

*B*eginning in the 1960s, these patterns began to change. Driven by the development of the birth control pill, women's liberation, and the sexual freedom of the "hippies," young people in particular began to demand more freedom in their sexual behavior and lifestyle. Age of first intercourse dropped for both males and females. And perhaps partially due to the hypocritical attitudes of adults who discouraged distribution of contraceptives to teenagers, teenage pregnancies boomed.

The economic changes in the U.S. which began in the 1970s added fuel to these trends. No longer were the majority of American families able to survive on a single income. Women poured into the workplace. The new economic freedoms and changes in the legal code making divorce easier allowed many unhappy marriages to dissolve. But now many fear that the changes have gone too far, and that even couples who want to stay together may not survive the hard times. It seems to many

Chapter Preview:

Overview of Modern Families

Family Trend Quiz

Focus: Gay Families

Article: "What it Takes: Why Happy Families Aren't All Alike"

people that the search for new freedoms and the attempts to solve age-old problems went too far, or created problems that were worse then the ones before. Some commentators even go so far as to say that the very survival of the family as an institution is threatened. What do you think? Take this quiz based on an article, *Prophets of Doom* by Edward Kain, and see whether these fears are true:

FAMILY TREND QUIZ

1. The divorce rate in the U.S. was highest in which of the following years?
     a. 1935 b. 1945 c. 1955 d. 1965

2. What percentage of women worked outside the home at the beginning of the century?
     a. 2% b. 5% c. 10% d. 20%

3. TRUE OR FALSE: Due to the great increase in divorce, children are much more likely to live in single parent households than 100 years ago.

4. TRUE OR FALSE: One hundred years ago, most families lived in three-generational households, as opposed to now when grandparents are likely to be placed in nursing homes.

5. TRUE OR FALSE: Over the past century, fewer and fewer believe in marriage so the number of singles is increasing.

6. TRUE OR FALSE: Few poor families live below the poverty line for five years or more.

Before giving the answers, you should know that if you didn't do well, you are not alone. Edward Kain gave this test to hundreds of students and professionals and found that the majority did not score well. What this suggests is that most people are fairly uninformed about history of the family and its problems but are "well-informed" about the stereotypes of families past and present, as promoted by

politicians, talk-show hosts and other purveyors of gloom and doom. Following the answers will be some explanations.

ANSWERS:
1. b   2. d   3. f   4. f   5. f   6. t

1. Most people think 'c' is the correct answer, believing that the farther from the good old days, the worse things became. Actually 1965 had the lowest divorce rate. The highest was in 1945, when soldiers returned to marriages hastily arranged before going to war or disrupted by WWII, and found them unworkable. In the thirty years since 1965, divorces have generally, though not consistently, increased each year. Most experts believe social disruptions affect the divorce rate, as societal stresses increase the pressures felt in marriages by increasing economic difficulties or creating changes in values or other disruptions.

2. We have an image that women started to work outside the home during WWII, but fully one-fifth of all women worked outside of the home at the beginning of the century. Many women worked in agriculture and as domestic servants, and many more worked in the newly emerging textile industry, and as teachers and clerks. Many other women who did not work outside the home, supplemented family incomes by working within the home, doing sewing, laundry and other part-time work.

3. This question throws nearly everyone. Kain points out that few people are aware of the profound effects on family life that have resulted from the decline in mortality rates due to modern medicine and health practices. While divorce has increased tremendously, it has been more than offset by the incredible decline in the numbers of parents who died at an early age, leaving behind vast numbers of widows, widowers and orphans.

4. For a number of years, most experts have believed that extended families were the norm until they were supplanted by the smaller, more mobile nuclear family during the industrial revolution. This view has recently been challenged by a number of recent studies which demonstrate that the nuclear family, at least in Northern Europe and America, was the dominant form even before industrialization. Given the predominance of the nuclear family, three-generational families being the majority is a mathematical impossibility since there are more children than parents with every generation. More likely was the temporary addition of a relative, whether sibling, parent, or even child which lasted until they married, remarried, or [at a much earlier age than now] died.

5. Despite the increase in divorce, and the increase in singlehood, most Americans believe in marriage. Nearly all singles would like to get married eventually, and 75% of divorcees remarry.

One hypothesis for the increase in singlehood is the growth of cohabitation. Most couples believe that "living together" will lead to marriage, but in two-thirds of all cases it does not. Probably the majority of singles who never marry will cohabit one or more times, but that cohabitation will end before marriage occurs.

6. Despite concerns about a "culture of poverty" or "cycle of poverty," very few families live below the poverty line [as officially defined by the U.S. government] for five consecutive years. Major studies by the University of Michigan showed that only 4% of families remain consistently below the poverty line. Most families move in and out of poverty as wage earners lose a job, get sick, divorced, give birth to an additional child or are rehired, get well or remarry.

□ Focus: Gay Families

One of the most striking examples of the variety of families is the appearance of the gay family. Of course, homosexuals have always existed, but only in the last three decades has there been open public acknowledgment of their presence. As gays began to come out of the closet, the public has been forced to accept a reality it once loathed. In recent years, public debate has centered on gay marriage, because of the expected Hawaiian Supreme Court decision to legitimize it. Like many native peoples, Hawaiians had no real anti-homosexual taboos. Fearing that decision, Congress in 1995 passed a "Defense of Marriage Act" prohibiting that decision from establishing a precedent in the other 49 states.

Estimates of numbers of gays and lesbians range from 3% to 10% of the population (Marmor, 1980). In 1987, there were over 1.5 million gay or lesbian couples living together. About 92,000 had children living with them. While the larger figure may be considered as an equivalent of heterosexual living together, or cohabitation, the smaller number must be seen as true families, as legitimate structurally as a two-parent heterosexual family.

There are numerous similarities between gay and heterosexual couples. Regardless of sexual orientation, intimate relationships provide love, sex, fulfillment and security. Likewise, the responsibilities of jobs, money, housework, childrearing are also the same. Gay and lesbian couples, however, are much less likely to adopt a traditional marriage model or traditional roles. Despite stereotypes of "butches" and "femmes," neither partner tends to see him/herself as acting out primarily male or female roles. Peplau (1988) describes the predominant model as a one of "best friends." This model may actually be more equal than in many heterosexual relationships, at least in terms of financial responsibilities and the division of labor around the house.

What is the result of having gay or lesbian parents? There is no evidence that having gay parents increases a child's likelihood of becoming gay. Nor is there evidence that lack of both sex parents causes problems in with developing proper role models. An opposite sex child may feel the lack of same sex parental companionship, but probably no more than a child with a single parent. Most important, of course, is the quality of love in the relationship.

It is clear that in many ways family life in the U.S. is less stable than it was in the 1950s. But it is not clear that the 1950s were really THAT much better. Depression, unhappy marriages, and physical abuse were common but unspoken problems in many families. Those with problems were stigmatized, and rarely knew where to seek help. In earlier periods, conditions were probably much worse. Our stereotypes focus on the family life of the middle class, but before WWII, the middle class was a small proportion of the population. For the poor and working classes of a hundred years ago, family life probably included poverty, work weeks of seventy to eighty hours, child labor, sudden deaths of spouses and parents, high infant mortality, and many other hardships.

Perhaps the best response is given in the title of Ben Wattenberg's 1986 book, *The Good News is the Bad News is Wrong*. Wattenberg uses numerous statistics to show that contrary to popular opinion, family life (among other things) in the United States nowadays is not as bad as commonly thought.

References

Baca-Zinn, M. and D.S. Eitzen. 1993. *Diversity in Families* (3rd ed.). New York. Harper Collins.

Jones, C.L. et al. 1995. *The futures of the family*. Englewood Cliffs, NJ: Prentice-Hall.

Kain, Edward. 1990. *Prophets of Doom*. New York: Lexington.

Peplau, Letitia. 1988. "Research on homosexual couples." In John DeCecco (ed.) *Gay relationships*. New York: Haworth.

Popenoe, David. 1993. "The American family in decline, 1960-1990: a review and reappraisal." *Journal of Marriage and the Family*. August.

Wattenberg, Ben. 1984. *The good news is the bad news is wrong*. New York. Simon & Shuster.

Whitehead, B.D. 1993. "Dan Quayle was right." *Atlantic Monthly*. April.

❏ What It Takes: Why Happy Families Aren't All Alike

Dr. Robert Manis

A couple of Christmases ago, my siblings and I were visiting our parents, complete with aunts, uncles, cousins, husbands, wives, significant others, children by past marriages, and all the *accoutrements* of modern family life, when my father, then nearing eighty and the patriarch of the clan, surveyed the scene and the sunset and offered a toast: "To the best family anyone ever had." Not that we're probably that much different than many families across the country. But not that we're like what anyone of us thought families should be. Neither my sister or I ever had children. Two of my cousins never married, despite being in their late 40's. Two of my cousins married three times. Another had a couple children out of wedlock. One cousin died of AIDS. Another had problems with drug addiction.

In short, we've had practically every problem any American family that lived through WWII, Happy Days, Hippie Days, Boogie Nights and all the way to the 90s could've had. What makes families into good families, despite whatever happens through the "vicissitudes of life"? Is it love, money or simply keeping the family unit intact? I started asking friends, family, and students a number of questions to try to find some answers. Here's what I did and didn't find out.

Every semester I ask my students how many of them come from divorced families, and nearly every semester the answer is just the same: about half. I then ask how many wished their parents were still together, nearly all the forest of hands drops. I ask why, and they answer, "We weren't happy," or "We're happier now." Clearly, the answer isn't just keeping families together come hell or high water like the Moral Minority like to insist. But what is it? I've strung together some of the stories that I've heard. It may not be fully scientific, but I'll wager it's valid. Let me know what you think.

Father's Day

Carol and Jay have a son named Mike. So do John and Annie. In fact, it's the same Mike. Like the pic "Father's Day" with Robin Williams and Billy Crystal, Mike has two fathers. He also has two mothers. Mike, now 16, has lived with John and Annie most of the last six years; before that he lived with Carol and Jay. During summers, he lived with the other couple. When he lives with one couple he often spends weekends with the opposite one. Nothing is too formalized, the couples regularly confer to see what each has planned. How does it work?

"Great," says Carol, and adds only half-jokingly, "I want to lead workshops on the positive side of divorce."

"When John and I divorced, I took Michael. It was a lot of work. But with John married to Annie and me with Jay, it's a quarter as much, and half as much as when we were married.

"When John had other girlfriends after the divorce it was often uncomfortable when we met up," she continues. "But Annie and I already knew each other before she met John. She made a real effort to stay friends, and now we're all incredibly close."

She and Jay have no plans to get married, despite being together nearly ten years.

"Been there, done that," she says. She also has kept her married name.

"I like it better than my maiden name, and I got pretty used to it during eight years of marriage.

Jay doesn't mind not being married, either. "It doesn't change a thing," he comments.

John and Annie are also happy. John and Annie have been together over a decade and have been married for five years. Annie's approaching forty and is thinking about having one of her own children.

"I've been too busy to think about it, but now's the time. It's tough to think about all the work without Carol and Jay being there to help out so much. I guess I'm spoiled."

Annie attributes the two couples' closeness to communication and respect.

"I've made every effort to communicate and to listen to Carol. Even though we knew each other, it would've been easy to let things come between us, at one time or another."

John concurs: "Annie is very into communication, and she really made it happen. It was also very good that we're all reasonable people and no one has that bad a temper," he laughs.

In another year and a half, Mike will go to college. "I hope we always live near each other," Carol says. "We're such good friends."

The Immigrants

Isabella came from Mexico at age thirteen. "When my brothers and I were very young, we didn't have much of anything. We lived in an adobe hut that my grandparents let my parents borrow. My mom used to make us clothes out of old cloth that people would give to her. We each had a pair of shoes to wear, but those were just for Sundays when we went to church. The rest of the week we would go barefoot, not that we minded.

"We also had very little things to eat. Sometimes we would go for weeks on tortillas, beans, eggs or soup."

Everybody helped with the work. Her father and brothers would get up early to work in the orchards or go looking for work. Mother and sisters would clean, sew and when the men came back in the afternoons, prepare fruit and take it to sell in the plaza.

"But one thing was for sure, even though we didn't have much to eat, we would all have breakfast and dinner together, even if it was the same thing for days: eggs and beans." Then everyone would go to the parents' room and play games that her mother made up.

"Even though we didn't have many things, we were very happy because we had each other. Especially, we had the love of our family which made us stronger."

At thirteen, Isabella's family moved to Los Angeles. Her father worked in construction and they began to afford more things. They have a house with one room for each person. Almost each has a car, clothes of their own, and a job.

"Now all of us work and have different days off and different shifts. It's hard to sit down and have a meal together. But we still try have a dinner together once a week.

"I believe we are a happy family. We have our problems but we always find a way to work them out."

Gay Dads

Lori's parents divorced when she was eight, nearly twenty five years ago. "I didn't really know why because they never fought. Friends of mine whose parents divorced said their parents always fought. I didn't know my father was gay until I was 16, when I wanted to move in with him.

"When I look back, I must have been really thick-headed or else it didn't matter because I never thought about his sexuality one way or another. I even had a friend ask if he was gay, and that still didn't get me thinking about it."

Lori lived with her father and his partner until she was nineteen. Then she moved out on her own. To her, her two dads were a lot like any other couple. They had their ups and downs, their fights and good times.

"When I compare my home life with that of other people there is either not a lot of difference or else it's like night and day. What I mean is that every family, no matter what its composition, goes through its growing pains just like every other family. The only ones that are any different are the ones that are completely dysfunctional."

Lori is married now and has a daughter. Because her parents handled their divorce without bitterness, she doesn't feel it affected her view of marriage.

"My parents divorced because my father finally came to the realization that the heterosexual lifestyle was not for him. There weren't any fights my brother and I were aware of, and no one playing child against parent. They handled everything maturely and away from us, and were both always there for us. If anything, it affects my husband more because he's afraid I'm not as stable in my upbringing as he was."

When her father died, Lori traveled hundreds of miles to be at his bedside. She talked to him, told him she loved him and forgave him for any time he had hurt her, and told him she hoped he forgave her.

"I had been afraid to touch him because of all the tubes and monitors, but before I left I grabbed his hand and gave it a squeeze and said my final farewell. Even though he couldn't speak I knew he could hear every word I said."

Best Friends

Jan's mom and dad divorced when she was nine years old. Her father moved away and didn't help out at all with the finances, so her mom had to work as much as two full-time jobs and a part-time one to support them both. "My mom always did the best she could considering the circumstances. There were many times when we would go without a movie or a dinner out, but I always had my favorite food as a kid, macaroni and cheese."

Despite all the jobs, Jan and her mom had quality time together. "She would make sure we had at least one day a week to go to the park or take a drive to see my grandparents. We had plenty of weekend trips to baseball games or Magic Mountain. She always was there for me anytime I needed her for advice or just to talk."

The big wake-up was when Jan was twelve. "Little did I know what mom had in store for me. One day I woke up, and mom told me she had saved all she could for a vacation at Disney World in Florida. Just the two of us. We had the best time. For one whole week, it was just her and I, by the pool or eating ice cream. I never wanted for anything when it was just us."

Although there were times when Jan wished her mom could've been home a bit more, she has no regrets. "I just hope when I have children, I can give them the love and security she gave me.

"A family is love and trust. My mom was and is everything I couldn't get from anyone else. I believe that as long as you show love and affection to the children and really let them know you are doing your best for them, the 'ideal' family is whatever you make of it."

Adding It Up

So what does it take to have a happy family? Like I said, it doesn't have to be a conventional "Leave it to Beaver" or "Ozzie & Harriet" family. While it's true that it's easier to have a simple two-parent & children family, it doesn't by any means guarantee happiness. Nor does being different preclude it. According to psychologist Wilfred Leslie, "A two-parent family with kids is like a body with all its arms and legs. Just because you lose a leg doesn't mean you'll be unhappy or unhealthy, it just means you'll have to work harder."

Love, trust and respect are important elements, according to students I've talked to. So is flexibility, according to a psychologist in Roberta Israeloff's "Happy families are not alike," an article which set off my speculations. Happy families may not be alike in their external appearances, but they do seem to be alike in how they feel. Communication features strongly in most student responses, as does open display of affection.

Most of all, a willingness to work things out is mentioned time and again. Every time a family is able to work out a problem, it strengthens the confidence it can survive. Even divorce does not have to end the bonds, if everybody is willing. That may seem strange to many, but the truth is that when children are involved, relationships do continue. It may be true that many ended marriages, at least among those not plagued by serious problems like abuse or alcoholism, could benefit by the understanding shown by the couples depicted here.□

-Robert Manis is the author and editor of this text.

DEFINING TERMS

Demographics

Lifestyles

"Blended Families"

Cohabitation

WHAT DO YOU THINK?

1. All in all, do you think the American Family is deteriorating?

2. Do children raised in unusual families face severe handicaps other children do not? Why or why not?

3. Is it better for children to be raised in a single parent family than in a family where there is conflict or lack of love? Explain why.

☺ **MEDIA WATCHER:**

What TV shows depict contemporary American families?   How much like your family are they?

🜨 **VIDEO VIEWER:**

Rent the video "Pleasantville." What is it saying about the traditional American family? Is it being fair? Why or why not?

Module Three

The Family: Institution, Roles and Rules

Institutions

*W*e have often heard the family called an institution, but perhaps have never understood what it means. An institution is not a building, but a habitual way of doing things, strange as it may seem. Families are repeated ways of doing things, such as bringing up children, relating to one another, that people do. You can never see a family, only the people in it, and what THEY do. There are other institutions in society, such as education, religion, government, and the economy, and each of them is simply what certain people habitually do.

What all these institutions have in common is that they fulfill certain social needs. They may do so in a variety of ways, such as in the differences between polygamy and monogamy, or the economic institutions of socialism and capitalism, but they fulfill similar needs or functions, in this case the distribution of goods and services. They may not do them equally well, as we found out when the Berlin Wall came down in 1989.

Chapter Preview:

Institutions

Roles

Rules

Roles and Family Background

Article: "Same Family: Different Lives"

Article: "Birth Order and Family Differences"

*A*s mentioned earlier, the family as an institution provides certain functions that are essential to society:

♦ taking care of children
♦ regulating sexual behavior
♦ providing love and nurturance
♦ teaching children to fit into society

Without these needs being provided, human social life would be considerably harder.

This is not to say that any institution is indispensable. Until modern times, many societies existed with only the most rudimentary forms of many institutions (with the exception of the family, the oldest institution). Now many people believe that the family itself is being threatened. Can society exist without the family? Possibly so, probably not.

Roles

I've mentioned that institutions are simply ways of doing things, patterns of behavior. It's useful to think of institutions in this way because it points us to an interesting concept which forms the building block of institutions, the "role." Everyone has heard of roles, particularly in connection with the parts people play in movies and tv. That is exactly what a role is, a part someone plays. More precisely, it is the way someone is expected to act as a person in a certain position. Hamlet is supposed to act like Hamlet, a parent is supposed to act like a parent, a teacher is supposed to act like a teacher, and there's an amazing amount of agreement as to what that is. The specific expectations or rules about how to fulfill a role properly are called "norms," which comes from the same word as "normal." A person who fulfills the norms or rules of his or her role is considered "good" or "normal." A good kid goes to bed by 10 PM, a good parent doesn't whip his kids, and so on.

Of course, in reality, people break the rules all the time. There is a lot of leeway within each role, too. As long as you fulfill the major expectations of your part, you can do whatever else you want. Besides the major family roles like parent, child, brother and sister, etc., there are stylized roles that people often take on. These roles are absorbed from the labels other family members apply to each other over a period of time. Quite often, the recipient comes to accept the label and act it out more or less willingly. Sometimes, too, a family member takes on such a label from an outside source such as television, school or friends. Here are some common labels that family members often accept into their roles.

◆ Baby of the family -- Usually reserved for the youngest, he or she gets special treatment in return for staying immature.

◆ Parent's Pet -- Seeks rewards and approval for being mature, following parental rules, taking responsibility, and making sure others follow the rules, too.

◆ Scapegoat -- All the family problems can be blamed on this person, who, often because of low self-esteem or some other problem can't defend himself/herself.

◆ Tyrant -- Whether parent or child, this person seeks to enforce their will through anger, threats and intimidation.

◆ Hermit -- This person reacts to some unpleasant family dynamic or unresolved issue by self-isolation.

◆ Black Sheep -- A non-conformist who dares to go against family conventions.

◆ Rebel -- Stronger version of the black sheep, the rebel angrily rejects social and/or family norms, often getting into trouble of various sorts.

◆ Politician -- Smiling, negotiating, this person seeks to be liked and to smooth over difficulties.

These are just a few of the possible roles family members may enact. Some may act out different roles at different times.

Rules

Roles themselves are constructed out of norms and rules. While some of these are common to all families, here again there is a certain leeway. In a sense, families are like miniature societies which can make up their own rules and laws. These rules tend to come about in a couple of ways. First, they may be brought into the family from the parents' original families. These types of rules predominate when the children are young. Rules like these can be about bedtimes, chores, disobedience and the like.

The second way these rules come about is through evolution and negotiation, starting with the father and mother working out which way to deal with their own issues and how to bring up the kids. The kids, too, have a part in the development of rules. They cause rules to be developed by the problems they bring up. Many problems aren't anticipated by either parent--realities force the development of new rules or the re-interpretation of old ones. As the children get older, they often become a positive force in renegotiating rules, wanting more freedom, testing the limits, even challenging the parents' authority. Different rules can sometimes occur for different members of the same family: one child can force a change in bed-times, be excused from eating foods or performing certain chores. Quite often these differences are gender- or age-based, but that doesn't mean the children will accept them easily. "Mom always liked you best," is the age-old and usually untrue complaint that starts many attempts at renegotiating the rules. Adolescence with its new risks and responsibilities is yet another opportunity for social change within the family unit.

It's interesting to think back to the rules we grew up with. Maybe we can remember all the times we said to ourselves about rules we didn't like, "I'd never be so unfair to my kids." But then maybe we can also remember our parents' warning to us, *"Wait 'til YOU have kids!!!"*

Roles and Family Background

Because there is a great deal of freedom in how people play roles, and in fact, how well their roles are performed at all, there is a great variety in how families perform their functions. We call this **family background.** The events that occur, as well as the attitudes, behaviors, and values passed on, have a strong influence on the children's later development into adults. A number of factors are important: parental attitudes towards children, the opposite sex, intimacy; parental values towards work, education, morality; and parental behavior or example with regards to communication, and their own values. It is useful to look at the factors because it helps us to understand how we have been influenced, so that we have more control over our lives and the directions it may take.

Parental attitudes -- One of the most important contributions parents can make to the children is to let them know they are loved, valued, cared for, and accepted. Parents who demonstrate these attitudes through praise, encouragement, and showing interest help children develop self-esteem and confidence. Parents who reject or overly criticize their children can contribute to feelings of ill-worth or dependence that may show up as anger or clinginess in later relationships. Parental attitudes towards sexuality or the opposite sex also can have strong effects. A parent who strongly feels that "sex is dirty" or "all men are pigs" can contribute to a child developing ambivalent attitudes toward men or sex.

Parental Values -- Parental values are also significant in their effect on children. Most important are values placed on work and education. Numerous studies have shown significant correlations between such things as educational attainment or income and early family emphasis on those values. Religious values are also extremely important. The majority of children remain within the religion they were brought up in, and report that values held by their religion continue to influence them throughout their lives.

Parental behavior -- We are all familiar with the concept of the **role model**, a person whose position influences us by their example. Consciously, or not, we often imitate the behavior of such people. Probably the most powerful example of role models are our parents. If we have a positive image of them we may deliberately try to be like them, or at least we may mentally use them as reference points in making decisions. If their image is negative, we may use them as an example of what we reject. And if their image is mixed, they may produce an ambivalent response. There is also a subtler effect: we may mentally link our parents behavior, not only with ideas of the way people ought to be, but with the way things are. For example, a son with a critical mother, or a daughter with an unavailable father may come to believe that women are hard to please or that men are cold. Sometimes these patterns are reinforced in later life, because the child may be drawn unconsciously to partners that are like the parent.

Communication styles are one area that is strongly affected by parental example. According to Rice [1996], the patterns of communication that exist in a family may be replicated when the children establish families of their own. Styles of communication may range from open, honest communication to hostile to superficial to complete avoidance of communication. Clearly, children brought up in communicative homes have a great advantage in their later relationships.

Other important areas of parental behavior are work habits and sex role behavior. Children whose parents have poor work habits may grow up without the discipline to create successful careers. Similarly, parents whose behavior strongly reflects traditional sex role stereotypes may make it more difficult for their children to adapt to the changes occurring in sex roles.

It can be extremely useful to look at the family backgrounds in which we have been brought up, and to compare them with others, and even more than useful, it can be critical in helping us understand or even avoid conflicts with partners in our relationships and marriages.

References

Lamanna, M.A. and Agnes Riedmann. 1994. *Marriages and families: Making choices and facing change.* Belmont, CA: Wadsworth.

Macionis, John. 1996. *Society: the basics.* (3rd ed.) Upper Saddle River, NJ: Prentice-Hall.

Rice, Phillip. 1996. *Intimate relationships, marriages and families.* Mountainview, CA: Mayfield.

◻ Same Family, Different Lives

Bruce Bower

Psychologists uncovered a curious feature of military morale during World War II. Those in branches of the service handing out the most promotions complained the most about their rank. The investigators cited "relative deprivation" as an explanation for the trend. Essentially, it's not what you have, but what you have compared with others in the same situation.

Relative deprivation achieves a more profound influence through the daily battles and negotiations that constitute life in the nuclear family, maintain researchers in human behavioral genetics. Each child in a family harbors an exquisite sensitivity to his or her standing with parents, brothers and sisters, and thus essentially grows up in a unique psychological environment, according to these investigators. The result: Two children in the same family grow to differ from one another in attitudes, intelligence and personality as much as two youngsters randomly plucked from the population at large.

While one-of-a-kind experiences and perceptions of family life combine with each child's genetic heritage to create pervasive sibling differences, shared genes, which account for half the genes possessed by all siblings save for identical twins, foster whatever similarities they display, argue scientists who apply behavioral genetics to child development.

The emphasis on children's diverse experiences cultivating sibling differences seems ironic coming from scientists dedicated to estimating the genetic contribution to individual development. Yet behavioral genetic data provide a compelling antidote to the increasingly influential notion among psychiatrists that defective genes and broken brains primarily cause mental disorders, asserts psychologist Robert Plomin of Pennsylvania State University in University Park, a leading researcher in human behavioral genetics. Ongoing studies also challenge the assumption of many developmental psychologists that important family features, such as parental education, child-rearing styles and the quality of the marital relationship, affect all siblings similarly, Plomin adds.

"What runs in families is DNA, not shared experiences," Plomin contends. "Significant environmental effects are specific to each child rather than common to the entire family."

In a further challenge to child development researchers, Plomin and psychologist Cindy S. Bergeman of the University of Notre Dame contend that genetic influences substantially affect common environment measures, such as self-reports or experimenter observations of family warmth and maternal affection. "Labeling a measure environmental does not make it environmental," they conclude in the September *Brain and Behavioral Sciences*. "We need measures . . . that can capture the individual's active selection, modification and creation of environments."

Not surprisingly, the trumpeting of "non-shared" sibling environments and the questioning of traditional measures of the family milieu have drawn heated rebukes from some psychologists. In particular, critics claim that behavioral genetics studies rely on statistical techniques that inappropriately divvy up separate genetic and environmental effects on individual traits, rather than examining more important interactions between genes and environment.

Human behavioral genetics use family, adoption and twins studies to estimate the importance of genes and environment to individual development. Family studies assess the similarity among genetically related family members on measures of intelligence, extroversion, verbal ability, mental disturbances and other psychological traits. Adoption studies obtain psychological measures from genetically related individuals adopted by different families, their biological parents, and their adoptive parents and siblings. Researchers assume that similar scores between adoptees and biological parents reflect a greater genetic contribution, while adoptees showing similarity to adoptive parents and their children illuminate environmental effects. Twin studies compare the resemblance of identical twins on various measures to the resemblance of fraternal twins on the same measures. If heredity shapes a particular trait, identical twins display more similarity for it than fraternal twins.

Psychologist John C. Loehlin of the University of Texas at Austin directed a twin study published in 1976 that greatly influenced human behavioral genetics. Averaging across a broad range of personality measures obtained from 514 identical and 336 fraternal pairs of twins culled from a national sample of high school seniors, Loehlin's group found a correlation of 0.50 for identical twins and 0.28 for fraternal twins.

Correlations numerically express associations between two or more variables.

The closer to 1.0 a correlation figure reaches, the more one variable resembles another, say one twin's IQ and the corresponding twin's IQ. A correlation of zero between twin IQs would signify a complete lack of resemblance with twin pairs, as different in intelligence scores as randomly selected pairs of youngsters.

The Texas researchers doubled the difference between identical and fraternal twin correlations to obtain a "heritability estimate" of 0.44, or 44 percent, an estimate of how much genes contribute to individual differences. This means that genes accounted for just under half of the individual personality differences observed in the sample of twins. Thus, environment accounted for slightly more than half of the twin's personality variations.

A further finding intrigued the scientists. The correlation on personality measures for identical twins only reached 0.50, suggesting the environment orchestrated one-half of their personality differences. Since these twins carried matching sets of genes and grew up in the same families, only "non-shared" family experiences could account for such differences, Loehlin's group argued.

Subsequent twin and adoption studies carried out in Colorado, Minnesota, Sweden and England confirmed the importance of the non-shared environment for most aspects of personality, as well as intelligence and mental disorders such as schizophrenia, Plomin asserts. He and psychologist Denise Daniels of Stanford University reviewed much of this data in the March 1987 *Brain and Behavioral Sciences*, followed by a book on the subject written with Penn State psychologist Judy Dunn titled *Separate Lives: Why Siblings Are So Different* (1990, Basic Books).

All the correlations and heritability estimates boil down to a simple point. Plomin maintains: Allegedly shared family influences, such as parent's emotional warmth or disciplinary practices, get filtered through each child's unique perceptions and produce siblings with strikingly diverse personalities. For example, a shy 9-year-old who gets picked on by schoolmates will react differently to an emotional, permissive mother than a gregarious 7-year-old sibling who attracts friends easily.

Many factors divide siblings' perceptions of family life, Plomin says, including age spacing, peer and school experiences, accidents, illnesses, random events and, to a lesser extent, birth order and sex differences. Each sibling's temperament and behavior generate specific perceptions and responses from parents that further shape non-shared environments.

As researchers in molecular genetics vigilantly pursue genes that predispose people to a variety of mental disorders, psychiatrists should not neglect the importance of the environment specific to each child in a family, contends Plomin and two colleagues, psychiatrist David Reiss of George Washington University in Washington, DC, and psychologist E. Mavis Hetherington of the University of Virginia in Charlottesville, in the March *American Journal of Psychiatry*.

The three researchers bluntly warn psychiatrists enamored of the new genetic techniques that biology alone cannot explain the development of serious mental disorders. For example, a large, ongoing study in Sweden conducted by Plomin and several other researchers has found that when one identical twin develops schizophrenia, the other twin contracts the disorder about one-third of the time. Heredity shoulders considerable responsibility for fomenting schizophrenia, Plomin acknowledges, but an individual's experience of family life, peers and chance events plays at least as strong a role in triggering the devastating fragmentation of thought and emotion that characterizes the disorder.

Research directed by George Washington's Reiss, and described in his article with Plomin and Hetherington, suggests non-shared experiences protect some siblings, but not others, from alcoholism when one or both parents drink alcohol uncontrollably. Family members often shield the protected child from alcoholic behavior during that child's most cherished family practices, such as Christmas celebrations, Reiss' team finds. In this way, the protected sibling gradually learns to minimize brushes with the corrosive effects of alcoholism within and outside the family, the investigators observe. Upon reaching adolescence and adulthood, the protected sibling maintains limited family contacts to avoid the influence of an alcoholic parent and often marries a non-alcoholic person.

Given the importance of non-shared environments, developmental researchers need to study more than one child per family and devise better measures of children's perceptions of family experiences, Plomin contends. He and Bergeman find that several self-report tests currently used to assess the home environment largely ignore unique individual experiences within the family and rely on measures that show substantial genetic influence. In one case they cite, unpublished data from a study of 179 reared-apart twin pairs (both identical and fraternal) and 207 reared-together twin pairs indicate that genes account for one-quarter of the individual differences plumbed by the widely used Family Environment Scales, which is generally regarded to measure environmental influences. These scales include ratings of emotional warmth, conflict, cohesion and cultural pursuits within the family.

Even the time children spend watching television, a seemingly vacuum-sealed environmental measure employed in many studies, significantly stems from genetically influenced characteristics, Plomin and his colleagues argue in the November 1990 *Psychological Science*. Parental restrictions do not exert strong effects on children's television viewing, since about 70 percent of parents put no limits on how much time their offspring can spend watching the tube, they state.

Plomin's team tested 220 adopted children three times, at 3, 4 and 5 years of age, as well as their biological and adoptive parents, younger adopted and nonadopted siblings, and control families with no adopted children. Biological parents and their children adopted by others spent a surprisingly similar amount of time watching television, indicating an important genetic influence on the behavior, Plomin's team asserted. Shared home environment, such as the television viewing habits of parents, also influenced children's television time, but to a lesser extent.

The results do not imply that some people follow a genetic imperative to sit glassy-eyed in front of the television for hours, day after day. "We can turn the television on or off as we please, but turning it off or leaving it on pleases individuals differently, in part due to genetic factors," the investigators conclude.

Some scientists who have long labored to understand family influences on psychological development take no pleasure in the conclusions of behavioral genetics researchers. Psychologist Lois W. Hoffman of the University of Michigan in Ann Arbor offers a critique of research highlighting sibling differences in the September *Psychological Bulletin*.

Behavioral genetics tends to overestimate sibling differences because it concentrates on self-reports of personality traits, rather than on observations of coping skills and social behavior typically relied upon by developmental psychologists, Hoffman holds. A child may exaggerate differences from siblings on self-reports, whereas behavioral observations by experimenters may turn up sibling similarities in aggression or other attributes, she maintains.

Even in behavioral genetics research, significant sibling similarities apparently due to shared family environment turn up in political and religious beliefs and in general interests such as music, Hoffman adds. Some family environments may more easily produce similarities among siblings than others. When both parents share the same values, attitudes and child-rearing styles, the chances increase that their pattern of behavior will rub off on all their children, in Hoffman's opinion.

Behavioral genetics researchers also incorrectly assume that only strong correlations between the personalities of adoptive parents and their adopted children reflect an environmental influence, the Michigan psychologist contends. Parental influences can weaken parent-child correlations on all sorts of personality measures, she points out. For instance, domineering, powerful parents may produce an anxious child, and an extremely self-assured, professionally successful parent may make a child feel inadequate.

Behavioral genetics comes under additional fire for its reliance on statistics that treat genetic and environmental influences on personality separately. This approach simply lacks the statistical power to pick up the interactions between genes and environment that primarily direct physical and psychological development, rendering current research in human behavioral genetics meaningless, argues Canadian psychologist Douglas Wahlsten of the University of Alberta in Edmonton. Much larger samples might begin to pick up such interactions, he adds.

Behavioral geneticists rely on statistics derived from a technique known as analysis of variance (ANOVA). This method is used throughout psychology to calculate whether a significant relationship, or correlation, exists between experimental variables, by comparing variations in individual scores from a group's average value. Statisticians developed ANOVA in the 1920s as a way to estimate whether different types and amounts of fertilizer substantially increased the yield of various agricultural crops.

When applied to human personality and behavior, an ANOVA-based approach treats heredity and environment as mutually exclusive influences on personality, Wahlsten argues. Psychologists possess no conclusive test of interactions between genes and environments. But evidence of their interplay, as in the widely accepted theory that specific genes combine with particular family experiences to produce a psychotic disorder, may begin to emerge in behavioral genetics studies employing samples of 600 or more individuals, Wahlsten maintains. Mathematical formulas used in conjunction with ANOVA stand a better chance of ferreting out gene-environment interactions in extremely large samples, Wahlsten concludes in the March 1990 *Brain and Behavioral Sciences.*

Psychologist Daniel Bullock of Boston University takes a bleaker view of ANOVA, citing its neglect of the intertwined forces guiding personality development. "The special status of ANOVA in psychology is an utter anachronism," he contends. "Many past claims by behavioral geneticists are unreliable."

Plomin rejects such charges. "To say that genetic and environmental effects interact and therefore cannot be disentangled is wrong," he states.

Twin and adoption studies consistently find strong separate effects of genes and non-shared environments on personality and other developmental measures, even when researchers painstakingly seek out possible interactions of nature and nurture, Plomin points out. Investigators may devise more sensitive statistical tests to illuminate cooperative ventures between genes and family experiences, but that will not invalidate the insights of behavioral genetics, he maintains.

That includes the discovery that what parents do similarly to two children does not importantly influence personality or problem behavior in the long run; rather, each child's perceptions of what goes on in the family prove critical. Appreciating the differences of offspring based on their individual qualities, with minimal preferential treatment of one child over another, seems a good general rule for concerned parents, Plomin says. Parents should recognize that siblings as well as "only children" harbor a keen sensitivity to their standing within the family, he adds.

"If we are reasonable, loving, but not perfect parents, the children will grow up to be themselves all different but okay," says psychologist Sandra Scarr of the University of Virginia, a behavioral genetics researcher. "Children experience us as different parents, depending on their own characteristics, and we simply cannot make them alike or easily spoil their chances to be normal adults."□

– Reprinted with permission from Science Service, *the weekly newsmagazine of science, copyright © 1991.*

❏ Birth Order and Family Differences

John C. Pulver, M.S., *Licensed Marriage and Family Therapist*

As the only girl in a family of three siblings, you are constantly amazed at the difference between your two older brothers, Josh and Brent. It seems to you that coming from the same set of parents there would be a greater similarity, but alas, no matter how you look at it, Josh and Brent look like they came from not only two different families but, at times, it seems they do not even live in the same universe! How different are they, you ask?

Josh who is 17 is always involved with anything physical and has lettered in three sports. He takes his studies seriously and was a member of the debate team last year. He is outgoing and can really be the life of any party when he decides to be. Dad is enjoying coming to most of his games since he, too, participated in sports as a child. In most ways you could say that Josh is a model child, one that would make most any parent happy they had decided to have children in the first place.

Brent, 15, is often found in his room in some kind of "mind meld" with his computer. He is not very interested in joining the family for Josh's games; in fact, he isn't even interested in sports in the least. He thinks school is boring, barely gets acceptable grades and only seems to communicate when something major goes wrong in the family. Being quite reserved, Brent is not the type to engage you in a conversation about anything, let alone be interested in debating with you on any topic. He is content to go with the flow, usually taking a back seat to Josh.

In spite of any genetic differences between these two individuals, a key element within the sociological perspective that may illuminate some understanding of their differences is the concept of social context. Josh and Brent are both "socially imbedded" within the family, they do not operate as islands in the middle of nowhere, but as human beings interacting with and being influenced by others. How do they interpret their environment? How does their environment shape their choices or the range of their choices? What roles have they decided to play within this family? These and other similar questions regarding the development of roles and behavior can be understood in part through the psychology of Alfred Adler, which since the early part of the 20th century has undergone much application in child rearing and school settings and has spawned a large amount of research.

Adlerian psychology emphasized a number of key elements in the development of a self:

✦ Individuals have a need to feel connection in some way with others.

✦ Each person strives to find a "place" within a social setting where he or she can develop an identity.

✦ How each person determines their place can be influenced by the reactions of others and their own interpretation of other's attitudes.

✦ Each individual will strive to establish this position, whether it is through positive, functional means, or through dysfunctional or negative means.

✦ Each individual experiences their social setting differently through their own perception.

✦ Within the family each individual in a sense has a different set of parents due to their social placement within the family.

✦ Is the family atmosphere cooperative or competitive? Is there a particular gender that is valued more than the other?

Developing out of some of these elements came an important perspective on understanding the differences between Josh and Brent. Each family became seen as an entity which forms a kind of "Family Constellation" consisting of a father and mother with children who may be born creating a birth order which can be used to gain insight into the experiences of each of the children. Each child is then seen as having their own unique social experience within the context of this family, and each child sees and experiences the family differently from the perspective of their ordinal place. To focus on how these positions provide different experiences creates a key that can help unlock an explanation for the differences between two children within the same family, such as Josh and Brent.

As we look at the experiences of a first-born child, a second-born child, a youngest child, an only child or a child within a large family with many siblings, it must be remembered that the person is attempting to achieve a place in the family, to connect with others, and responds not only to the expectations and treatment of their parents, but also that of other family members and siblings.

These "perceptual conclusions" then form the basis for some of the behaviors, traits and attitudes that different children will manifest within the family.

Some guidelines for determining where a child actual fits within a family context are as follows:

✦ In families with larger amount of siblings there is not just one constellation of an oldest child, several middle children and then a youngest. These families often break into two or more separate constellations.

✦ If there is 4-5 years difference between you and the next child up or down, you may function as an oldest or only child.

◆ If a child had other step brothers or sisters added, determine how the constellation was for the most influential years, and make a judgment on that basis.

◆ In large families of children, determine if they divided into groupings for play or interaction and look for the children who manifest leadership qualities within that grouping.

Remembering that each child decides his or her place within the family, based upon their own perceptions of where they fit and the expectations of other family members, we will now look at some general insights into each position.

First Child or Oldest Child

First children tend to be very authority conscious, leadership oriented, bossy and are often held up as the family example or hero. They have the unique advantage of having a period of time where they had all the parents attention and did not have to share it. They are the "family guinea pigs" in the sense that parents are first-time parents when they are born. They tend to be demanding of themselves and others, perfectionists who do not like making mistakes and often rise to leadership positions in organizations. They generally like responsibility and have usually been given a good amount of it early in life. Many respond to their parents expectations, and some in less functional families actually take over the role of the parent. They are independent and like to be in charge.   Many oldest children with siblings spent time caring for younger children which further developed their sense of responsibility.

Oldest children sometimes will take responsibility for things that had little to do with them. They can also blame themselves excessively when things do not go well in the family. There are lots of photos in the family albums of first-born children!

Middle Children

A middle child, and particular a second child, has to make a choice of whether to follow in the footsteps of the oldest and compete or to establish some other sense of identity on their own. They can suffer from being compared to the oldest. They hardly ever get to do anything first.   In families with a competitive atmosphere, these children can spend endless hours trying to compete with or keep up with the oldest, leading to feelings of discouragement. Or they can strike out in an opposite direction to establish their place or identity. When these children are in photographs, they are usually pictured with other siblings.

Middle children can develop of sense of being the "peacemakers" in the family, they are usually cooperative and are often "not seen" by others. They have an issue with fairness since the oldest has received privileges before them, and sometimes they are compared to them regardless of whether they do good or bad things. Middle children often feel like they receive more chores. When a second child is born, it is said they he or she will "dethrone" the oldest, creating another child for the parents to pay attention to. This can lead in some cases to jealous behavior toward the second child. Sometimes middle children are teased and treated badly by the older sibling. Middle children have the advantage of watching someone else grow and then learning from their success or failure.

As they grow, middle children are less likely to aspire to positions of leadership than older children, but they are experienced by others as solid, dependable workers who are loyal and easy to get along with. As future spouses they "roll with the punches" better than siblings in other positions.

Youngest Children

Folk wisdom would have us believe these children are the spoiled ones. They are referred to as the "babies" of the family and still can have that term applied to them even as adults! They are often given more attention than the middle children and are sometimes held back in the growing-up process. They can experience challenges in developing an identity since older siblings have already taken various family niches. Other family members tend to give them too much assistance by readily supplying advice and tying their shoes for them all the time when they are little. They are almost always in the position of being taken care of. Youngest children often have less expectations than the older children and are disciplined differently. They have many others to watch to see how they would like to act.

Youngests sometimes feel dependent on the other members of the family and lack confidence in their own decisions. They have little experience in caring for others unless the family sets up experience for them. They can learn to manipulate others in the family into doing what they would like. They can be the last one to find out anything that is being planned or any forthcoming change within the family. They are sometimes treated as though they do not have the competence or maturity to handle things. In most families they have more access to financial resources and experience their parents as being more relaxed than the other siblings do.

Only Children

The experiences of oldest children and only children are similar, except the only child has the advantage of remaining the center of the parents attention permanently. They have all the resources of the family focused toward them, but they also have all the expectations of the family to live with.

Only children tend to associate with adults as they grow up, missing significant cooperative experiences with other children. They often feel alone. Some feel as though they had to grow up too fast. They are leadership oriented and responsible, but like the oldest do not care for making mistakes. They are highly independent and individualistic. In families where siblings are many years apart there can be "functional onlys" where each sibling functions separately from all others as though they were each isolated from one another. Only children can find a real difference between the "center of attention" world of their home and the "you're one of the bunch" world outside the home. They sometimes lack the skills of interaction with the group. Only children will often rise to leadership positions as adults, having lived in the adult world all their lives.

Twins and Disabled Children

The resulting place in the family for twins depends primarily upon how each perceives him or herself and upon the atmosphere within the family. Identical twins can have some special difficulty in families where identity is primarily a competitive effort. In some cases twins will act more like a first and second child or follow a pattern where one is dominant and the other recessive. Both of these point to the interpretation each person makes of their role and how to achieve their place.

Disabled children function according to the atmosphere of the family and the attitudes of the family members. The natural tendency to focus on the needs of the disabled child give them a position similar to a youngest child in some families. The expectations of adults as perceived by the child often is a key in how he or she will establish their place.

So What about Josh and Brent?

We might assume that Josh is responding to the usual expectation from his parents that he be the leader of the siblings and also an example. He is getting reinforcement from his father for his participation in sports. He has been given that special attention initially and is responding to a leadership role. His interest in debate may be reinforced by his ordinal place in the family since being right may be important to him as well as relying upon authority to establish the correctness or incorrectness of a given position. His continued excelling maintains his special place as a child who is making his family proud.

Brent, on the other hand, has a dilemma on his hands. Does he try to compete with Josh for attention in sports or in grades? How does he get a sense of identity separate from Josh? He chooses to excel in computer skills, perhaps so he can achieve expert-status in an area not conquered by his brother. In most ways Brent appears to have decided he is not up for competing with Josh for a favored place in the family and may be actually trying to invent his own ways of receiving some attention and focus. Even his lower grades may be a way for him to gain family focus. If you talked to Brent you might get insight into his behavior by having him talk about his parents' expectations and how he views his older brother.

Applying Birth Order Theory to Your Life

Using the information listed above you will first need to determine what your position

is in the birth order of your family. Determine whether there was any preference given to girls or boys in your family. Was your family a competitive type or a cooperative type? As you think about your own experiences, ask yourself the following questions:

1. What was expected of you in your family when growing up?

2. How were you treated by your parents and other brothers and sisters?

3. What advantages and disadvantages do you feel your position gave you?

4. What conclusions about relationships and people do you think you came up with out of being in this position?

5. Do you think you can identify a particular "style" that comes out of being in this position? Or maybe an approach to things or a philosophy of life?

6. If you are presently married or in a cohabitation relationship, how do you think the birth order of you and your partner affects what is going on in your relationship?

7. How are your experiences or approaches within the workplace related to your experiences within the family? □

—Used with permission.

DEFINING TERMS

Institutions

Roles

Attitudes

Family Constellations

WHAT DO YOU THINK?

1. What other institutions could be modified to fulfill the functions of the family?

2. Which position seems stronger with regards to sibling differences: nature or nurture?

3. What rules can you think of in your family?

4. What beliefs and values did (does) your family hold?

 **VIDEO VIEWER:**

Rent the film "Ordinary People." What roles do the various family members play? How does it contribute to conflict?

☺ **MEDIA WATCHER:**

"Dysfunctional Families" have been a hot topic for a while. What have you seen in the news or other programs about this topic?

Part Two
Sex, Sexuality, and Gender Roles

Module Four

The Biological Differences
Between the Sexes

---

*I*t all boils down to a single gene on a single chromosome. While biologists have long known that women have what is called XX chromosomes and males have XYs, it was not until 1990 that British scientists isolated the single gene that makes the difference. Essentially, each female has all the genes for being male except that one, and each male has all the genes for being female.

This single gene activates all the others into the complex task of turning a fetus into a boy. One final factor is required--an elevated level of testosterone secreted by the fetus' own undescended testes. In the rare cases in which the tiny body does not respond to the hormone, a genetically male fetus develops sex organs that look like a clitoris and vagina instead of a penis. Though they look and act female, they are genetically male and unable to bear children. Curiously, other little girls who are genetically female, but who, due to another genetic abnormality, have elevated testosterone levels, have been found by scientists to prefer playing with boys' toys (Gorman, 1992).

*B*oth men and women have both men's and women's hormones--androgens, including testosterone are the male hormones, and estrogens, the female--in differing amounts. Without testosterone, neither sex would experience much libido.   The differing testosterone levels between male and female probably explain differences in sexual desire and aggressiveness between the sexes. Giving each sex an excess amount of the other's hormones would cause females to gain some facial hair and men's breast sizes to somewhat increase.

If one looks at an internal view of the male and female reproductive tracts, one is struck by how much the apparent opposites look alike. This is because the basic structure as developed in the early fetus is the same. It is only the effects of the hormones that produce the external differences (Wells, 1991).

How Much Difference?

But how much does biology explain the differences between the sexes? Most of the differences discovered are statistically quite small. While men are generally taller and

Chapter Preview:

Biology of Sex Differences

How Much Is Explained?

Article: "Bad Sex: A Guide to Sexual Problems and How to Solve Them"

stronger than women, the differences within each sex are far greater than the average difference between the sexes. Differences in sexual response are as significant within each gender as between them. Men tend to be more easily aroused than women, but women may be able to experience greater total sexual response than men. Many women are able to experience multiple orgasms, and although men are able to have repeated orgasms, there is usually a waiting or refractory period necessary between orgasms. Differences in sexual response, though, vary tremendously between individuals --far more than the average difference between the sexes (Gorman, 1992).

Most cognitive differences are even smaller. While men tend to do better at spatial analysis and numerical/abstract reasoning, women are better at verbal abilities and deciphering emotions. Whether this is due to biology or upbringing is difficult to tell. Recent research has focused on the hypothalamus, a little organ that sits at the top of the brain stem. In most animals, it is larger in males than in females. Its function is to strongly activate a person toward satisfying hunger, thirst, desire, or anger. In 1991, one scientist provoked a controversy with his announcement that a region in the hypothalamus was twice as large in heterosexual men as in women or gays. Other scientists have disputed his findings (LaVey, 1995).

Another group of scientists have been trying to determine whether the corpus callosum, a bundle of nerves that connect the right and left hemispheres of the brain is larger in women than in men. If true, it might explain why women are often better able to verbalize emotions than men, since the left hemisphere is associated with logic, and the right with feeling. Until recently, scientists were hampered by the need to use autopsied material which degenerates too quickly after death. In 1992,

UCLA researchers used brain scans to determine that parts of the corpus callosum were as much as 23% larger in women than in men. A University of Washington researcher who attached electrodes to different parts of the brain under local anesthesia during neurosurgery, found that women's language centers were located near the front of the brain, while many men's were located nearer the back. Curiously, in people with higher verbal IQ's the differences were much smaller--both sexes' centers moved to more intermediate locations.

Despite the growing evidence of differences, the actual differences between the sexes may be shrinking. A University of Wisconsin researcher found that since 1974, overall gender differences for both math and verbal skills have decreased dramatically. Nevertheless, some differences persist -- studies have found that men still are better at rotating objects, while women continue to excel at finding and remembering locations of objects. Some believe this difference reflects evolutionary pressures which forced men to become better at handling weapons, while women needed to forage for food.

While the differences are real, the causes and consequences of biological differences can easily be exaggerated. Women can read maps, at least some of them, and men can read emotions, or at least some can. Further, both men and women can be taught to overcome their shortcomings. Biology is not destiny, and rather than seeing it as a limitation which cannot be overcome, it should be seen at most as an explanation for what is. □

References

Gorman, Christine. 1992. "Sizing up the sexes." *Time*. January 20.

Lavey, Simon. 1995. *The sexual brain*. Boston: MIT Press.

Wells, J.G. 1991. *Choices in marriage and family*. Alta Loma, CA: Collegiate Press.

Zilbergeld, Bernie. 1992. *The new male sexuality*. New York: Bantam.

❑ Bad Sex: A Guide to Sexual Problems and How to Solve Them!

Dr. Robert Manis

Viagra $9.95!!! The ads blare. Young people may laugh or even blanche at the notion of the older generation lining up to get prescriptions to be able to have sex, but the fact that Viagra has knocked off Prozac as the most prescribed drug in America shows that sexual problems are no laughing matter. From impotence, to premature ejaculation, to inability to orgasm, sexual problems are less the exception than the rule, and give lie yet again to the notion of rampant sexuality promoted in the movies and on TV.

Sexual problems may be physical or psychological, but best estimates are that nearly 70% of all couples experience sexual problems at some point in their lives. That means that if you are out with two of your buddies, odds are if you've never had a sexual problem, they both have. During any given year, about one in three men report reaching climax too soon, and nearly the same number of women report frequently inability to reach orgasm. Actual figures may even be higher if, as we might suspect, some people are being less than honest about their problems.

Amazingly, most problems go untreated. Whether because of expense or embarrassment, or simply the difficulty of locating solutions, most couples ignore or improvise their own solutions. Some problems do go away or get better with time, but many are "solved" by simply withdrawing from sexual life, either temporarily or permanently, either fully or partially. Others are handled by accepting "that's just the way things are."

Types of sexual dysfunction

In discussing sexual problems, we need to distinguish between the various types. The most widely used system of classifying sexual dysfunctions is from the American Psychiatric Association's Diagnostic and Statistical Manual of Mental Disorders, also known as the DSM. The DSM classifies sexual disorders into four categories:

[1] **Sexual desire disorders**. These generally involve a problem with sexual interest, desire, or drive, in which a person might experience lack of desire or an aversion to sexual contact. Also within this category would fall the opposite, people with compulsive sexual problems, people who used to be called "nymphomaniacs" or "sex addicts."

[2] **Sexual arousal disorders.** These are problems in which people consistently or recurrently are unable to become adequately aroused to enact or sustain sexual relations. For men, this refers to inability to achieve or sustain erections, while for women it typically involves insufficient lubrication despite normal desire.

[3] **Orgasmic disorders.** The most common category of sexual problem, these include too rapid climax or trouble reaching orgasm.

[4] **Sexual pain disorders.** Both men and women may suffer from painful intercourse. The causes, however, may be different for men than for women.

Causes and Cures

Professor Davis Mannino reports that during his Peace Corps tour of duty in Penang, Malaysia in the 1960s, a popular drink for his friends was "Cobra Blood," a potion that included snake blood, liver bile, booze and some sweetener, which when downed was supposed to increase sex drive and cure impotency. Going one step further, Richard Marchinko's bestseller "Rogue Warrior," includes an episode of drinking actual cobra venom, still within the venom sac and suspended in whiskey! (Snake venom isn't poisonous unless it enters the body through the bloodstream--hopefully, drinkers don't have any ulcers!) Neither provided much benefit, but they did produce monumental hangovers. More common is the use of oysters, ginseng, sushi and other foods and herbs from all over the globe, to improve sexual functioning.

Orgasmic disorders. What does work? Let's NOT go in order in discussing these. If you are like most people, you are most likely to have experienced an orgasmic problem (#3). The good news is that in 95% of all cases the problem is curable, usually without professional help. For both sexes, the problem is usually tension-related, though the specifics and the cure are somewhat different.

For men, premature ejaculation can occur from over-excitement, stress or tiredness, or performance anxiety. It can also become a "self-fulfilling prophecy" in that the more he worries about it the more likely it is to happen. Premature ejaculation can be treated in a number of ways. The medical profession seems to be moving toward drug therapy using Prozac or related drugs. These work by reducing desire, the chemical equivalent of thinking about baseball! But they can make erection more difficult, and can cause mood changes.

Many doctors recommend behavioral therapies. These include the "squeeze technique" pioneered by Masters & Johnson, where the woman masturbates the man until just before ejaculation, then firmly squeezes the tip of the penis, preventing ejaculation. When done correctly, this prevents ejaculation. After a while this technique is transposed to intercourse, and the partners decouple so the man can get his "squeeze!"

Because this requires some supervision, many therapists have moved to the "start-stop" technique. Best explained in Bernie Zilbergeld's "The New Male Sexuality," this method teaches orgasmic control by teaching the man when to stop stimulation just before orgasm. He starts be learning how to control himself during masturbation, then during petting, and finally during intercourse. He also recommends men experimenting with different motions and positions that enable better control. One man I know reports that the female on top position allows him the most relaxation, while another prefers crouching. Another man told me that a side to side motion drove women wild but kept his hand off the trigger, so to speak. Look at some sex manuals for ideas, and buy Bernie's book!

The leading edge in sex therapy, though, comes from an unusual source. Called Tantra or Neo-tantra, some clever New Agers have combined contemporary sexology with the sexual science of ancient India and China. Books like Margo Anand's *The Art of Sexual Loving* show how you can use sound or exhalation to reduce tension and last longer. They also stress the relaxation and control of specific muscles like the pubococcycx (PC) muscle. This muscle, located between the genitals and anus, is the one that controls peeing. You can learn to identify it by starting and stopping the flow while urinating. Once you know where it is, you can exercise it any time of the day. Pretty convenient! Women can do these exercises too, to increase their pleasure and that of their partners. Ejaculation can be prevented by contracting the PC muscle, while strongly blowing out air in exalation, or several other methods including stroking the inside of the thighs to relax them, and especially by pulling back the scrotum gently or by pressing and vibrating the vas deferens (the tube the sperm travel in to the penis) right between the scrotum and the anus.

As with the start-stop method, this is best practiced first in masturbation, then with a partner, and finally during intercourse.

For women, treatment of orgasmic difficulties is quite different. Women who have never experienced orgasm may harbor negative sexual attitudes that can cause anxiety or inhibit response. Treatment may therefore include exploring and dealing with those attitudes. Most therapists follow Masters & Johnson's approach of using sensate focus exercises. These exercises are designed to increase sexual relaxation and reduce pressure by taking the emphasis off orgasm and placing it on pleasure. Sensate focus means both partners are simply asked to focus on stimulating and exciting the other person sensually, usually taking turns, so that person can simply relax and enjoy. The clitoris is usually not stimulated early, because it may produce a high level of stimulation before the woman is prepared. Instead, teasing and exciting are emphasized. Orgasms can't be forced, but when a woman feels free to focus on her own sensations, without anything being demanded of her, she'll generally be able to reach orgasm. Other therapists focus on masturbation as an important step. Women are encouraged to give themselves permission to explore their bodies, massage themselves, use fantasy, and in general, find out what works for them. Once a woman is capable of regularly producing orgasm, the focus shifts to partner

sex, and the woman teaches the man what she likes best. She may also stimulate herself clitorally during intercourse. Communication is also often stressed. Couples are taught that eight simple words are the key to improved communication during sex. OK, here they are: faster, slower, harder, softer, up, down, left, right. Do you think you can remember them? Couples are also encouraged to talk about sex outside of the act, to tell each other what they like and wish to do. Sometimes, this gets them back into bed! Oh, well.

Sexual Arousal Disorders. When we are aroused our bodies normally respond with **vasocongestion,** the swelling of genital tissues with blood that causes the erection of the penis and the engorgement of the vaginal area. The inability to gain or maintain an erection is what is called impotence. The occasional inability to gain an erection isn't uncommon and like premature ejaculation may be caused by stress, tiredness or performance anxiety. Repeated problems, however, nearly always have a physical cause. The decline of testosterone after age 40 is frequently the culprit. High levels of cholesterol may be even a more common factor. Interestingly, Nobel Prize winner Linus Pauling found that sugar intake was even more predictive of high cholesterol than was red meat. Be safe and cut down on both. Viagra, of course, is the hot new drug on the market, but is not recommended for people on the common heart medicine nitroglycine. Another option is testosterone hormone replacement, which by the way, does not involve gonad transplants, simply a patch much like the nicotine patch. There is a possibly increased risk of prostate cancer, so many endocrinologists recommend DHEA or pregnenolone, hormonal building blocks which are available over the counter. These are not recommended for anyone under 40, however, and probably should not be undertaken until after a hormonal test by your doctor. The inability to adequately lubricate is the most common physical female arousal problem. This may be due to diabetes or more likely decreased estrogen due to aging. Hormone therapy with estrogen, progesterone or DHEA is often successful, and of course, lubricants like K-Y gel are a simple solution. Psychological factors like those mentioned in the previous section can often cause arousal problems as well.

Sexual Pain Disorders. Sexual pain can afflict both men or women. It is a sign that something is wrong. Sexual pain is about four times more frequent among women than men. It may be caused by allergies to spermicides or even condoms. Pain during deep thrusting may be caused by inadequate lubrication, endometriosis or pelvic inflammatory disease [PID] or vaginal infections or STD's. It may even be caused by a too-large penis. If the latter cause can be rejected, a visit to the doctor can forestall serious future consequences. If size is a problem it can be mitigated by going slowly and using lubrication. A frequent cause of sexual pain for women is vaginismus, the involuntary contraction of pelvic muscles that surround the outer third of the vaginal column. This occurs at the time of attempted penetration. The woman is generally not aware that she is contracting her muscles, and may desire intercourse. The causes of vaginismus are usually emotional. The woman may have a history that includes rape, incest or abortions. She may have been brought up to fear men or intercourse. Vaginismus may cause or be caused by premature ejaculation. Treatment usually consists of therapy combined with relaxation and sensate focus. Sexual pain is less common among men. A common cause is dehydration. If some pain occurs and does not go away after drinking a few glasses of water

and urinating, he should visit a doctor. STD's and prostate problems are probable causes.

Sexual desire disorders. After all this discussion, you may feel like sex is now the last thing on your mind. Fortunately, unless you have a desire disorder, you'll be back to normal probably within an hour or two. But if you're not, read on.

There are two opposite types of sexual desire disorders: Low desire which is called hypoactive sexual desire [HSD] and extremely high desire or compulsive sexual behavior [CSB]. Hypoactive sexual desire may be caused by physical or emotional factors. Hormonal deficiencies, genetic or due to aging, may be the cause of the physically based problems. Drug or alcohol use or prescription drugs including anti-depressants like Prozac also can reduce desire. These can be treated by hormone replacement therapy or Viagra, or by changing medications. Psychological factors can include a heavily negative sexual upbringing. If parents imbue the children with strongly negative attitudes about sex, this can cause actual repression of sexual feelings. Traumatic incidents like rape or incest can also have this effect. More common is the withdrawal of one partner from sexuality because of problems in the relationship. All of these problems can be solved through therapy.

I should say here, that it is quite common for partners in a relationship to have differing levels of desire. These may not surface at first, when the novelty and excitement of a relationship are at its peak, but as both people relax into their more normal rhythms of sexuality, these differences start to appear. That does not mean that either person has a desire disorder. There's no standard as to what is normal. Usually, therapists recommend some kind of compromise.

Compulsive sexual behavior or CSB, is nearly always caused by psychological factors, usually in the person's upbringing. Like HSD, CSB is often caused by repressive sexual upbringing. In this case, the repression causes a sexual obsession. Persons with CSB may masturbate many times a day, have multiple affairs outside marriage, or tie up their phones with 900# calls. A small proportion of CSB victims cross the line into hard-core criminal deviations, voyeurism, pedophilia, exhibitionism and the like, but most people prefer the plain vanilla type--just taken to an extreme. Although it's popular to refer to CSB as a "sex addiction," most therapists still consider it an anxiety disorder. The desire-lowering effects of Prozac and other serotonin inhibitors makes this a promising new therapy, but most experts believe psychotherapy is also an important factor. CSB sufferers have layers of guilt, shame and loneliness often piled upon the earlier levels that first caused their problems.

Whatever your problem, the good news is that nowadays, it is treatable. The primary problem is ignorance and embarassment. But the truth is that no one should be embarassed to have a problem that is in its essence, not their fault. So here's to a future, where, as Garrison Keillor used to say about the children in mythical Lake Woebegone, "Everyone is above average." ☐

The American Academy of Clinical Sexologists (202-462-2122) and the American Association of Sex Educators, Counselors and Therapists (send an SASE with $2 to 435 North Michigan Ave., Suite 1717, Chicago, IL 60611) will provide names of qualified local sex therapists.

DEFINING TERMS

Testosterone

Estrogen

Arousal

Dysfunction

Compulsive Sexual Behavior

Hypoactive Sexual Desire

WHAT DO YOU THINK?

1. What accounts for the supposedly stronger sex drive of men than women? Are there limitations that men have sexually that women don't? Explain.

2.   What are some common sexual problems? List at least three. How can they be helped?

3. What are the strengths and weaknesses of biological studies of the differences between the sexes?

4. Does sexual experience before marriage provide a good indication of post-marital sex? Why or why not?

⊛ VIDEO VIEWER:

Rent "Angels and Insects." What does the film suggest accounts for male and female behaviors? Do you agree? Why/why not?

☺ **MEDIA WATCHER**

Do TV shows and movies show much about sexual dysfunctions? In what tone do they treat it? Give examples.

5. Make two lists: What you think turns men on, and what you think turns women on.

A. Men   B. Women

Module Five

Sex Role Socialization

*I*t starts with a pink or blue blankie at the hospital. Socialization into our gender roles, begins at birth and is reinforced throughout our lives. Sex role socialization is undoubtedly the strongest form of socialization we receive. Starting at the hospital, it is perpetuated by parents, television, and school. Socialization is defined as the process by which a society's beliefs, norms and values are imprinted in the minds of its members. Socialization begins at birth and continues throughout life. Sociologists believe that the earlier a particular socialization process occurs, and the more wide-spread it is, the less conscious we are of its effect and the more powerful it becomes. Traditionally in American society, sex role socialization has divided human characteristics into those seen as masculine and feminine. The list (below right) is a representative example:

*T*hese traits are somewhat opposite, and tend to limit the self-expression of both sexes by essentially ruling out half of human emotional expression for each gender. These norms are enforced by society's disapproval and shaming of those who cannot or will not conform. Technically these differences are known to sociologists as gender, which is to

FEMININE	MASCULINE
dependent	independent
emotional	rational
intuitive	analytical
nurturing	competitive
sensitive	tough
sexually alluring	sexually aggressive

sex, literally, as feminine is to female. But in general, people use the terms sex roles and gender roles interchangeably

Nowadays, few people believe the traditional notion that women are somehow inferior or that they shouldn't be allowed to do the things men can. Nevertheless, young people are often surprised to find out that vestiges of sexual prejudice exist in many people and even in themselves. How can this be the case?

Chapter Preview:

Overview of Socialization

Sex and Gender

Focus: "What Planet Are You From, Anyway?"

Article: "Football and Modern Masculinity"

Article: "Love In the Afternoon"

Researchers have discovered numerous subtle ways in which society reinforces sex role differences. Parents tend to treat boys and girls differently, rewarding boys for creativity and independence, while rewarding girls for helping behavior, such as helping in the house.

In pre-schools and early grades, girls are rewarded with approval for working closely with the teacher, and are often ignored when acting out. Little boys whose play tends to be more aggressive, are "rewarded" with negative attention--being shouted at, rather than ignored. Remember that for children negative attention is better than no attention at all, so this attention tends to reinforce their behavior to some degree.

Probably the most powerful and pervasive agent of socialization in modern society is television. From an early age we are bombarded by thousands and thousands of images teaching us what men and women are like. Often these images show stereotypical pictures of sexy girls and powerful men. Advertising uses these images to lure us into buying things by playing on our desires and our insecurities.

Dr. Jean Kilbourne, producer of the film *Killing Us Softly*, states that the cumulative effect of these images has been to devalue women and to teach us that the traits defined by society as feminine are inferior. Most of us are aware of the costs of sexism against women, but it has its costs against men as well. Sociologists have determined that men are many times more likely to be victims of heart attack, depression, alcoholism, suicide, murder, or to be murderers themselves--all possible consequences of the devaluation of supposedly feminine characteristics like emotional expression. Curiously, what is seen as feminine and masculine does vary somewhat between cultures.

Doctoring is seen as a feminine profession in Russia, and visitors to the Ivory Coast in Africa might be surprised to see men engaged in the very masculine activity of washing clothes in the river.

□ **Focus: What Planet Are You From, Anyway?**

Not only are sex role stereotypes promoted by parents, teachers, storybooks, movies, and television, but often most strongly by children themselves. Most children are raised in almost completely self-segregated environments, where boys do boy things and girls do girl things.

According to linguist Deborah Tannen, boys and girls are in effect raised in two separate cultures, two different worlds for most of their early and most formative parts of their lives. When they try to get together as adults in marriages and relationships, the result is often misunderstandings and conflict. Tannen studied men's and women's conversations and interactions both separately and together and found out that quite often each sex had quite a different agenda from what the other thought was going on.

According to Tannen, most men are socialized through games and male play into competition. They often come to think of themselves as part of a somewhat hierarchical social order, where they are either, in her terms, "one-up" or "one-down." Conversations are negotiations in which they either playfully or for real try to achieve or maintain the upper hand, or at least protect themselves from others' attempts to put them down. For men, life is a struggle to preserve independence.

Women, on the other hand, tend to see themselves in a network of connections. They are socialized through girls' games and helping around the house to value connectedness. Conversations for them are negotiations for closeness and support. Women try to protect themselves from others' attempts to push them away. For women, life is a struggle to preserve intimacy and avoid isolation. While not all men and women fit neatly into these categories, these themes showed up repeatedly in Tannen's research.

Two Examples:

♦ *"Put down that paper and talk to me."* In public, men tend to dominate conversations. They speak often, and at greater length. They tend to interrupt more often than women. Yet many women complain that at home, men become silent, burying their heads in newspapers, or watching television. Why is it that men dominate in public and disappear at home? Tannen suggests that for both men and women, home is a place to be offstage. But that offstage feeling has a different meaning for men and women. For men, getting home means freedom from having to prove and defend themselves through talking. They are free to remain silent and just "be together." For women, however, home is a place where they are free to talk--unlike public where they may be somewhat intimidated, and where they feel the greatest desire to talk--with those they feel closest to. For them, being home means the freedom to talk without being judged.

♦ *"What do you want from me anyway?"* Many men are mystified by women's "troubles talk." They offer helpful advice, often only to get rejected, sometimes with anger. Tannen gives the example of a woman who had minor breast surgery, and was disturbed by the scar. When she talked to her friends they offered support by saying things like, "I know, I was upset too, when it happened," and "I know, it's like having your body violated." But when she told her husband, he responded, "You could have plastic surgery to cover up the scar." While she found her friends' comments

comforting, her husband's comments upset her. Not only did she not hear what she wanted--that he understood her feelings--but, worse, she felt that he wanted her to undergo more surgery. "I'm not having any more surgery, and I'm sorry you don't like the way it looks." He, in turn, was puzzled by her anger at his response. Like many women, she wanted the gift of understanding, and like many men, he responded with a gift of what he felt was helpful advice. Men are socialized to take action, to solve problems, while women are more socialized to nurture and comfort. Tannen feels that by knowing these gender differences, couples can begin a process of communication that leads to greater understanding by recognizing the effects of socialization. □

References

Crook, R. & K. Baur. 1996. *Our sexuality*. (6th ed.) Pacific Grove, CA: Brooks/Cole.

Kilbourne, Jean. 1985. "Still killing us softly." (film) dist. by newsreel, San Francisco, CA

Lips, H.M. 1993. *Sex and gender*. Mountainview, CA:Mayfield.

Tannen, Deborah. 1990. *You just don't understand: Men and women in conversation*. New York: Morrow.

❑ Football and Modern Masculinity

Dr. Robert Sands

The author, anthropologist Robert Sands, researched junior college football by becoming one of the team. Looking at mechanisms of cultural identity, Sands paints a picture of college football players, once secure in the identity of masculinity bestowed on them by playing, now caught in a cultural and athletic paradox. To be a good football player requires behavior and a mind set that no longer is widely acceptable in contemporary society. Straddling a line between a culture of where controlled violence and physical punishment is mandatory and a surrounding culture, where sensitivity to those less fortunate is encouraged, players construct an identity fraught with social and cultural tension. Masculinity just ain't what it used to be.

Out the locker room door, we flinched at the bright sun and then all eighteen of us we were down the concrete winding stairs that led onto the parking lot where the ticket office was. A big crowd of parents and kids pushed us through the big gate that led onto the stadium floor. Slowing slightly to give the rest of the sophomores time to catch up and then we crossed the nine lane synthetic tartan track and reached the turf, a group of helmeted players ready to do battle and challenge the odds. We marched across the field to the sidelines opposite the huge, old 10,000-seat concrete grandstand, where already there was a large group of red clad Bakersfield fans. The Vaquero contingent was slow in arriving, fashionably late and in half the numbers of the Bakersfield supporters. No surprise to us. Usually, at our home games, the visiting team usually had more fans than we did.

One of the officials met us at the 50-yard-line and told us only four could walk all the way to midfield to meet the Bakersfield captains. The rest would have to stop at the near hash. Mike Hayes, a starting cornerback, lone halfback Twuan Hill, Jarrett Thiessen the monsterback and I lined up with the rest falling in behind us. We grabbed hands and waited for the official to lead us out. A minute passed before the Bakersfield contingent was ready to go. We stood there, each lost in our own thoughts, silent, our hands resting in each other's grasp. Not conscious of what this particular display of male bonding would be thought of outside this stadium, at a different time and place, the anthropologist in me rudely intervened and pushed aside the player in me. I remembered a particular passage from a book I had just recently read.

Mariah Burton Nelson, the author of *The Stronger Women Get, The More Men Love Football,* wrote of bonding in male athletes by describing the cover photo of H.G. Bissenger's *Friday Nights Lights,* three high school football captains striding through the stadium tunnel on their way to the pregame ceremony, as an irony, a social-sexual paradox in an otherwise hyper-masculine activity. "Were these same young men," said Nelson, "to hold hands in a different setting on a city street . . . without their football uniforms, they would be thought of as gay. They might be taunted by other men-- football players perhaps. Yet in this picture their hand-holding projects a solemn, unified sort of group power that conveys both threat and affection. It illustrates the fact that male power is based on male bonding. Together they feel powerful. Together, they act powerful."

Standing there, my hands wrapped in two different hands, I felt some of that unified power. A feeling of togetherness to approach a monumental task, a giant obstacle, and to gather strength. I didn't feel a power that held dominion over women. My thoughts were not of us males dominating women by our linking of rough and calloused hands. I could feel the texture of Jarret's skin that lay in mine, and its roughness reminded me of the feeling of security I felt when my father's giant paw, giant to a six year old, used to settle around my hand. It wasn't threatening; it was comforting in its maleness.

However, Nelson continues, "together, they fall in love--with power, with masculinity. They also fall in love with each other." I wasn't ready for some psycho-sexual analysis of hand-holding and attempted to push the thought from my mind. I didn't need to look at Twuan on one side of me and Jarrett and Mike on the other side to know that I was not in love with either of them or any others on the team. In some real way, Nelson's male-bashing is a treatment and condemnation of male athletes. Look, she is saying, only in hyper-masculine sports like football can a man physically show another male how he feels without fear of negative labeling.

"While sport offers a man a place to worship traditional manhood, paradoxically it also offers a man a place to loosen the rigid masculine role without losing status," wrote Nelson. Mary Boutilier and Lucinda San Giovanni add that men "can embrace each other unself-consciously, holding and hugging, touching and kissing without threat of ridicule and suspicion. They can express fear, hesitancy, pain and doubt, and be nurtured by other men. They can be irrational, cooperative, sentimental, and superstitious in the accepting presence of male camaraderie. In sum, in the absence of women, they can allow themselves to express what sexist ideology insists must be suppressed if they are to lay valid claim to being 'real men.'"

Pat Griffin, a lesbian athlete and writer, in her book, *Strong Women, Deep Closets*, takes a similar tack: "It is not a coincidence that expressions of male-to-male physical affection

and love are acceptable in few other contexts. In athletics, men can admire other men's bodies and their physical accomplishments openly without arousing suspicions about their heterosexuality." More simplistically, Nelson says, "Much of sport . . . is an elaborate stage set to enable men to feel."

Allen Dundes, a folklorist, contributed a thought-provoking piece for a volume I edited on anthropology, sport and culture based on his belief that football was a ritual that allowed for the expression of male homosexuality combat rites. Dundes finds these rites not unique to American culture, but rather, fairly common in other cultures. Echoing other feminist writers, Dundes also suggested that beyond serving as a male initiation right, football promotes the continuation of a male preserve that manifests both the "physical and cultural values of masculinity." In the speech and behavior from penetration of one's end zone to the postural stances of lineman and the center, football, he suggested is full of homosexual connotations. Yet Dundes doesn't stop there; he sees football as "a ritual combat between groups of males attempting to assert their masculinity by penetrating the end zones of their rivals . . . The ritual aspect of football provides a socially sanctioned framework for body contact and is a form of homosexual behavior." Although these male initiation rites are a doorway to manhood in many cultures, football players, especially college and professional players, due to financial incentives, extend and retard this period of adolescence for many years.

Yet, to avoid the nature of bonding and the physical requisites that accompany such behavior is to fall into the trap that Nelson and many other feminist writers accuse sport in general, and football, in particular, of doing: creating a safe, artificially constructed haven where a man can show and express real emotion and attachment to other males without being labeled a homosexual. I know that the turf is a rectangular harbor, where the emotion and feelings of males find asylum, and I wonder, what is wrong with that? Human ritual, and football can be considered as such, an activity that supersedes normal or profane reality, has been designed over the thousands of years of human evolution to accommodate behavior that is necessary for the function of culture, but finds its home in a meta-existence, above and beyond normal reality. Once philosopher of sport, now famous sports attorney, Howard Slusher suggests that religion, and associated rituals play less and less an important role in human's existence, and sport is one of those "rites" humans now turn to to impose order on a chaotically changing world. Why should males, or for that matter females, today be exempt from that same evolutionary need? Why not let order come to chaos through a ritual that stretches back in our evolution?

Male athletes are stuck with a label of closeted homosexuals by many feminists. In a twist of logic, lesbian athletes and women athletes on the whole, are now finding out the strength, power and bonding that participating in sports can bring to the athlete. Writes Griffin, herself a lesbian and athlete/coach, "Women in athletics develop strong relationships with other women as teammates, friends, and lovers; they challenge, comfort, and support each other . . . . The truth is that women do develop passionate feelings for other women in the sport context, and for some women these feelings are sexual." Now women find out sport is a venue, removed from real life, and yet part of real life, that offers them a sanctuary to express affection and comradery.

The academic liberal inside me acquiesces to their logic, but the player in me tries to escape it. I can rationalize, telling myself that it isn't the game that I have come to cherish that creates the homophobic, masculine-only locker room feelings. It is the players and the coaches and the men who sit back in their easy chairs and in smokey bars that create the need to ritualize male affection. The game, the comradery, the surge of adrenaline, the goal of team victory all are connected together in some ritual Zeitgeist that propels the players forward and at the same time, as each sport reflects the contemporary behaviors prevalent in society and culture, brings out the worst in those who play and watch.

In the minute before marching toward midfield, 18 young men and one older man held hands in full view of 2000 fans. And this wasn't the first time we held hands. We held hands in practice and games in the offensive huddle. We held hands during team prayers. We hugged players with a happy embrace after a good play and mauled them when they scored a touchdown or made an interception or recovered a fumble. We consoled players after mistakes by draping an arm over a shoulder and telling them to shake it off. We grabbed a player's face mask or shoulders to make them focus after losing their cool during a play or on the sidelines after coming off the field. And after the game, some would walk toward the locker room with arms draped over shoulders reveling in that emotional high of a victory or the bittersweet feeling of a loss, where your heart and soul are telling you that the you and the team screwed up, but your body is arguing that you gave it your all.

Very vividly, I can recall the end of the San Francisco-Minnesota *Monday Night Football* game on December 18, 1995. Two old warriors, quarterbacks Steve Young and Warren Moon, met in the middle of the field at the end of the close game. One white, one black. Young is a devout Mormon, and Moon just recently spoke out and begged forgiveness for his alleged spousal abuse. Uniforms covered with moist turf, sweat glazing their faces, steam rolling off their helmetless heads in the late evening Bay fog, they met and embraced and then pulled away, but kept their arms resting on each other's shoulders. The *Monday Night Football* camera remained on this image for what seemed like hours, but was probably only a minute. The viewer could not hear what they were talking about, but whatever, the game, the season or just renewing a friendship, the affection and respect each had for the other was there for 20 million viewers to see.

Defined during this context of spent souls and bodies, exhaustion taking its toll, there are feelings of love, of deep respect, of a camaraderie that transcends the profane and passes between players. But with society constructing such loaded and dangerous labels and rigidly defining acceptable behavior, is it any wonder that none of us 18 hand-holding sophomores would ever admit that this display was nurturing or even slightly affectionate. It has to remain unlabeled, undefined, underscoring the brutal, violent and lightning quick context of what Nelson calls the "manly sports" like football. In those seconds of charged combat, I don't wonder if grabbing a fellow player is socially acceptable; I grab a player because I feel. I bow to the elation of the moment and let the wave of emotion wash over me and it feels good. My mind does not categorize and compartmentalize my actions.

In that instance, those brief seconds of time swallow up social boundaries and my heart is allowed to run rampant. Is football solely an elaborate stage constructed so that these moments of passion can be allowed to surface? So according to Nelson, I went through months of training so that I could stand here holding hands with two other guys and not feel uncomfortable. Nelson and others dwell at length on the physicalness of male sport but conveniently, or maybe without knowing, overlook that oftentimes sport is a celebration of achievement, where one or a group triumph and the passion is not the end result of participation, but is rather something that sweetens the already enjoyable experience.

Aware of all attempts to explain the meaning of one player hugging another, I stood on the sideline, knowing that in the ensuing march to midfield, it would be wrong not to hold hands. It was the final piece to complete the experience, not the experience itself. Whether the experience is called love or whatever, I couldn't deal with it now. I had other things to think about, so I banished Nelson from my thoughts, knowing that in the future, the anthropologist in me would have to deal with her claims. □

—Excerpted from Gutcheck: An Anthropologists's Wild Ride into the Heart of College Football. *by Robert Sands, Ph.D. Used with permission.*

☐ Love in the Afternoon: Love, Marriage and Family on Daytime Soap Operas

C. Lee Harrington, Ph.D.

Associate Professor of Sociology, Miami University, Oxford, Ohio.

> "They do a lot more than just sell soap!" You may have heard this famous line that refers to the influence TV and other media have in our lives. These media influence how we see ourselves and others and how we think about the world in many ways. And because they must portray our world in colors we can accept, they provide a reflection, though perhaps distorted, of that world. —The editor

Soap operas are important to examine because of their longevity in the television world, their amazing resilience, and the extreme loyalty they generate in their viewers. According to Carole Smith, ABC's head of daytime research, "The ongoing nature of soap opera [provides] an involvement you can't get from other types of programming. People identify with these characters [to an extent] you can't get [elsewhere], no matter what the competition is. They gossip about it, and it becomes a community within itself, to say nothing of being extremely fun to watch" (quoted in Valerie Davison, "Is the Soap Bubble About to Burst?", *Soap Opera Weekly,* September 16, 1997, p. 38). Approximately 22% of the U.S. adult population today watches soap operas regularly, translating into 42 million viewers (Lynn Liccardo, "Who Really Watches Daytime Soaps?", *Soap Opera Weekly,* April 30, 1996, p. 37). In terms of sheer numbers of viewers alone, then, soaps are an important focus of inquiry into contemporary images of love, romance, and family life.

The reigning queen of daytime television, "All My Children's" Erica Kane, keeps getting married and married and married. At last check the character's full name was Erica Kane Martin Brent Cudahy Chandler Montgomery Montgomery Marek. In fact, the names Roy Roy could be added somewhere in the middle. Erica twice married writer Mike Roy, but neither marriage was legal. Is this the image of faith and commitment that "All My Children" is trying to promote? Is this what soap operas are all about? Actually, no. Fairly traditional notions of family, domesticity and community have always been at the core of daytime soap operas, since they first appeared on radio in the 1930s. The staple of early radio soaps such as "Ma Perkins" were one-on-one discussions between the self-reliant widow, Ma, and other characters on the show. The scenes usually took place in the same setting, Ma's kitchen, and the program invariably closed with Ma dispensing words of wisdom. This advice was

ostensibly directed at the other character, but was really intended as "self-help" instruction for the listening audience. Soaps have always taken their role as moral guide seriously; even after their transfer from radio to television in the 1950s, they continued to focus on the moral order that upholds small (albeit fictional) American communities.

To most critics, however, today's soaps look anything but "moral," depicting an image of domestic life much different from the traditional ideal. Much like Erica Kane, most characters have multiple marriages, and pre-marital and extra-marital sex are routine. This is ironic, perhaps, given that the search for "my one true love" still dominates most characters' everyday lives. How do soap writers reconcile this disparity? Today's soaps have also been criticized for portraying an increasingly unrealistic notion of family life: the vast majority of characters are white, heterosexual, upper-middle class adults in their 20s, 30s and early 40s. Why isn't there more diversity on soaps, like there is in real life? We will answer that question shortly.

Portraying life-long commitment

Perhaps the biggest challenge faced by daytime soap operas is portraying lasting, committed love relationships. Soap characters, much like characters in popular romance novels, are motivated primarily by a desire to find True Love--they might hold jobs as doctors, lawyers and forensic psychiatrists, but it is affairs of the heart which dominate the narrative. What pleases soap audiences more than anything else is the long, slow tease of two characters falling in love, acknowledging their love for one another, overcoming whatever hurdles might stand in their way, and finally making it to the alter and a lifetime of wedded bliss. But, as any good soap fan knows, they never stay married. Why not? The biggest problem is the medium itself; since soaps are a serial format, with a new episode shown every day, 52 weeks a year, writers are constantly searching for new stories to tell. For reasons that are sometimes hard to understand, simply "being married" doesn't make for a very good storyline. While it might be exciting and fulfilling in everyday life, soap writers have a harder time sustaining that excitement in fictional narratives, and audiences tend to get bored with seemingly contented couples. Actors themselves know that having their character get married is often the "kiss of death"--after wedding night scenes and a great honeymoon, they are relegated to the back-burner as more exciting storylines take over.

As a result, most of soaps' made-for-each-other Supercouples--such as Roman and Marlena on "Days of Our Lives," Jax and Brenda on "General Hospital," and Brooke and Ridge on "The Bold and the Beautiful," find their marriages beset by an increasing number of problems that threaten their relationship. And by problems I mean problems: an ex-spouse comes back from the dead, a long-lost child shows up on the doorstep, or a terminal disease threatens the couple's eternal happiness. Significantly, however, these problems are external to the relationship, at least initially. The couple does not discover that their love was fake; rather, they are split up by circumstances beyond their control. This way, the ideal of true love is maintained: nobody's really at fault for the break-up, the characters are morally freed to search for love elsewhere, soap writers have new stories to tell, actors move back to the front-burner, and the audience--who likes watching the "falling in love" part of love the most--is once again happy.

Aging on the soaps

"I think age still influences whether you'll get front-burner storylines or not. I've certainly had less story as my character has aged . . . society's vision of romance and fantasy is very limited. Most people don't find it sexy to see two wrinkled faces smooching," (Nada Rowand, who played Kate on ABC's now-defunct "Loving," quoted in *Soap Opera Weekly* May 9, 1995, p. 33-34).

One of the biggest criticisms soap operas receive today is that the fictional communities they portray--such as Llanview, Salem, Sunset Beach or Springfield--are filled with people who all seem alike, especially in terms of age and race. For example, most characters are young adults in their 20s, 30s and early 40s. Infants and children are fringe characters, at best, appearing as part of custody-battle storylines or popping up on holidays to open presents. Frequently, children undergo what TV critics have termed RACS--Rapidly Aging Child Syndrome. A 5-year-old character is shipped off to Aunt Sally's for the summer, and comes back three months later a hormonally charged 16-year-old, ready for teen romances and a quick segue into adult storylines. Actually, teen storylines on the soaps are a fairly recent emergence, traced back to producer Gloria Monty's work on "General Hospital" in the late 1970s-early 1980s. Soaps were experiencing a decline in popularity, and Monty is credited with revamping the genre by populating it with teen characters (most famously Luke and Laura) to attract the younger audience during school breaks, as well as adding action and science-fiction elements to attract more male viewers. But critics argue that teens and young adults have taken over daytime drama, leaving older characters and actors with little to do. Leading characters in their 60s or older are a rarity. The "last chance" for soap characters to find erotically-based love seems to be in their 40s, though it is difficult to tell, at times, just how old certain characters are supposed to be (such as "Another World's" Felicia or "One Life to Live's" Viki).

Writers and producers insist, however, that they are working to create more age-realistic storylines that are exciting for actors and viewers alike. With the demographic changes in the U.S. population creating an older and older viewing audience, television executives are increasingly interested in telling stories that speak to real-life experiences of aging viewers: stories about Alzheimer's, nursing home abuse, elderly stroke victims and aging-related impotence are all recent additions to the soap opera tapestry.

This is not to say that aging is defined by problems, of course--soaps do portray love and commitment between older couples, such as that between Edward and Lila on "General Hospital"--but that love tends to be affectionate rather than sexually intimate. As the quote above suggests, our general cultural bias against aging and the aged in the U.S. is accurately reflected on the soaps; while we know that most people remain sexually active as they grow older, many viewers are still uncomfortable with watching it on-screen.

Race and ethnicity

A 1994 study conducted by Sharon Bramlett-Solomon and Tricia Farwell found that of 3,360 scenes showing intimacy during an 8-week period (including hugging, kissing, intimate touching and verbal intimacy), only 12% involved non-white characters. None of the couples depicted were interracial (see Alan Carter's "Separate But Unequal," *Soap Opera Digest*, March 24, 1998, p. 34).

Similar to the age bias in soap operas is the overwhelming "whiteness" of the fictional worlds they portray. For example, while Blacks make up approximately 12% of the U.S. population and comprise as much as 20% of the soap viewing audience, long-term Black characters remain rare. According to critic Alan Carter, the two actors' unions in the U.S. (SAG and AFTRA) point to increased numbers of Black actors working in the soap genre, but many of those roles are very small, and "the character has no life, any real or lasting connection to the story or anything meaningful to say." If other roles are meatier, they are often stereotypical. Black characters might be brought on solely to create trouble for the (white) heroes and heroines of the show, and stereotypically portrayed as drug dealers, hit men, or sexual criminals. Or, Black characters are written such that they interact only with other Black characters. As the quote above suggests, interracial contact between soap characters, particularly romantic or intimate contact, is either rare or nonexistent.

Other racial/ethnic minorities, such as Asian-Americans and Native Americans, are largely absent from the soap world. The one soap opera that was premised on a more racially-realistic community, NBC's "Generations," was canceled after just a few years on the air. What explains this absence of diversity? Some believe the audience is to blame, saying that viewers find the traditional soap world "comfortable" and would stop watching if there were dramatic change of any kind, including alterations in the racial composition of the fictional community. Alan Carter points out that there are few Black writers in daytime television and no Black executive producers or head writers. Do white writers feel uncomfortable writing "Black" stories? Would they rather write for white characters instead? Daytime insiders insist that there is no such thing as "Black" or "white" stories--rather, good stories are race- or color-blind.   As actor Tonya Lee Williams (Olivia on "The Young and the Restless") stated in a magazine interview:

"I don't like it when shows take a religion or [race] and make that the story. If you're Asian, you don't have Asian problems, you have real problems. When your boyfriend runs off, it's not a racial thing. You can't play a black person having turmoil. We don't have black turmoil.   Our problems are the same as everyone else's," (quoted in "It's Not Just Black and White" by Carolyn Hinsey, *Soap Opera Digest*, April 12, 1994, p. 60).

We are, in fact, slowly seeing a change to more racially realistic storytelling. Reflecting the changing ethnic composition of the U.S., for example, is the increasing number of Latino and Hispanic characters on the soaps, most notably on NBC's "Sunset Beach" and ABC's "One Life to Live." If this trend continues, we will indeed have soaps that "look like" America, rather than the predominantly white communities portrayed at present.

Sexual orientation

"It's one thing to explore homophobia. It's quite another to explore the life of a gay couple--a life that includes sex and such problems as whether or not to adopt gay children.   I doubt that day will come," (television critic Mike Logan, quoted in *TV Guide*, September 25, 1993, p. 37).

Another absence on soaps--and the most striking absence of all, in many ways--is the overwhelming heterosexuality of daytime communities.   Gay and lesbian characters (especially the latter) remain extremely rare on the soaps, even though they comprise as much as 10% of the U.S. population (this is the figure cited most often by gay rights activists). The number of gay characters ever depicted on soaps can probably be counted on two hands. I

remember watching "All My Children" about 15 years ago when a kind of "pseudo" gay character arrived in Pine Valley. She was a psychologist (if my memory's right), and a core character, Devon, became attracted to her -- but there was never any intimacy, the word "lesbian" wasn't uttered, it was decided that Devon was not gay after all but merely "confused," and the psychologist quickly exited the canvas.   Have there been any lesbian characters on soaps since then, whether real or implied? I'm not entirely sure, but I think not. There have, however, been a handful of gay male characters -- but, like the psychologist, their romantic life is very sanitized. They rarely have relationships, or even dates. If they are in a relationship, viewers might never see their partner. If the partner is seen, the couple is not shown having sex, kissing, or even holding hands. They're together, but certainly not in a realistic way.

According to scholar Joy Fuqua, ("'There's a queer in my soap!' The homophobia/AIDS storyline of 'One Life to Live'," in *To Be Continued: Soap Operas Around the World*, edited by Robert C. Allen) the biggest problem with representations of homosexuality on soaps is that gay and lesbian characters are defined entirely by their presumed "problem." Their storyline quickly comes to be about their sexual orientation. For example, consider "One Life to Live's" celebrated early-1990s storyline about the gay teenage character Billy Douglas. Billy's sexuality was revealed as part of a long-running, intricate storyline about homophobia and the meaning of community. However, as soon as the homophobia problem was "solved," Billy quickly disappeared from view. He has popped up on a few AIDS-related episodes of the show, but otherwise, "case closed."

According to Fuqua, soaps have yet to figure out how to incorporate the everyday lives of gays and lesbians--including their search for romance, intimacy and family--into a fictional world dominated by heterosexual courtship and marriage. As Michael Logan suggests above, that incorporation might never be possible because of potential audience rejection of the storyline and characters. More importantly, however, homosexuality seems to violate the implicit premise of the genre as a whole: a search for true love between a man and a woman.

Conclusion

In short, contemporary soap operas do have problems with their depiction of love, romance and family life. The fictional worlds they portray, while familiar and comfortable to many of us, are an increasingly inaccurate representation of reality. The U.S. is undergoing significant demographic changes: an aging population, a rise in the numbers of "out" gays and lesbians, and an increasingly non-white population, among other things. Soaps have shown in the past that they are committed to responding to real-world issues--consider, for example, the number of timely, socially relevant storylines on daytime television, ranging from breast cancer to gang violence to prescription drug abuse--and their challenge today is to create characters and stories that reflect, in a more realistic way, who we actually are. □

–Used with permission.

DEFINING TERMS

Socialization

Sex Roles

Masculinity

Femininity

WHAT DO YOU THINK?

1. How does socialization explain the differences between men and women? Does it do a better job of explaining than biology? Why or why not?

2. What's your reaction to the quote below from "How to Get the Man of Your Dreams" in the September 1994 issue of *Cosmopolitan:* ".... when all else fails, try the age-old failure-proof mantra of seduction . . . 'Come here . . . . Go away . . . . Come here . . . . Go away . . . .'"

 **MEDIA WATCHER:**

Check out some "talk shows." How are men and women portrayed on them?

3. Explain how each of the following "agents" of socialization affects our notions of gender and gender roles: parents, friends, school, media. Give an example of each. Which is strongest? Why?

VIDEO VIEWER:

Rent a romantic film from the 1940s and one from the 1990s. Compare how sex roles have changed.

4. Make two lists on this page: [1] your "pet peeves" about the opposite sex, and [2] what you think their "pet peeves" are about you.

Module Six

Dating and Courtship

---

*M*odern societies which have abandoned the practice of arranged marriages face the problem of how to get couples together. Dating is the uniquely modern contribution to the process which has traditionally been called courtship. In earlier times, courtship occurred when a suitor appeared at the family residence of his desired. He met her parents and they kept company, highly chaperoned at first, then more loosely later. Such activities as dances and sleigh or wagon rides evolved to give the courters opportunities to caress and hold each other without social disapproval.

In other modern countries, group activities are the norm. The wife of Boris Yeltsin, the Russian President, reminisced that they rarely spent time alone together, preferring to socialize in the large but tight group of friends that went to school together. "It was as if we were all married together," Nina Yeltsin recalled. In many parts of Europe, the nightly "promenade" figures prominently in courtship and socializing. Whole families and groups of young people walk up and down the main street at night, pausing at cafes to eat and drink and socialize. For singles it is an easy way to make and deepen friendships with the opposite sex.

*I*n the United States, with its greater distances and diminished community life and widespread automobile ownership, dating has taken on a special significance. Even here, however, dating is a relatively recent phenomenon. Before WWI, courtship consisted mainly of the young man paying formal visits to the young woman and her family. This was called "keeping company" and could only be done by obtaining the parents' permission. Chaperones were often present to ensure good behavior, although as courtship developed, it could be arranged for the couple to discreetly slip away.

Modern dating emerged because of a number of social changes including the industrial revolution, which brought people together into the cities; the establishment of free public high schools which brought young people together outside of parental control; the development of the automobile; and the beginning of the women's right movement in the 1920s which freed women from earlier restrictive forms of behavior.

Chapter Preview:

Overview of Courtship

Dating

Rules of Modern Courtship

Focus: Breaking Up

Article: "The Changing Nature of Relationships on Campus"

Dating

Dating reached its apex in the 1950s when a fairly discernible pattern of stages began to emerge. Group and double dating began in 8th and 9th grades, followed by "random" dating, steady dating, getting "pinned," engagement and marriage, each stage a year or two apart. By the end of the sixties, this system began to break down, a victim of the greater informality of the "hippie" years, replaced by "hanging out." In the last twenty-some years, both patterns can be seen, with predominance fluctuating depending on the time period and the geographic region. Currently, dating seems to be dominant in the later high school, and post-college years, while hanging out is common among early high-schoolers and college students.

"Rules" of Modern Courtship

Whether "dating" or "hanging," the modern form of courtship proceeds by a couple of rules.

First, **propinquity,** the principle of nearness. People are most likely to meet people that are near to them geographically, economically, religiously, etc., and despite the notion that "opposites attract" they are more likely to get along over the long term. This is because they share common experiences and values. This doesn't imply that inter-racial or inter-religious pairings are bad or doomed to fail, but rather they simply have greater gaps to bridge.

Second, **the rating-dating complex.** First noted by Willard Waller in the 1930s, it's been replicated many times. People consciously or unconsciously rate prospective partners in terms of their desirability, and rarely continue to date people whom they perceive to score lower than themselves. It sounds cold, but it's true. Of course, many people don't rate themselves accurately, so there can be situations where a person is aiming too high and ends up alone, or

aims too low and ends up with someone unsuitable.

☐ Focus: Breaking up is hard to do

Nowadays, people are pretty optimistic about the chances for their success in romance. Up until recently this was not so; in previous centuries romance was often seen as leading to tragedy as in *Romeo and Juliet* or Goethe's early novel, *The Sorrows of Young Werther*. Nearly all romances fail. Some crash before they get off the ground, and others sputter out early. Most serious dating relationships end within two or so years. Even if a relationship succeeds at becoming a marriage, it still faces a 50% chance of divorce. While much has been written about divorce in the popular press, breaking up is a phenomenon sometimes ignored, but frequently experienced.

In 1979, Boston University researchers studied couples dating exclusively. By the end of two years, nearly one half had broken up. Couples had the best chance of staying together if they were equally matched from the start: equally committed, equally attractive, and of similar backgrounds.

Very few of the breakups (7%) were mutual. Women were generally more eager to break up than were men. Interestingly, couples rarely agreed on what was the cause of the breakup--or even how suddenly or gradually it came about!!!

Not surprisingly, it was easier being the leaver, than the one being left. Leavers felt guiltier, but otherwise considerably less lonely or depressed than those left. In fact, reactions tended to be mirror opposites--often the happier one person was to get out, the worse the partner felt about the breakup.

For the person being left, the pain and shock of being left can be substantial. There is a loss of intimacy and companionship, and often a loss of an imagined future, a dream.

Rejection can be damaging to self-esteem, since the partner's love and esteem over time tends to become an important part of the lover's self-image. Finally, for many people rejection can bring up deep abandonment anxieties left over from childhood. These anxieties may or may not be conscious, but they can greatly intensify a later rejection by a partner.

Given the great pain inflicted by breakups, one might think that the person leaving would try to make every effort to ease the pain on their lover, but this is frequently not the case. Breakups are often accomplished on the telephone, even via answering machine!!! In any case, they are usually announced as a fait accompli, a done deed, often without previous warning. After the breakup, the leaver may avoid the leavee, increasing the degree of rejection. One therapist calls the modern form of breaking up "nuking" the other person. We "nuke" the other person when we kick them out of our lives, and blame them for our dissatisfaction. It seems strange that we should act so uncaring to a person we once cared for. Perhaps a little etiquette should be taught:

♦ Make every attempt to resolve any problems through communication. Many problems are solvable, even when they don't seem like it. Others are simply misunderstandings.

♦ Don't use breakups as a weapon in arguments. Breaking up is a big decision and should be done in a rational state of mind, not an angry one.

♦ The decision to break up should be as mutual as possible. Thorough discussion can help both sides to better see whether breaking up is the best choice.

♦ Take your time breaking up. Making a gradual time-line to separate helps the other person adjust, and makes sure the leaver is not avoiding important issues.

♦ Establish clear boundaries. Make sure each person understands what is appropriate behavior under the circumstances.

♦ Don't rush into another relationship. Even if you are breaking up to be with someone else, it is better wait until you are emotionally complete with your former partner. □

References

Cate, R.M. & S.A. Lloyd. 1992. *Courtship.* Newbury Park, CA: Sage.

Hatfield, Elaine & Richard Rapson. 1993. *Love, Sex and Intimacy.* New York: Harper Collins.

Hill, Charles et al. 1979. "Breakups before marriage." in G. Levenger & O.C. Moles (eds.) *Divorce and separation.* New York: Basic Books.

Whyte, M.D. 1990. *Dating, mating and marriage.* New York: Aldine de Gruyter.

❑ The Changing Nature of Relationships on Campus: Impasses and Possibilities

Stephen J. Bergman and Janet Surrey

Stephen J. Bergman and Janet Surrey are on the faculty of Harvard Medical School and the Stone Center, Wellesley College.

Old models of male-female relationships are breaking down. In the past, role differentiation helped define what was "male" and "female" and helped shape the male-female relationship. Although it was important for women to be educated, often a woman's "role" was to support a man's self-development and career. Healthy development was defined primarily as "male" development: a strong, independent "self" that could connect with others only after achieving a degree of separation and maturity. (The epitome of this was the Freudian model of development.) Deviation from this "separate self" model, by man or woman, was seen as pathology. Campus counseling centers by and large endorsed this model. "Relationship" was seen as the coming together, in role-defined ways, of two separate "selves."

But this model will no longer serve. In society and on campus, the old paradigms of roles and identities tied to gender are no longer the reality. In all aspects of society, male-centered models are being challenged. Campuses are at the forefront of these challenges as many young adults struggle to create and develop new forms of relationships.

In her 1976 book, *Toward a New Psychology of Women*, Jean Baker Miller challenged whether the male model fit women's experience. For the past 15 years, we and others at the Stone Center (Wellesley College) have been developing a new paradigm of psychological development, shifting from a "self-centered" model of healthy development to a "relationship-centered" model. The work has focused primarily on shaping an accurate description of women's psychological development. Recently, the relational paradigm has been applied to male development. Gilligan and Belenky have also developed this model.

The Stone Center model

The relational model differs markedly from old models of development. First, it suggests that the primary motivation for all humans is not Freud's "sex and aggression," but rather a desire for connection. Second, it suggests that healthy growth takes place "through and toward connection," rather than in isolation or in the fashioning of a separate, isolated self. And finally, in a paradigm shift, it suggests the existence of a third element, "the relationship," a process that encompasses the sense of "self"

and "other." "The relationship" reflects and informs all participants. Each person's reality can be seen in a "relational context," the field of connection between and among people, which extends to the greater community and society.

We have come to believe that to work on gender issues within relationship, it is useful for men and women to work on these issues not only individually, but also in groups. In groups of men and women discussing cross-gender relationship, it soon becomes apparent that an individual concern, which may have been thought of as "pathological" and therefore kept hidden, is in fact a concern shared by other men and women; further, what were thought to be an individual couple's difficulties in relationship are found to be difficulties inherent in all cross-gender relationships. Once these difficulties can be seen as shared, they can be "de-pathologized," and dialogue can begin. We feel strongly that to look at these issues, men and women on campus must work together, and we have found that once a climate of mutuality between men and women has been created, difficult issues, among them, sexuality and violence, can be addressed.

The male-female workshop

Using the Stone Center model, we have worked for the last ten years to bring the genders together, offering workshops on "The Woman/Man Relationship: Creating Mutuality." (Our work thus far has focused particularly on the obstacles to mutuality in heterosexual relationships.) We offer a vision of "relational mutuality," a model of engagement around gender differences. Each time we hold this workshop, we find that almost without exception, it is the first time that men and women have been brought together for the specific purpose of attending to gender differences and working through the conflicts toward mutual understanding and action.

First, in a brief didactic session, we describe the Stone Center paradigm, which helps participants shift their focus to "the relationship." We try to enhance attention to and awareness of the relationship and the qualities of connection or disconnection in the relationship. For example, we ask each person to think of an important relationship and imagine its color, texture, sound, and climate, as well as an animal that might be a metaphor for it. This shift of focus from the individual to the relationship is very new for most people who have grown up in western industrialized cultures like the United States'.

Next we separate the men and women in different rooms, and in small groups of three or four they come up with consensus answers to three questions:

1. Name three strengths the other gender group brings to relationships

2. What do you most want to understand about the other gender group?

3. What do you most want the other gender group to understand about you?

After separate group discussions about the questions, the men and women come back together. Without having told them in advance, we seat the men and women in two semicircles facing each other. We then ask them to discuss their answers.

Immediately, things get heated. The men are often fearful; the women are usually curious. We asked one male college student who looked particularly anxious to describe what was going on. He said, "I'm afraid that something might happen." A woman responded enthusiastically, "I'm hoping that something might happen!" Thus, some familiar and important differences begin to emerge as men and women try to engage in relationship. The men start to feel what we have called "relational dread," and they start to withdraw; the women

start to feel angry, and they either pursue or give up. This impasse is familiar to participants from their own relationships, where things spiral out of control and get stuck in a hostile standoff. We have termed this a "relational impasse": it exists neither in the man nor in the woman, but in the relational space in which they meet.

We have called the three impasses we have identified Dread/Anger, Product/Process (where the men are trying to complete the task, while the women want to keep opening up the process), and Power-Over/Power-With (where the men experience conflict as a threat or as an attempt to control and as something that should be resolved through some rule or criterion, while the women want everyone's voice to be attended to and retreat from what seem like definitive stands). Any or all of these impasses may occur in any particular aspect of relationship. Think, for example, of how Dread/Anger, Product/Process, and Power-Over/ Power-With might get played out around sex. For example, a man may approach a woman sexually:

Woman: "I can't just go right into something physical; I need to feel connected to you first."

Man: "That's what I'm trying to do; making love is how I connect."

Woman: "But I need to connect with you in order to make love."

We have held these workshops on various campuses, ranging from a liberal eastern school where the group started out fragmented along ethnic, racial, gender, sexual, and class lines and was embroiled in an ongoing debate about "political correctness," to a conservative midwestern school where the concerns were less political. In each workshop, strong feelings are generated: fear, anger, confusion, hopelessness, and yet there is a sense of freshness and newness in actually talking together about these feelings, especially when the students begin to discuss their responses to the question, "What do you most want to understand about the other gender group?"

Some of the responses of these college students are as follows:

Men's questions to the women:

"Why are you so angry?"

"How often do women feel threatened by the presence of a man? Or a group of men?"

"What is your intense need to talk about feelings?"

"Do I need to prove myself to you?"

"Do women feel they are holding up the emotional end of relationships, and do they want to?"

"How does your emotion affect connections?"

"Why are you more curious than we are? Why do you value means over ends?"

"Can you really accept vulnerability in a man?"

Women's questions to the men:

"How can you compartmentalize your thoughts?"

"How deep does male bonding go? How close are male-male relationships?"

"Are you ever conscious of being a member of the dominant sex? Do you go through the same self-questioning that we do and that we think you don't? Do you depend at all on outside approval and affirmation for your confidence?"

"Why is it hard for men to express their emotions?"

"Why is it so hard for men to deal with other people's emotions?"

"Why, if men have a need for connection, do they act directly against their primary need?"

"What is the meaning of men's silence?"
"How do we get your attention?"

Out of the dialogue around these questions, several main areas of conflict between male and female college students become apparent.

Stereotyping and political correctness

Political correctness has been well discussed. (See, for example, *Educational Record*, Winter 1992.) One solution to the conflict is to try to equalize everything and deny any differences in experience. (This may be a reaction to the history of inequality, where difference was used hierarchically and the dominant race or gender or class exerted power over the subordinate.)

While it is crucial to begin the discussion about breaking down stereotypes, it is equally crucial to acknowledge differences in experience, perceptions, and power.

Denial interferes with dialogue, engagement, and real understanding. The problem is not "diversity" versus "PC," but rather how to open the dialogue about difference. It is essential to begin to distinguish "stereotype" from "difference."

In our workshops, issues of stereotype are raised immediately. Often, women will ask questions such as:

"Are you men ever conscious of being a member of the dominant sex?"

"Why is it hard for men to express their emotions?"

"Why do men separate love and sex?"
"When are you men going to wake up?"

These questions from the women often evoke anger in the men, who answer:

"Don't stereotype me. I'm not into that macho thing."

"Don't blame me for the things that other men do."

Often, when the men list women's "strengths," they say things like "women are nurturing" and "women take care of the details of the relationship"; this tends to make women angry because they are unwilling to be thought of mainly in these traditional "female role" ways.

In this atmosphere, we find that it is difficult to ask about each others' experiences and listen to the answers. It becomes clear why stereotypes tend to prevail when men and women are placed in situations where there is no chance for dialogue, no opportunity for the movement of relationship--that is, when there are disconnections between men and women. In disconnection, stereotypes become more powerful; if there is an opportunity for mutual connection, stereotypic thinking and language become less evident. This is certainly true of gender/sexual stereotypes, and it probably is true of others. In American culture and on campus, there seems to be an unspoken fear that addressing difference will lead to stereotyping. In fact, our workshops suggest that it may be just the reverse: exploring difference together breaks through stereotypes. As we help students pursue the dialogue, they begin to discuss the deeper roots and effects of these images of being "nurturers" or "macho."

Violence and date rape

There is an increasing incidence of alleged violence and date rape on campus, and a sense that more women are beginning to speak out about rape, harassment, and abuse. But women still feel that it is risky to speak out--and with good reason. The Anita Hill phenomenon showed just how difficult it is for a victim to be believed, and how the victim who speaks out may find herself the target of anger. A woman

may conclude: "It's all right to speak out, but it can get you in a lot of trouble--you may not be believed."

Men, too, are placed in a difficult position. They are confused and annoyed about this issue: on the one hand, they feel accused, and on the other, they feel that it is difficult to take a moral stand against the problem without dissociating from their gender: "Yeah, some men do that stuff, but not me."

In one workshop, at a point when the men and women were caught in an impasse around this issue of violence, one man helped break through the impasse by frankly relating a dilemma he had recently experienced:

Man: "I was walking behind a woman student at night on a dark path, and I didn't want to scare her. But I didn't know whether to stop and let her go ahead so that I wouldn't frighten her, to walk up to her to make her feel more safe, or just to walk normally and let what would happen. She heard me. When she turned around, I saw on her face a look of real terror. I thought to myself--What? She's scared of me? And then, for the first time, I really got it. I mean, I realized how much fear of physical violence women carry around with them all the time."

Woman: "You mean you didn't know?"
Man: "Not 'til that night, no."

Responding to the man's gentle authenticity, the other students raised similar concerns. The men identified with the dilemma. The women, feeling understood, were able both to hold to their experience and to empathize with the men's experience. Together, they discussed aspects of this difficult issue, moving back and forth between individual and societal arenas. It became clear to the students how the power of the dominant group (men) over the subordinate group (women) can often be invisible to the dominant group. The extension to racial, ethnic, sex, and class divisions was apparent. The discussion led to a listing of proposals to deal with violence and date rape on campus: men offering to escort women, initiating discussion groups to further explore the issue, etc.

Our workshops have also shown us how infrequently men and women discuss sexuality. Each gender is curious about the other's sexual style, and sometimes the facts are at odds with the stereotypes. One men's group asked the women, "Do you like to flirt? What is a sure sign [that you are interested in a man]?" "What are your signals and standards of attractiveness?" "How do you feel about taking an active role in initiating relationships and sex?" One man said, "The big lie is that we men are the pursuers, but the fact is, the woman's the one who opens the door." A women's group asked, "Why are men intimidated by women when we're expressing our sexuality?" "What's with this breast fetish?" "Why are male bodily functions so important to you?" "Why do men separate love and sex?"

Given this basic level of uncertainty about the other gender's sexuality, it is not surprising that impasses arise. And when a man feels trapped in an impasse, especially if alcohol or drugs are involved, violence can arise. (Violence could, in fact, be reframed as the ultimate disconnection.) In the workshops, the exchange of questions and answers between genders can result in remarkable movement toward mutuality in a short period of time. It is astonishing to see just how far a simple exchange of previously "hidden" information about the other gender can go. For example, the men asked the women: "How often do you feel like a sexual being?" A woman answered: "We are multifaceted, changing creatures, and our sexuality is different from yours--we can be highly sensual and sexual, but we're not necessarily pleased in the same ways, nor do we have the same appetites, as men. For us, sex is not a linear activity." From this interchange, the group had a fascinating discussion about how to understand the other gender's sensuality and sexuality.

Backlash

Over the past 12 years, as American society has fragmented along lines of income, race, ethnicity, and class, there has been a violent increase in hostility toward women, described in Susan Faludi's prize-winning book, *Backlash*. A reciprocal backlash against men was fired up by the Anita Hill--Clarence Thomas hearings: "Men just don't get it." The economic climate has increased pressures on students, promoting an atmosphere of every person for him- or herself and fueled by anxiety about getting a job.

The isolation of both genders is intense, as is the private devaluation of genders in stereotypical ways. Groups of men, in particular, "get into" this devaluation of women. Recently, in a college workshop, a woman asked her boyfriend, "Why do you get so different, so weird, so unaffectionate toward me, when you're with your friends?" Other women asked, "How do you feel about status differences with women partners?" and "Do you know what it feels like to make 67 cents on the dollar?" At another college workshop, we heard about a hidden microphone at a college fraternity that picked up incredibly sexist language and hateful remarks. Once again, disconnection inflames isolation and backlash.

The way to "reconnect" is to express the anger and fear and to work to understand the other gender's experience and perceptions. It is increasingly clear that the way through is not to further solidify gender identity--to become "more female" or "more male"--but to value and learn how to make mutually empowering connections, not only within gender, but across gender.

Often, both women and men will raise the question, "But we don't want men to become more like women--are you talking about the 'feminization' of men?" If asking men to be more "relational" is called "feminization," we are all in big trouble. We are bringing men and women together to work on the "relationalization" of all.

The economy, commitment, and identity

The past decade has seen a dramatic worsening of the economic climate. For college students, this means increased pressure to get a good job, which in turn promotes an atmosphere of competitiveness rather than cooperation. There is tremendous anxiety, in both college and graduate school, about being able to make a "good living."

These tensions have profound effects on the qualities of relationships. College is a transition period, in which relationships are based on work identity, concerns about personal identity, and the formation of the so-called "adult" identity. We would reframe these concerns not only in "self" terms, but in "self-in-relationship" terms. As they set the stage for adult growth, college students both absorb the current culture and are the creators of it.

The Reagan-Bush era focused on the old notion of "self." At best, it fostered a kind of heightened individual achievement; at worst, it fostered a greedy discounting of the value of personal relationships. In individual relationships on campus, both women and men express a terrible fear of "getting involved." One man asked, "Why do you have such lofty expectations about relationships?" Another asked, "If you had on your tombstone: 'She was wonderful at relationships,' would you be satisfied?" A woman answered: "It would be great - but I'd like a second line: 'She pitched in the World Series.'" A woman asked, "What are your needs in a relationship? Does a relationship ever matter as much as a career?"

In college, as in society, pressures abound, competition is fierce, and the ethos is "do it for yourself," for your own development. But how can these be reconciled with commitment? Most college students want to be committed to a person--in fact, they want to be committed not only to a person, but to a relationship--and yet they are truly afraid of making the commitment.

Women in particular have been struggling long and hard for "self-hood," which often is based on the male model of success. In an eastern women's college, women are expected to put their own careers first: "If you are going with somebody, and you both get into grad school in different parts of the country, there are no more of the old rules, which said that women were supposed to follow the men's careers. But there's no new model of relationship. It's everyone for herself." This leaves students with a terrible fear and doubt about whether to get involved and committed. Women and men want relationships badly, but they are told to put their own careers first.

Again, we might reframe this by teaching men and women how to enter into a dialogue that includes but transcends "self" and reframes "identity" in terms of "what will make this relationship truly mutual and foster the healthy growth of both participants."

The shift toward mutuality

In the workshops, once the work begins and the impasses develop, when the male and female students persist in a dialogue around their differences, a shift in the "sense" of the group invariably occurs. Suddenly, the men and women are working together on the questions, helping each to find out about the other's experience. We have called this a "shift toward mutuality." Men and women have described this experience of mutuality in these words:

Release, comfort, caring, safety, sharing, peaceful, easy, enjoyment of different styles, hopefulness, mutual nurturance, energizing, movement, insight, softening, appropriate confrontation, dynamic process, clearer recognition of others' experience.

Even in groups that start out angry and fragmented, this shift occurs. There is a great sense of relief, movement out of the impasses and stuck places, away from shame and blame, and toward a new sense of possibility.

In an atmosphere of mutual endeavor, almost any topic can be discussed productively, including sexuality, violence, stereotype, backlash, and commitment. In this atmosphere of mutual connection, stereotypes fade. In their place we see mutual inquiry, authenticity, and empowerment. Often, this results in men and women working together to take action on campus.

We have found that the possibility of moving from separation to mutuality is always present when men and women get together. The openness, the desire to work together, the strong feelings, and the vitality of college students make them an excellent group in which to begin the work of redefining the nature of cross-gender relationships. □

— From the winter 1993 issue of Educational Record. *Copyright © 1993, American Council on Education. Reprinted by permission.*

DEFINING TERMS

Courtship

Propinquity

Rating-Dating Complex

Mutuality

WHAT DO YOU THINK?

1. How much of your reality is portrayed in the article. Give examples of similarities or differences.

2. What are "norms" about dating in your circle of friends?

4. What are the best and worst parts about dating as you've experienced it?

3. In what ways does dating help males and females to "grow up"?

5. If a girl says "no" to a boy's advances, should he stop immediately, or can he wait to find out if "she's serious"? Why or why not?

⊛ **VIDEO VIEWER:**

Rent "Grease." What are some of the dating rituals depicted?

Are the two main characters changing to impress each other, or are they simply broadening their horizons? Explain your view.

☺ **MEDIA WATCHER:**

View some sitcoms about young people. Is the dating scene portrayed similar or different from your peers? In what ways?

Part Three
Love and Intimacy

Module Seven

The Emotions

*D*espite all the talk about it, we don't know much about emotions. Even a survey of marriage and family textbooks would be unlikely to find a discussion of emotions. We all have them, and despite the thousands of scientific articles written on the mind, relatively few have been written about the emotions. This is strange because sociologist Max Weber commented nearly a hundred years ago that rationality was the least common source of behavior, coming after habit and emotion. Nevertheless, over the last twenty years, a few researchers in and out of academia have made important contributions to our understanding.

Biologists have long classified emotion as a form of "arousal." This essentially means that emotions are based on an increase of chemical and metabolic functions. These occur through the stimuli of perception, thought, or contact. All animals are known to experience the "fight or flight" syndrome, which is its simplest state. Most animals seem to exhibit some form of "love" or nurturing, but we cannot tell whether it is a real emotion or simply instinctive behavior.

*I*n humans, dozens of emotions can be listed: envy, jealousy, disgust, happiness, boredom, frustration, love, greed, sadness, fear, terror, embarrassment, etc. According to Thomas Scheff, a sociologist at University of California, Santa Barbara, these emotions can be reduced down to combinations of several core emotions: love, rage, fear, grief, and guilt. Most other emotions are either combinations of those four or are "lite" versions of a single emotion. Some examples of the latter are "sadness" instead of "grief," or "anger" instead of "rage." Other emotions such as shame or envy are complex emotions that combine feelings of guilt or rage with thoughts about what others think or have. In that sense, they are "social" emotions, and they provide certain social functions.

Chapter Preview:

Overview of Emotions

Functions of Emotions

Romance and Jealousy

Article: "What's Love Got To Do With It?"

Article: "Jealousy: Is It All Bad?"

Functions of Emotions

It is possible, in fact, that most emotions provide important functions. Fear warns us of danger, anger can be used to protect us from attack, and guilt can protect us from harming others.

Sociologist Gordon Clanton points out that emotions provide an alternative to accepting a reality. He points out that if you don't want to accept that someone has something you don't you can feel envy, or anger if they prevent you from getting what you want. Expressing emotions also is a way of using power short of physical force. Anger can be used to defend oneself or put pressure on another, crying can be used to gain sympathy, and so on. Scheff points out that shame is often used to prevent people from breaking social norms.

Emotions have their down sides as well, as we all know. They can prevent us from enjoying ourselves, they can cause us to do violent or irrational things, but if repressed, they can affect us without our knowing it. Scheff suggests that there is a proper distance we can create so that our emotions can move through us naturally without causing problems. He calls this being a "participant-observer." If a person is simply being a "participant," he or she is too close to a particular emotion and may tend to wallow in it. However, remaining too distant, being an "observer," is what allows people to repress their emotions and not deal with them.

According to Harvey Jackins, the founder of the Co-counseling movement, emotions can be released by creating a similar balance. Getting a person in touch with their feelings, then contradicting the negative thought that prompted the feeling, triggers a spontaneous release of the emotions. Both Scheff and Jackins point out similar releases to the various emotions, laughter for shame, heat for anger, trembling for fear, crying for grief, and yawning for physical tension.

The biggest barrier to releasing our emotions, according to Scheff, is itself an emotion--shame. This emotion causes us to worry about how others see us, and to stifle our own emotions. Scheff theorizes that one reason why comedians are popular is they allow us to laugh at ourselves and discharge our embarrassment. In any case, it is only by breaking through the shame barrier, going beyond our embarrassment, that we can clear up the emotions that lie within.

Romance and Jealousy

Mention romance and people picture candle-light and valentines, princes and happily-ever-after. Mention jealousy and people think of ugliness and anger. The two passions represent the light and darkness, the angels and demons of love and relationships, our hopes and our fears. But both romance and jealousy are more complex than they seem, and our views of them have changed over the years. Most of us think that our romances will turn out well, and the more romantic our relationship is, the better. This contrasts strongly with the view held by most peoples over the last few centuries.

While it is true that most partners in most cultures loved each other, marriages in many cultures were arranged and expected to last a lifetime. They were valued more for stability than their passion. The mythologies of these cultures often emphasized the tragic nature of passion which led young people break rules and customs and act unthinkingly. Suicide was considered the likely outcome for those whose passions led them to seek love at the expense of practicality.

This view of romance was also held in medieval Europe. Andreas Capellanus wrote in the twelfth century, "Everybody knows that love can have no place between husband and wife . . . For what is love but an inordinate desire to receive passionately a furtive and hidden embrace?"

The knightly ideal of chivalry met its apex in the unconsummated love of the knight for the wife of his lord and master. Since love couldn't survive the taint of day-to-day living only unconsummated love could endure. Perhaps also influenced by religious condemnations of sexuality, the highest and pure love was one from a distance. Romantic passion could only have a tragic ending as with Romeo and Juliet, Hamlet and Ophelia.

Jealousy, too, has been subject to rewriting. Once seen as a clear indication of true love, it has been recast as "the green, two-headed monster." Changes in our beliefs and values have caused these passions to be seen in a new, but not necessarily more accurate, light, as the following two articles explain.□

References

Amadeo, John. 1994. *Love and betrayal.* New York: Ballantine.

Clanton, Gordon & L.G. Smith. 1987. *Jealousy.* Lanham, MA: University Press of America.

Goleman, Daniel. 1995. *Emotional intelligence.* New York: Bantam.

Jackins, Harvey. 1982. *Fundamentals of Co-counseling manual.* Seattle: Rational Island.

Scheff, Thomas. 1986. *Sociology of emotions.* Unpublished manuscript.

❑ What's Love Got To Do With It?

Nancy Marriott

Love between the sexes--it sends our spirits soaring, our blood pulsing and our emotions reeling out of control. In the name of love, we wage wars, forsake our homeland, throw away fortunes--it even brings Presidents to their knees (as well as interns), making fools and victims of us all. Blindly, we subject ourselves to the gamut of human emotions from ecstasy to torment, all for love. Poets and songwriters, Hollywood scriptwriters, and pulp novelists would all be in a fine mess without it. Plus, it makes the world go round.

But given some of the consequences of our love-inspired excesses, why do we bother? We can get on with the task of reproducing humans quite easily without falling in love, and many argue we'd be better off to skip the messy business altogether. After all, isn't love merely a contrivance, a fantasy concocted by human beings over the centuries, a cultural delusion that originated in the 12th century with wandering troubadours and knights in shining armor? Cynicism aside, where is there any proof that the injunction to love and be loved obligates us to endure the suffering we go through in the name of love? A less pragmatic view holds that romantic love is innate, an undeniable aspect of what makes us human. If love were simply a mass hallucination, one which sprang up when civilized societies first had time to indulge in flowery prose, wouldn't it have fizzled out long ago? But it hasn't, and today love is more widespread than ever. A recent study coordinated by anthropologists at the University of Nevada and Tulane University shows romantic love is a universal phenomenon that exists in at least 147 of 166 cultures studied. It may look different, but just because the indigenous love-struck don't have the resources for candy and flowers, doesn't mean romance is absent. In many cultures, romantic love and marriage don't even go together, the latter serving mainly to cement territorial agreements or business interests. But love pops up anyway, and sometimes in all the wrong places.

Until recently, hard core scientists have avoided getting on board this debate, preferring instead to leave the task of understanding human emotions to the softer sciences: psychology, sociology, anthropology. The reason for this reluctance is that love and the emotions are not easily analyzed and dissected, and science requires precise measurement to show a phenomenon is "real." Love falls well outside what has been the limit of the reigning paradigm of reductionism, which strictly distinguishes between mind and body, emotions and physiology. But all this is changing. Scientists across a broad range of disciplines have had a change of heart about love. One reason is women have entered the scientific arena and are less willing than their male counterparts to regard human emotions as unfit for the laboratory. AIDS, too, prompts that we try to understand this force that potentially binds couples faithfully and discourages casual sex. Then there's the "paradigm shift," a change that many perceive occurring in the mass consciousness of our world, which has its roots in quantum physics and is shaping how we view reality at all levels of our culture. With it comes the emerging belief that nothing exists in a vacuum, that even as objective observers we contribute to the definition of what is "real." As the paradigm shifts, we will see an affirmation of the interconnectedness of mind and body, as well as all of life.

Today, the new research coming from the biological sciences--neurophysiology, biochemistry and psychopharmacology (the study of the body's own natural drugs)--forces us to look at this most common yet mysterious of human experiences with new respect. Mounting evidence shows that biochemistry underlies our emotional behavior throughout every stage of human love and intimacy. From that very first skipped heartbeat, we are literally awash in natural drugs, produced in the brain as well as glands and organs throughout the body, which regulate the emotional states we experience.

A most noticeable effect of this biochemical phenomenon is the "love buzz," the natural high we feel when we first fall in love. In *Anatomy of Love*, Dr. Helen Fisher explains how many of the chemicals coursing through the blood of the newly smitten are cousins of the amphetamines. Phenylethylamine (PEA) gives us that silly smile we might flash at a total stranger, while dopamine helps us choose between potential mates and gives us a heightened response to one specific individual. Norepinephrine spurts from the adrenal glands to provide the rush of excitement and anticipation we experience when thinking of that special person. Once we're hooked, our bodies become flooded with monoamines, chemicals which cause the pupils to dilate, giving lovers that dewy-eyed, come-hither look.

Together, this panoply of chemicals makes our hearts pump faster to send blood rushing to the face and to stimulate sweat glands that produce that moist "glow" people have when they're newly in love. The oil glands in the scalp are also triggered, which gives the hair extra shine and creates a halo-like effect. But the high is short-lived, and it soon takes more and more of the biochemicals to produce the love buzz. In fact, so addictive is this chemical high, that it creates romance junkies, people who crave the intoxication of falling in love and move frantically from affair to affair just for the rush.

Fortunately, nature's design has provided an alternative and saner option, once the love buzz has begun to fade. Behavior in more long-term relationships is supported by other kinds of biochemicals, most notably, the endorphins, which are secreted by the pituitary gland, as well as by sex glands, and even throughout the gastrointestinal system. Discovered as the body's own natural morphine, the endorphins are natural pain killers, those happy juices that sustain long distance runners to reach their goal, an ideal chemical to support long-term marriages. Unlike the amphetamines, the endorphins have a soothing and stabilizing effect, fostering intimacy and bonding over time. They, too, are addictive, causing us to repeat behaviors for which they are the reward, such sexual intimacy and family bonding between parents and children, brothers and sisters.

So, if love is innate, a hardwired biological fact, the question then begs: Are we all bound by biological determinism to be prisoners of love, ruled by our passions and denied the freedom to choose otherwise? No, says neurobiologist Candace Pert, who, in her 1997 book, *Molecules of Emotion*, describes how our behavior and our biochemicals are intricately intertwined.

"It's really a two-way street," she explains. "Depressing thoughts or toxic repressed emotions interrupt chemical pathways and can shut down the natural flow which regulates our systems for overall health. Then, our emotions affect our biochemicals to produce different physiologic states and behaviors. There's a feedback loop that operates both ways, making our behavior and our biochemistry mutually interrelated and interdependent."

And this raises one further question: If we are not biologically determined to love, then why, as a species, have we evolved such elaborate systems to support this behavior? What advantage could it possibly give us?

The answer comes both from the hard and the soft sciences. The connection between our physiology and our emotions is best explored through a new branch of science, psychoneuroimmunology, or PNI, the study of how our feelings and thoughts impact our immune systems. According to Candace Pert, one of PNI's founders, the biochemicals of emotion directly communicate with our immune system, and visa versa, through a "psychosomatic network" to bring about health or disease.

In *Love and Survival: The Scientific Basis for the Healing Power of Love and Intimacy*, author/doctor Dean Ornish documents the many studies done by epidemiologist (researchers who study population trends) which have shown that people who are involved in satisfying, intimate relationships enjoy better health than those who are isolated and alone. Ornish draws the conclusion that we live longer and healthier, as individuals and as a species, when we have love in our lives.

So maybe it's not a matter, as Darwin would have it, of survival of the fittest--the most competitive and the toughest--but survival of the most loving and intimate. Then, what love has to do with it is more than just a thrilling ride, a biochemical rush, but a matter of the continuing evolution of our species. Perhaps we should look at our world as one in which survival is not merely a matter of dog-eat-dog, but dog-love-dog, one where those who love the most live the longest and survive to pass on their genes to future generations. If that's the case, perhaps we should thank our ancestors for their romantic excesses, and forgive ourselves for our own. □

–Used with permission.

☐ Jealousy: Is it all Bad?

Maria Manuela

Luisa always thought that jealousy was crazy. "Maybe it started when my cousin Marta got married when I was fourteen. I remember Johnny and her going out as boyfriend and girlfriend. Johnny was very nice with everybody, polite and funny. But as soon as they got married, he changed completely."

He didn't let Marta go anywhere or talk to anybody. "At a picnic, Johnny kept shouting at her for talking to different guys, even though most of them were married, too. After the picnic, my sister and I stopped over to drop off some plastic ware and found her crying and bleeding. He hadn't hit her as we first thought, but Marta had gotten so frustrated at his screaming at her, she punched her hand through a window. I'll never forget Johnny's face as we loaded her into the car to get her checked over at a hospital. He just smiled, as if it somehow proved him right."

Because of that, Luisa always said she'd never go out with a jealous man. But when she was a senior in high school, she met Ricky. For the first three months, she thought she was in heaven, but by the fourth month Ricky started acting strange. "After that, I don't remember a single day where we could go three hours without an argument. At the time, I had lots of friends from classes and from sports. Whenever they saw me, they all said 'hi.' But that was all it took. Soon people started telling me they weren't going to say hello to me anymore, because whenever they did Ricky got mad."

Ricky was a very jealous person. "He told me if I wore shorts or tight clothes and a guy would look at me, he would break his nose. Another time, we went to a restaurant, and I needed to use a pay phone. The one inside was broken, so I started to look around outside. I spotted one across the way, but before I could tell Ricky he started shouting, 'Why the hell do you have to look at that guy?' and walked away. I didn't know what he was talking about. I looked back at the phones and saw a couple next to them in a corner. I didn't know if that was who he was talking about, but I didn't see anyone else there. Because of all this I started isolating myself from everybody except my family and Ricky."

The last straw was on prom night. "We were dancing, and I was daydreaming, and without noticing it, I looked away. All of a sudden, Ricky dropped my hand, stopped dancing and walked away. I asked him what was wrong and he answered, loudly, 'You know what's wrong. I wish you would at least respect me and not look at other guys when I'm with you.'

"I had no idea who he meant. Everyone was looking, so I told him I was leaving. He followed me to the parking lot and continued to shout. Finally, some police came over and asked if I was alright. That was my cue to escape. I later found out he was upset because one of my male friends was dancing with his girlfriend too close to me."

After that, as you can imagine, Luisa had a real allergy to jealousy. Imagine her surprise, then, when she found jealousy creeping into her own behavior in her marriage.

"It started when my husband, who I married in college, got a job in another city. The plan was for him to find a house, and then I'd come later. But somehow things didn't feel as smooth as I wanted. The thought of him alone in a new place provoked not pity, but fear. I thought of him meeting strangers in bars. The first weekend he came home to visit he seemed distant. My mind started doing strange things. It erupted at a party in the neighborhood. He spent quite a lot of time talking to a young woman that worked in his old building. On the drive home, I confronted him. He accused me of being jealous. I denied it."

The next night as she put him on a plane, she began to freak out. "How could I trust him? I thought of making phone calls at odd hours to his hotel room to see whether he was there. I confess I did call once, though I hung up after the first ring. I also worried every time I called him at a normal hour and he was out. Then it hit me: What's so wrong with being jealous anyway?"

Nothing, according to San Diego State sociologist Gordon Clanton, who wrote the book on jealousy (Jealousy, University Press of America, 1980). What the problem is about is . . . when you feel it and what you do about it. Jealousy got a bad name in the 1960s, when freedom and sexual experimentation were in their heyday. Previously, believe it or not, jealousy was seen as a sign of love.

Nearly everyone feels jealous at some time, say psychologists and sociologists. It is based on the fear of losing someone you love. In actuality, jealousy generally decreases after people marry, according to a longitudinal study by R.D. Storaasli and H. Markman, who tracked 130 couples through dating, engagement, marriage and childbirth. This is undoubtedly because they feel more secure in their relationship. However, should insecurity pop up again for other reasons, psychologists say, jealousy can as well. Just ask Luisa.

"I'm not proud of what I felt or what I almost (and actually once) did," she says. "But I did bring it up, and amazingly my husband understood. That's why I married him. Of course, it helped to bring it up in the right way. As my problem, not his. I owe that to Ricky, who certainly taught me what not to do."

"There's two big questions about jealousy: Number one, is it OK?, and number two, can it be controlled? The answer to both is yes," says Clanton. He suggests we think of jealousy as a continuum. At one end is what he calls normal jealousy, the protective feelings that arise from a situation that is threatening to the relationship. On the other side is neurotic jealousy, which is triggered when a person is already insecure.

"Quite often, it's difficult between a real and imagined threat. Insecure people have an even tougher time distinguishing," he continues. That's why communicating about jealousy is so important. However, our judgements about jealousy nowadays get in the way. It is all seen as a neurotic form of possessiveness, especially if it's the other person doing it.

Clanton notes that the accused person generally sees the issue in terms of trust. "They feel that their partner should trust them no matter what. That's generally pretty unreasonable."

"The jealous person is usually the one who asks the second question," notes Clanton. "They often feel that because they are feeling a strong emotion they should let it out, preferably whenever they want. They ask how can I control this strong an emotion? I ask them if they were in a car having an argument, and the car got pulled over by the cops, would they stop the argument? Nearly everybody would. Of course, they would go right back to the argument once the police left. But it illustrates the point that all emotions are controllable."

Jealousy can also erupt in non-sexual situations. One common situation is with the advent of a new baby. The husband may become jealous of all the attention the baby it getting. Jealousy may also be a factor in many in-law tensions.

In essence, there are two factors: perception and behavior. Is what you perceive a real threat or is it pretty farfetched? Are your actions appropriate, or are they extreme? Violent abusers in domestic cases are often guilty of both, according to C.S. Feazell and associates who did a major study in 1984. On the other hand, the average spouse, boyfriend or girlfriend should probably be cut a little slack. Blaming people for their jealousy just tends to send it underground where it can linger and fester. And quite often, a guilty philanderer might be quick to accuse the victim of jealousy. Which is all the more reason to bring normal jealousy back out in the open.

Psychologists often recommend something like the following approach: "I'm feeling jealous and I don't want to. Could you explain what is going on with . . ." That is usually enough to solve most problems.

People with a more serious problem might want to seek help in sorting it out. According to a 1987 study by psychologist Elaine Baxter, possessiveness, jealousy and other perceived threats to autonomy were contributing reasons for breaking up in 27% to 30% of relationships. Not all of those cases are because of excessive jealousy. But many people are also hyper-sensitive to perceived jealousies. Which is all the more reason for talking things out. □

–Used with permission.

DEFINING TERMS

Endorphins

Psychoneuroimmunology (PNI)

Destructive Jealousy

WHAT DO YOU THINK?

1. How does knowing about the "chemistry" of love affect your perception of it?

2. What, if anything, would be wrong with engaging in a series of short-lived marriages based on romantic love? Why?

3. In real life, how can you distinguish good from bad jealousy? Give examples.

 **VIDEO VIEWER:**

Rent "Moonstruck." List all the emotions felt by the various characters. Which emotions are viewed positively, which negatively? Why?

4. How do you know if someone is "the right one"?

☺ **MEDIA WATCHER:**

On sitcoms, which emotions are expressed, and which repressed? Which are comforted and which criticized?

5. Make two lists: (1) the qualities of person who would be your perfect date, and (2) the qualities you would desire in a marriage partner. Put one list in each column on this page.

Module Eight

Types of Love

---

*T*he word "love" has a lot to do. Generally, the more we talk about a certain idea, the more words we develop to describe it. It's said that Eskimos have some thirty or more words for snow. Not so with love. We use the same tired word to describe our intense passion for a lover, as our addiction to ice cream. We use the same word to describe our feelings for our lovers as our mothers and our pets. Perhaps it would be useful to know what we are talking about?

Psychologist Robert Sternberg has identified three components of love: intimacy, passion, and commitment. Each aspect involves different parts of the self, namely the emotional, biological, and mental. Depending on the presence and strength of each element in a particular relationship, we can describe the different kinds of love people feel.

Aspects of love

*I*ntimacy is described by Sternberg as a feeling of deep attachment, closeness and warmth toward another. We usually enjoy being with them, and understand and empathize with them, accepting their faults and failures and appreciating the good qualities. We trust them. Feelings of intimacy generally take a long time to develop. They develop because we are able to feel vulnerable with the other, yet trust them not to hurt us.

Passion is a feeling of strong physical attraction, which is largely based on the biological drive for sex. Feelings of strong passion that are gratified tend to decline in intensity because the novelty wears off, and because the biological stimulators, the hormones, decrease. A love relationship will end when the passion decreases if feelings of attachment, empathy and understanding have not developed.

Commitment is a conscious decision to maintain a relationship whether for life or for a certain period of time. It is a key to stability in relationships, because feelings tend to fluctuate. Commitment may involve a dedication to the relationship simply because of the other aspects of love, or because of internal needs, values or morals, or external constraints like social or economic pressures.

Chapter Preview

Aspects of Love

Types of Love

Styles of Love

Article: "Some Enchanted Evening"

Article: "Lovers or Friends"

Types of love

Liking is the basic feeling in friendship. It is based on warmth, closeness and even attachment, but there is no sexual attraction or long-term commitment. Close cross-sex friendships are not uncommon, but they can be sticky if attraction develops, or outsiders become suspicious.

Romantic Love is a combination of intimacy and passion. This type of love is common while in high school or college, and has become more prevalent in other age groups as well. It, however, does not include commitment, either because one or more partners feels too young, or the partners feel too different, or even that one feels disillusioned with love in some way.

Infatuation is a kind of love characterized by intense physical attraction. It is "love at first sight" and tends to be obsessive, especially when it is not returned. The object of these feelings tends to be idealized, and shortcomings are minimized or even ignored. Because of its unrealistic nature, infatuation does not include real intimacy or commitment. Getting to know the person better often diminishes the feelings, as reality sets in.

Empty Love relationships occur when people remain committed despite a lack of intimacy or passion for their partner. The major reason for continuing the relationship is duty, loyalty, dependence or gratitude. One common example is couples who remain together for the sake of their children. Another is in long-term relationships where the feelings have died, but the couple remains together for economic reasons. Still another may occur when one partner or both have developed romantic relationships outside the marriage.

Companionate Love relationships develop when passion is diminished, but the sense of attachment and commitment remain. It is often characteristic of elderly couples, but can occur when people marry for friendship or companionship. Most people in this kind of relationship report themselves as being quite satisfied. Some, however, stray looking for romance or lost youth.

Fatuous Love is a kind of love that involves both passion and commitment, without real intimacy. This can occur when people become involved very quickly, or when they lack the ability to develop empathy and understanding with each other. This can happen in rebound relationships, long-distance relationships or other situations where normal constraints do not occur to slow down and develop the relationship.

Consummate Love is a complete kind of love, characterized by all three components of love. The relationship tends to be secure and gratifying. Although passion may diminish with age, it does not disappear altogether. In fact, attachment and commitment often increase as the time and energy devoted to the relationship make it more and more irreplaceable.

Some experts feel that Sternberg's typology of love is simplistic. They point to a history of research that contains five or six different types of love that may be blended together in each person's feelings. The following discussion is based in part on Lasswell and Lobsenz's (1980) *Styles of Loving*.

Styles of Love

According to Lasswell and Lobsenz, lovers may blend any combination of the following styles of loving, but they tend to predominantly fit into one or two categories in most cases

Erotic love: This is the romantic, erotic love that is portrayed in songs and movies. Characterized by strong emotion, intense attraction, it can arouse joy, ecstasy, and exhilaration. It can also arouse fear, jealousy and depression if feelings are not mutual or are even so suspected. There are strong elements of sexual attraction, physiological manifestations like palpitations of the heart, trembling, breathlessness, and a certain amount of idealization of the love object.

Friendly love: This type of love is based on feelings of friendship. Ease of communication, similarity of interest, and a sense of compatibility contribute to feelings of respect and liking for the other person. Liking in a relationship brings a certain relaxation and comfort that affords security and dissolves tension.

Playful love: Playful love sees love as a game or challenge. There are probably elements of competitiveness in most persons that may surface in love relationships. Certainly the problem of getting one's needs met is more complex when there is another to think about, and playful love seeks to make sure one gets one's way through teasing, flirtation, game-playing. In modern American culture, this aspect is often seen as manipulative, but in other cultures it is often seen as a necessary means of keeping a relationship interesting, balanced, and satisfying to both partners. Playful lovers, however, tend to be more focused on the excitement and challenge of love, and find commitment difficult and uninteresting.

Dependent Love: This type of love develops when one feels that one's needs are met by a particular person. In its simplest form, it is the kind of love a baby feels for the mother who feeds, clothes, and holds her. It is also the kind of love that develops between adults if they have intense needs that have been denied in the past. This may occur because the lover is a dependent type of personality or simply because their partner brings out a part of the personality they are not in touch with, as when a hard-working man falls for a woman who

recognizes his capacity to be a playful, uninhibited lover. Dependent lovers can be extremely possessive and jealous.

Pragmatic love: The pragmatic lover focuses on the practical aspects of a relationship, and on the desired qualities of a prospective partner. Called "love with a shopping list," this type of love is very realistic, and people who love in this manner know exactly what type of person they want, and are willing to wait until they find him or her. Feelings fade, according to this type of lover, but if the relationship is based on a good match of desired qualities, stability is more likely.

Altruistic love: This is defined as an unselfish concern for the well-being of another, the investment of one's emotions and energies in caring for another individual and seeking what is best for them. By nurturing and doing all that one can to make the other happy, the lover finds meaning and fulfillment. This kind of love blends respect and caring for the person with voluntarily taking a responsibility to give to the other whenever one can. At its best, this style of love engenders no feelings of martyrdom or being put upon. Rather it seems to rest in a genuine belief in giving, and a deep reservoir of loving kindness. This kind of unselfish love occurs far less in real life than might be imagined. Few people have the emotional strength to be so giving, and even if they do they may have hidden agendas about some form of "repayment." Nowadays, some even may suspect that this form of loving is "co-dependent." Nevertheless, many people do have elements of this style in their own form of love. □

References

Laswell, Marcia & Norman Lobsenz. 1980. *Styles of loving: Why you love the way you do.* Garden City, NY: Ballantine.

Lee, J.A. 1973. *The color of love*. Toronto: New Press.

Sternberg, Robert. 1988. "Triangulating love." from R. Sternberg & M. Barnes, *The psychology of love*. New Haven, CT: Yale Press.

☐ Some Enchanted Evening: Romantic Illusions and Disillusions

Dr. Robert Manis

If you're like most people you believe in love at first sight. You believe that there's someone who is right for you, and while you know that no one is perfect, you believe this person is about as close as they come, and would never, never betray, hurt, let you down, or be grossly impolite to you. Well, welcome to the real world.

Most of us don't believe in Santa Claus, but we do believe in the perfect relationship. We may never have experienced it, but we're sure it's out there. All our past relationships, well, maybe we thought they were love, but now we realize they were just infatuation. But this new person, he or she is so incredible . . .

Call it the "Cinderella Complex." We each think that someday we can attract a Prince/Princess Charming who will somehow overlook our rags and impoverishment and will lift us right out of the doldrums into a magical world. And the funny thing is, it sometimes seems to work. We meet someone, fall in love and it's great. Then we find out they cheat, drink, belch, talk too little or too much, are too independent or too clingy, too sensitive or too insensitive, or something. Maybe we just get bored. Then we break up and start all over again. Maybe for a while we're disillusioned,

but we never realize that the reason we're disillusioned is that we were "illusioned" in the first place. The Romantic Illusion. The illusion that there's a nearly perfect someone out there who will solve all our problems, overlook all our faults, and not bring up any difficult problems of their own to bother us.

"I'm not like that," we say. "I know that I'm not perfect (though my faults aren't that bad), and I deserve somebody attractive and loving, and I'm willing to work out things together and even solve some of their problems if they need me to."

There's only one thing wrong with our protestations. Reality. Lack of it, that is. Somehow, when reality sets in we will discover they weren't as attractive or loving, or able to work things out or willing to let us solve their problems, or if they were, maybe they think we weren't attractive, loving, etc. Why does this happen? Is it possible that setting our expectations so high sets us up for a fall? Is it possible that under the throes of hormones and brain chemicals, we delude ourselves? It is possible that, like so many other things, life is less about fulfilling our dreams than filling our needs?

One part of the problem is what's called the "halo effect." Long recognized in organizational psychology, it is the factor that causes us to jump to conclusions about others' personalities. What the halo effect does is to cause us to attribute other positive aspects to a person on the basis of only one or two observed good qualities. It often causes employers to hire on the basis of looks or a good impression, and it causes lovers to idealize their love-objects.

Yet another factor is what we might call the "romance industry." This includes not just the publishers of romance novels, but the movie industry, music business, TV commercials, perfume makers, doll manufacturers, and everybody else trying to make a buck by stimulating our romantic desires. While no one can claim that the romantic mythology is new to our time, never before has it assaulted our eyes, ears and noses so powerfully.

Perhaps you could say we are brainwashed. Influenced by mind-altering drugs (our hormones), relentlessly pounded by repeated images, what happens to us fits brainwashing's description. So we become like in the song: "might as well face it, we're addicted to love."

Yet there is a solution to the cycle of illusion and disillusion. And obviously, the solution comes from a more realistic view of love. If love is not seen as a solution to the world's problems, an escape from the mundane, or a flight to heavenly realms; then love's reality need not plunge a person to the depths of despair. If the love or the lover we experience is less than ideal, it doesn't mean that either we or they are inadequate, only human. We are here on this earth just a short time, too short to waste in wallowing in judgment or self-pity. Love, no matter how fulfilling, can't change that fact. When we accept love's limitations, we can more fully embrace its joys.□

□ Lovers or Friends?

Susan Sanders

Maybe its happened to you. One night you're eating popcorn with your best buddy of the opposite sex, when suddenly you get a glint in your eye, as you notice just how cuddly you never noticed he or she could be. And admit it, you always wanted Mulder and Scully to get X-rated, not just X-filed. In the film "When Harry met Sally," Billy Crystal and Meg Ryan have a deep friendship for years, then suddenly

one night when they're both single and lonely, they fall into bed. It nearly ruins their friendship, but in the end, they realize they're the person each wants to see first thing in the morning and talk to before they go to bed. It doesn't hurt that Billy has the best sense of humor this side of Philadelphia, and Meg Ryan is cuter than a silver button.

With all the barriers long since fallen about men and women hanging out together, and with no rules, and all the craziness out there in Dating Land, love with your best friend can seem like a good idea. And of course, after what happened to Julia Roberts in "My Best Friend's Wedding," you might not want to wait too long. Still, turning a friend into a lover can be a big risk as well.

Jackie and Phil were good friends at work, and starting out just talking on breaks. They were very comfortable talking to each other about just about anything. Eventually Phil asked her over ho his house to watch the Super Bowl. Jackie says, "I'm not much of a football fan, so I was being my normal self, as I am around friends, and I was making fun of the players and imitating the dances they do when the team scores a touchdown. If this had been an actual date I would never have done that. I would have just sat there and acted like I enjoyed the game."

They had a great time, and started spending time together. After months of hanging out together things to a sudden turn. Jackie continues," I was watching home movies at his house, when we began to wrestle. We were hitting and tackling each other, we he caught me by surprise and we started to kiss. It was completely spontaneous on both our parts."

"The rest is history," Phil chimes in. They are planning on getting married next year. Phil felt that being good friends first made it easier. "There was never any pressure to dress up or put on our best behaviors."

"I'd advise people to stop looking for a mate and just go out and have fun," Jackie adds, "Love will find you, you don't need to search for it."

But things don't always run so smoothly. Dana has been in a relationship with Mitchell for four years. She characterizes it as one of hard work. "We have a terrible time communicating, and I don't feel comfortable telling him all the things that I feel he should know."

On the other hand, she has a best friend Leon, with whom the communication is great. "Just the other night, I called him to say 'hi' and we were on the phone for four hours. Every time I told him I had to go, we would get onto another subject. We have the same spiritual and religious beliefs and enjoy the same types of outdoor activities. We always have a great time together."

On two occasions, Leon and Dana crossed over the line and became intimate. Once was when she and Mitchell had briefly broken up. "Both times we were out drinking all night and went home together. I can honestly say that neither of us have regrets, but I'm still not sure how I feel about the situation. The sex was neither bad, nor good, but in retrospect it was a little weird for me. I'm glad that it hasn't ruined our friendship, but I do worry a little about it.

"I have fantasized on several occasions what it would be like to be married to a person I am compatible with on so many levels, but one. Sex may not be the key to good relationships, but it does help. Sometimes I wish we lived in a polygamous society. I'd marry Mitchell and Leon both. All my needs would be met between the two of them."

Jim H. tells a different story. "I've been thinking of my female buddies I had in the past. The vast majority of the time we never crossed that line and became lovers. I've learned all about pain and loss in friendships that fell out

because of sex. The worst was with Paula. We were best friends and I guess I always was a little in love with her, because she was so sweet and funny. Finally, I started not being able to stand it, being so close to her all the time and not being able to touch her.

"I brought it up after buying her dinner, and taking her for a long walk. I guess her reaction was shock, and I was surprised by her adamant rejection. It really hurt me. I had been planning for a way to broach the subject for days and I was really crushed. I ended up getting mad, and walking off. After that she wouldn't talk to me. She just said that she didn't feel comfortable with me as friends, because she knew I wanted more. I think she was also hurt by how angry I got, and maybe it scared her.

"I really missed the friendship and wished I could go back in the past and change what went wrong, but I can't. I feel that too many times friendships are destroyed because the male or the female can't control themselves."

But that hasn't stopped him from having close female friends. "Today, my best friend is a woman and we support each other through our trials and tribulations. When we talk on the phone, we always say 'love you' at the end of the call and when she forgets to say it, I miss it. But that doesn't happen hardly at all. I love the friendship we share, and there is no doubt in my mind we will always stay only friends."

That of course is the big risk. That by wanting more you may end up with less. Not only losing a potential lover, but losing a close friend. But how can you know whether to take that big chance? Here are a few questions to ask yourself:

♦ **First, ask yourself why.** Are you stuck in a dating drought? Is your biological clock ticking with no one to turn you off (or on)? Are you in a low - self - esteem mode, where asking a new girl (or guy) out seems like jumping off the Hoover Dam? If you have no better reason, you'll probably regret risking your friendship impulsively.

◆ **Second, ask why not?** Remember why you limited yourself to friendship in the first place. Was one of you in a relationship? Did you see flaws you knew you couldn't handle? Did your religion or values differ too much? Was there just no attraction? Now ask yourself if that reason has changed. People grow up, and leopards do change their spots. If the tomboyish girl next door has turned into a real woman, or the perennially starving artist has gone out and gotten a real job, they just might be relationship material. Regrets can happen from opportunities NOT taken as well, so don't make the mistake of keeping someone in a box long after they've outgrown it.

◆**Are you sure it's the right thing?** It might be a good idea to start out with some long talks. You run a bigger risk than if you strike out with someone you don't know as well. If that doesn't work out, you can simply stop seeing her or him. But if this doesn't work, ask yourself if your friendship will be shot? And it's important not to get your expectations up before that long talk.

◆**Is it love or lust?** Probably most friendships with the opposite sex have an element of attraction in them. It's true that you see them at their worst--when they're hung over New Year's Day, covered in grease from fixing the truck, or sick with the flu--but you also see them at their best, carefree and natural. And remember that the understanding way in which he listens to your problems may vanish when the problems are about him.

Carlo and Jenny have been friends for years and talk on the phone every few days. "One night she called me up and asked me to come over. I said no because I didn't want to lose our friendship. Right now we can talk about anything. But the minute you sleep with somebody you lose your objectivity."

◆**How are your communication skills?** Both of yours, that is. You may need them if the transition from friends to lovers gets somewhat rocky. People have different expectations from friends than they do from lovers and you may be surprised to find out what they are. It pays to be thorough in sorting out your new relationship. Do you have the skills to do it, and does the other person? If not, you may want to back off.

◆**What's your back-up plan?** Before you go too far, it might be wise to talk about what will happen if things don't work out. Make an agreement to talk everything out so that you can still be friends. And make an agreement not to be attached to it working. If you can do so, even if the relationship doesn't last, the friendship can. And if it doesn't, you may have added a layer of depth, richness and caring beyond what was there before. Plus you'll have plenty to laugh about for years in the future. □

–Used with permission.

DEFINING TERMS

Intimacy

Passion

Infatuation

Cinderella Complex

Halo Effect

WHAT DO YOU THINK?

1. What makes you feel close to another person?

2. What style of love do you enact? What about your partner(s)? How does it work?

3. Psychologist Erich Fromm suggested that love is better thought of as a "giving" behavior, rather than a feeling that comes and goes. Which is better? Why?

4. Have you ever considered turning a friend into a lover? What happened?

 **VIDEO VIEWER:**

Rent "Crossing Delancey Street" or "When Harry Met Sally." What do these films say about preconceptions about potential partners? About friends and lovers?

☺ **MEDIA WATCHER:**

On what basis do TV characters fall in love? Are they the right reasons? Give examples.

Module Nine

What Is Intimacy?

*I*ntimacy is one of those things like motherhood and apple pie, that everybody believes in, or at any rate, says they do. Although people may disagree about what constitutes intimacy and how to attain it, few disagree that intimacy is a desirable, significant, or even critical ingredient in creating a happy life. Recent scientific research has confirmed that people who have close personal connections tend to be healthier, live longer, and feel happier than those lacking. Yet it is strange to think that, like many aspects of modern relationships, intimacy was not even an ideal in the Western World five hundred years ago, and even today is fully achieved rather infrequently. Many men, for example, still think of intimacy as meaning sex, and other than that view talking about it as a "girl thing."

*I*n non-western countries, the invisibility of intimacy as a concept is striking. Obviously, in poor countries, the struggle for survival takes precedence over higher-order needs like affection and intimacy, but even in a wealthy nation like Japan, intimacy has never been an explicit goal or norm. In fact, a brief look at Japan yields a clue to understanding the rise of intimacy. Japan is a densely-populated, closely knit society that is governed socially by a complex set of rituals that regulate conduct, affirm solidarity, and protect personal identity. Cross-cultural studies have shown Japan to be one of the most group-oriented societies.

By contrast, the United States is the most individualistic culture in the world, and other Western societies are not far behind. Sociological studies since Emile Durkheim's *Suicide* (1893) have shown that persons in individualistic societies tend to be much more vulnerable to loneliness than in other societies. British sociologist Anthony Giddens suggests the rise of intimacy as a concern in personal life is directly related to individualism and to the need for feeling in a highly mechanized, unfeeling society. Intimacy seems to provide a depth of feeling that attempts to replace a

Chapter Preview:

Overview of Intimacy

Types of Intimacy

Deepening Intimacy

Article: "Touch: Not Just a Girl Thing Anymore"

Article: "Intimacy: The Art of Working Out Your Relationships"

generalized decrease in feeling and closeness in society as a whole.

Types of Intimacy

There are obviously different types of intimacy. Probably the simplest way to cut the pie is to divide intimacy into two main parts: physical and emotional intimacy. The physical aspect may be further divided into two pieces: sexual and non-sexual. Physical intimacy is based on touch: sexual touching which leads to increased physical and emotional response on the part of both partners, and non-sexual touching which is seen as an expression of love with or without any anticipation of further emotional response. Emotional intimacy is the feeling of closeness. Like other forms of physical stimulation, the power of the sexual touching tends to decrease somewhat over time, as the body becomes acclimated to the sensations. This is one reason that the excitement of holding hands is soon replaced by kissing, then, petting, then intercourse. It is also why lovers sometimes become bored with sex and seek to rekindle their excitement with new partners.

Deepening Intimacy

This effect is much less pronounced for non-sexual touching, and in fact, works in the opposite direction with emotional intimacy. Emotional intimacy takes time to develop and builds slowly. Emotions can be more hidden, and to develop closeness means to remove walls that protect our feelings from being hurt. We are vulnerable, able to be hurt, exposed, shamed. This requires us to feel a certain trust before we will take that risk. Giddens notes a curious dynamic: we learn to trust when our vulnerability is not exploited, and our risk proves safe. So we are reluctant to risk, but it is the only way to develop trust. Thomas Scheff says that this is why intimacy develops slowly. People test the waters by revealing small secrets first, then if successful, gradually remove their masks. The good news is that emotional intimacy has no limits, at least theoretically, because honest risking can continue throughout a marriage or relationship. In fact, one school of marriage counseling suggests total and absolute honesty for long-term couples as a way of overcoming boredom and renewing intimacy. □

References

Durkheim, Emile. 1951[1893]. *Suicide.* New York: Free Press.

Giddens, Anthony. 1990. *Consequences of modernity.* Cambridge, UK: Polity Press.

Hatfield, Elaine & Richard Rapson. 1993. *Love, sex and intimacy.* New York: Harper Collins.

Hendricks, Gay & Kathlyn Hendricks. 1993. *Centering and the art of intimacy.* New York: Fireside.

❑ Touch: Not Just a Girl Thing Anymore

Lance Karlson

Touch is a funny thing for guys--you have only to look at a football game to see it--steroid-pumped giants crashing and thrashing at each other and occasionally slapping each other's butts in triumph. Or look at *Cheers* or *Seinfield,* the two most popular TV shows of the 80's and 90's. (Think about Norm and Cliff's A-frame hugs, or Jerry & George's inhibited love-pats.)   But it's not just homophobia.   Men are demonstrably less physically affectionate than women. A study of 1500 men and women by Michael McGill of Southern Methodist University found men to be less expressive of their emotions both physically and emotionally.

But that doesn't mean it's genetic. Most social scientists believe the way children are brought up accounts for most of the difference. Female children are cuddled more starting at birth. But as they get older, the differences get even greater--daughters receive considerably more affection than sons. Soon sons want less affection; they're being taught that hugging and smooching aren't manly. However, cross-cultural evidence shows it need not be that way. A traveler to a Middle Eastern or Asian country might be surprised to see two men walking down the street holding hands. Or consider the custom of the French, always kissing each other on both cheeks. In fact, Americans may well be one of the least touchy-feely cultures.

The truth is that touch is healthy, even necessary for life. As the psychologist Harry Harlow noted in his famous experiments with monkeys in the 1950s, touch-deprived monkeys tend to get depressed and sicken easier than

normal monkeys. We now know the reason why: According to Dr. Candace Pert, the discoverer of endorphins and the author of *Molecules of Emotions*, touch causes the release of many different neuropeptides, the chemical links between the body and the brain, that cause the body to be flooded with good emotions. In turn, these good emotions trigger the release of other neuropeptides that boost or support the immune system and other vital functions. It turns out that touch makes good sense.

Touch is often defined by sociologists and psychologists as a form of "non-verbal communication." While that's certainly true, it's a bit of an understatement. No words can convey the power of an embrace to succor a grieving friend, comfort a frightened child, or let a person know that you love them. Actions speak louder than words, we know from experience. And they're harder to fake as well. Which is why a simple embrace can mean so much at the right time.

Touch is generally not an issue when couples fall in love. Both partners generally are excited by each other's touch and respond to each other's excitement. But over time differences often emerge. Some are due to gender differences, but others to family backgrounds. Northern European families tend to touch least, Southern European and other ethnic families tend to touch more.   But differences may be specific; a particular family may be more or less touch oriented than another. Even identical twins can sometimes vary in how much they tend to reach out to be touched.   The problem is that once the differences start to emerge in a relationship, partners can feel confused: one feels neglected, the other might feel smothered.

It can be disturbing when one person wants much more affection than the other is willing to give or receive. It is easy to think that he or she "doesn't love me anymore." Usually, that's jumping to a conclusion. Most likely each member of the couple has reverted to their pre-partnering behavior. Additionally, each partner may have a different way of communicating. Recent research points to three distinct styles of perception and communication. Some people respond primarily to verbal messages, others to visual cues, and still others to kinesthetic or feeling cues. A person of the first variety, might speak and respond most to words of love. The second type of person may be more open to visible demonstrations of love, like doing a favor or buying a gift. The third type is most convinced by an actual embrace. Nothing conclusive has been demonstrated so far, but it may be that men in our society are more likely to be in the first two categories than are women.

Nevertheless, a person who isn't getting the physical affection he or she needs is likely to feel hurt and neglected. One common and vicious cycle therapists observe frequently is when a woman feels she isn't getting the affection she needs, she may turn off sexually. Now he may feel hurt and angry and withdraw even further, which puts off the woman even more. You can see where that's going to end up! The important thing to realize is that such a vicious cycle can easily be reversed by the simple act of increasing non-sexual affection. In this more positive cycle, increased affection leads the woman to feel better, and feeling better, she becomes more interested in connecting sexually, which makes her man feel better.

Another common dynamic that has self-fulfilling tendencies is what's been called the "two-step." Named after a kind of partner dance, it refers to the tendency of one person to back off when the other advances. Some people are more comfortable as the pursuer in a relationship and others feel better as the pursued. Or the couple may have simply gotten comfortable in a pattern of who pursues whom. The problem is that if one person is always the pursuer of affection they may feel dissatisfied, or alternatively if one person is always being pursued they may feel smothered.

This too, can become a vicious cycle. The way to change it is for either partner to reverse the dynamic. Usually, the best bet, though is for the pursuer to stop and wait until he or she gets pursued. This can do wonders for the self-esteem if it works, but there's a risk involved. "What if they don't pursue me?"

What can you do to resolve differences about touch? Myron Benton gives a number of suggestions. First, you must communicate, because you can't assume your partner knows, if you don't spell it out. You should also reinforce his behavior by letting him know how good it feels.

Don't assume the other person likes what you do. Some might like soft caresses, other a firm grasp--so communicate about that, too. Explore different forms of touch, like massage. As a child, I used to enjoy when my grandfather would scratch my back with a little wooden backscratcher shaped like an arm and hand. Benton also recommends the "pinkie-cuddle," intertwining the little fingers as a form of hand holding, that's more playful and less constrictive. It's especially well suited for those who are sensitive about public displays of affection.

The good news is that men are becoming more and more aware of the power of touch. Men are learning its OK to be affectionate even with each other. One man I knew years ago, from a strong military background, burst into tears when he realized he hadn't hugged his son for nearly ten years. That's much less likely nowadays. Even on the football field you're likely to see grown men embracing in joy and in consolation.□

–Used with permission.

❏ Intimacy: The Art of Working Out Your Relationships

Lori H. Gordon, Ph.D.

Confusion. Hurt. Silence. Missed opportunity. It is one of the ironies of modern life that many couples today are living together as complete strangers. Or worse, in great unhappiness. The data on divorce lead us to conclude that intimate relationships have been falling apart for the last 20 years or so. The truth is that couples have never learned reliably how to sustain pleasure in intimate relationships. The difference is it never mattered so much before.

Here at the close of the 20th century we have the luxury of living in splendid isolation. Unlike in more "primitive" cultures, most Americans no longer live as part of a large family or community where we develop a sense of comfort and safety, a network of people to confide in, to feel at home with. This, I have come to believe, is what has drawn many people into cults, the need to feel part of a bonded community, where there is a sense of being at home emotionally as well as physically. Our culture provides for meeting all other needs, especially the need for autonomy, but not for intimacy. Within this framework, couples today must provide for each other more of the emotional needs that a larger community used to furnish.

Compounding the wide-scale deprivation of intimacy we actually experience, our cultural talent for commercialization has separated out sex from intimacy. In fact, intimacy involves both emotional and physical closeness and openness. But we wind up confusing the two and end up feeling betrayed or used when, as often happens, we fail to satisfy our need for closeness in sex.

Shifts in our general views about what makes life worth living have also contributed to a new demand for intimacy. For many generations the answer lay in a productive life of work and service in which the reward of happiness would be ours, in heaven. That belief has broken down. People want happiness here and now. And they want it most in their intimate relationships.

Here, it's clear, we are unlikely to find it easily. Couples today are struggling with something new to build relationships based on genuine feelings of equality. As a result, we are without role models for the very relationships we need. And rare were the parents who modeled intimacy for us; most were too busy struggling with survival requirements. Yet the quality of our closest relationships is often what gives life its primary meaning.

Intimacy, I have come to believe, is not just a psychological fad, a rallying cry of contemporary couples. It is based on a deep biological need. Shortly after I began my career as a family therapist I was working in a residential treatment center where troubled teenage boys were sent by the courts. Through my work I began to discover what had been missing for these kids: They needed support and affection, the opportunity to express the range and intensity of their emotions. It was remarkable to discover their depth of need, their depth of pain over the lack of empathy from significant people in their lives.

It is only in the last 20 years that we recognize that infants need to be held and touched. We know that they cannot grow--they literally fail to thrive--unless they experience physical and emotional closeness with another human being. What we often don't realize is that that need for connection never goes away. It goes on throughout life. And in its absence, symptoms develop, from the angry acting out of the adolescent boys I saw to depression, addiction, and illness. In fact, researchers are just at the very beginning of understanding the relationship of widespread depression among women to problems in their marriages.

When I brought the boys together with their families through processes I had not learned about in graduate school, it transformed the therapy. There was change. For the adolescent boys, their problems were typically rooted in the often-troubled relationships between their parents. They lacked the nurturing environment they needed for healthy growth. What I realized was that to help the children I first had to help their parents. So I began to shift my focus to adults.

From my work in closely observing the interactions of hundreds of couples, I have come to recognize that most of what goes wrong in a relationship stems from hurt feelings. The disappointment couples experience is based on misunderstanding and misperception. We choose a partner hoping for a source of affection. love, and support, and, more than ever, a best friend. Finding such a partner is a wonderful and ecstatic experience the stage of illusion in relationships. it has been called.

To use this conceit, there then sets in the state of disillusion. We somehow don't get all that we had hoped for. He didn't do it just right. She didn't welcome you home; she was too busy with something else; maybe she didn't even look up. But we don't have the skills to work out the disappointments that occur. The disappointments, big and little, then determine the future course of the relationship.

If first there is illusion, and then disillusion, what follows is confusion. There is a great deal of unhappiness as each partner struggles to get the relationship to be what each of them needs or wants it to be. One partner will be telling the other what to do. One may be placating, in the expectation that he or she will eventually be rewarded by the other. Each partner uses his or her own familiar personal communication style.

Over the disappointment, the partners erect defenses against each other. They become guarded with each other. They stop confiding in each other. They wall off parts of themselves and withdraw emotionally from the relationship, often into other activities, other relationships. They can't talk without blaming, so they stop listening. They may be afraid that the relationship will never change but may not even know what they are afraid of. There is so much chaos that there is usually despair and depression. One partner may actually leave. Both may decide to stay with it but can't function. They live together in an emotional divorce.

Over the years of working with couples, I have developed an effective way to help them arrive at a relationship they can both be happy with. I may not offer them therapy. I find that what couples need is part education in a set of skills and part exploration of experience that aims to resolve the difficulties couples trip over in their private lives.

Experience has demonstrated to me that the causes of behavior and human experience are complex and include elements that are biological, psychological, social, contextual, and even spiritual. No single theory explains the intricate dynamics of two individuals interacting over time to meet all their needs as individuals and as a couple. So without respect to theoretical coherence I have drawn from almost every perspective in the realm of psychology from psychodynamics to family systems, communication theory and social learning theory, from behavior therapy to object relations. Over the past 25 years I have gradually built a program of training in the processes of intimacy now known as Practical Application of Intimate Relationship Skills (PAIRS). It is taught to small groups of couples in a four-month course in various parts of the United States and now in 13 countries.

There are no specific theories to explain why the course works. In time that will come, as researchers pinpoint exactly which cognitive, behavioral, and experiential elements (and when and for whom) are most responsible for which types of change. Nevertheless I, my associates, and increasing numbers of graduate students have gathered, and are gathering, evidence that it powerfully, positively influences marital interaction and satisfaction.

Studies of men and women before and after taking the course show that it reduces anger and anxiety, two of the most actively subversive forces in relationships. Judging from the hundreds of couples who have taken the PAIRS course, partners in distressed relationships tend to have more anxiety and anger than does the general population. Once they have taken the course there is a marked reduction in this state of anger and anxiety. What is most notable is that there is also a reduction in the personality trait of anger, which is ordinarily considered resistant to change. Learning the skills of intimacy, of emotional and physical closeness, has a truly powerful effect on people.

We also see change in measurements of marital happiness, such as the Dyadic Adjustment Scale. Tests administered before the course show that we are seeing a range of couples from the least to the most distressed. And we are getting significant levels of change among every category of couple. It is no secret that most attempts at therapy produce little or no change among the most distressed couples. Perhaps it's because what we are doing is not in the form of therapy at all, although its effects are therapeutic. In addition to improvement in many dimensions of the relationship, achieving intimacy bolsters the self-worth of both partners.

Love is a feeling. Marriage, on the other hand, is a contract, an invisible contract. Both partners bring to it expectations about what they want and don't want, what they're willing to give and not willing to give. Most often, those are out of awareness. Most marriage partners don't even know they expected something until they realize that they're not getting it.

The past is very much present in all relationships. All expectations in relationships are conditioned by our previous experience. It may simply be the nature of learning, but things that happen in the present are assimilated by means of what has happened in the past. This is especially true of our emotions: every time we have an experience in the present we also are experiencing it in the past. Emotional memory exists outside of time. It is obvious that two partners are conditioned by two different pasts. But inside the relationship it is less obvious. And that leads to all kinds of misunderstanding, disagreement, disappointment, and anger that things are not going exactly as expected.

The upshot is statements like "I can't understand women," "who knows what a woman wants," and "you can never please a man." All of the classic complaints reflect hidden expectations that have never surfaced to the point where they could be discussed, examined, kept, or discarded.

To add insult to injury, when one partner is upset, the other often compounds it unintentionally. When, for example, a woman is unhappy, men often feel they are expected to charge out and fix something. But what she really wants is for her partner to put his arms around her and hold her, to soothe her, to say simply, "I'm sorry you feel bad." It is a simple and basic longing. But instead of moving toward her, he moves away. And if when you are upset you don't get what you want from the person you are closest to, then you are not going to feel loved. Men, too, I hasten to say, have the same basic need. But they erect defenses against it for fear it will return them to a state of helplessness such as they experienced as children.

At the heart of intimacy, then, is empathy, understanding, and compassion; these are the humanizing feelings. It is bad enough that they are in short supply among distressed couples. Yet I have observed that certain careers pose substantial roadblocks to intimacy because the training involves education not in humanization but in dehumanization. At the top of the list is law. Built primarily on the adversarial process, it actively discourages understanding and compassion in favor of destroying an opponent. Careers in the military and in engineering also are dismissive of feelings and emotions. Men and women who bring what they learn from such work into a love relationship may find that it can't survive.

An understanding of intimacy has its own logic. But it runs counter to conventional wisdom and most brands of psychology. They hold that to understand the nature of, and to improve, relationships, the proper place to start is the self. The thinking is that you need to understand yourself before you can confide in a partner. But I have found just the opposite to be true.

An exploration of the self is indeed absolutely essential to attaining or rebuilding a sense of intimacy. Most of the disappointments that drive our actions and reactions in relationships are constructed with expectations that are not only hidden from our partners but also ourselves. From our families of origin and past relationship experiences, we acquire systems of belief that direct our behavior outside of our own awareness. It is not possible to change a relationship without bringing this belief system into our awareness.

But a man or a woman exploring their personal history experiences some powerful feelings that, in the absence of a partner to talk to, may make one feel worse rather than better. So the very first step a couple must take to rebuild intimacy is to learn to express their own thoughts and feelings and carefully listen to each other. A partner who knows how to listen to you can then be on hand when you open up your past.

Exploration of the self is an activity often relegated to psychotherapy; in that case a psychotherapist knows how to listen with empathy. But that is not necessarily the only way and at best is a luxury affordable only by a few. It is not only possible but desirable for couples of all economic strata to choose to confide in each other and build a relationship with a life partner rather than with a paid confidant. Both partners have an ongoing need to open up the past as well as share the present. But there are skills that have to be learned so that such interaction can be safe. Both partners need to learn how to listen without judging or giving unwanted advice. Disappointment in a partner's ability to hear is what often sends people to a psychotherapist in the first place.

All of us bring to our intimate relationships certain expectations that we have of no one else. On the positive side they usually involve undivided attention words and gestures of love and caring, loyalty, constancy, sex, companionship, agreement, encouragement, friendship, fidelity, honesty, trust, respect, and acceptance. We are all too alert to the possibility that we will instead find their exact opposites.

If we are not aware of our own expectations (and how they are affected by our history), there is no hope of expressing them to a partner so that he or she has a shot at meeting them. More often than not, we engage instead in mind reading.

Mind reading is often related to a past disappointing relationship experience. We tend to expect what we previously had the opportunity to learn; we make assumptions based on our history. And when in personal history there are people or situations that were the source of heartache, resentment, or anxiety, then any action by a partner in the present that is similar in some way often serves as a reminder, and triggers an intense emotional reaction. I call this "emotional allergy." As with other forms of prior sensitization, the result tends to be an explosive reaction, withdrawal, counterattack, and it is typically incomprehensible to a current partner.

If I had to summarize how to change the hidden expectations that work to distort a relationship, I would boil it all down to a few basic rules:

1. If you expect a partner to understand what you need, then you have to tell him or her. That, of course, means you have to figure out for yourself what you really need.

2. You cannot expect your partner to be sensitive and understand exactly how you feel about something unless you're able to communicate to him or her how you feel in the first place.

3. If you don't understand or like what your partner is doing, ask about it and why he or she is doing it. And vice versa. Explore. Talk. Don't assume.

Expressing your feelings about a given situation and asking for your partner's honesty in return is the most significant way to discover truth in your relationship. Instead, most communication between intimates is nonverbal and leans heavily on mind reading. The only thing you have to go on is your own internal information, which could easily be skewed by any number of factors. This is also why genuine responses are so important. Telling your partner what you think he or she wants to hear, instead

of what is really going on, complicates and postpones a useful solution to the problem.

Confiding is much more than being able to reveal yourself to another. It is knowing with absolute certainty that what you think and feel is being heard and understood by your partner. Instead. we tend to be passive listeners, picking up only those messages that have a direct bearing on ourselves, rather than listening for how things are for our partner.

Listening with empathy is a learned skill. It has two crucial ingredients: undivided attention and feeling what your partner feels. Never assume that you know something unless it is clearly stated by your partner. And you need to understand fully what your partner's thoughts and feelings mean to him or her. Instead of focusing on the effects of your partner's words on you, pay attention instead to your partner's emotions, facial expression, and levels of tension. The single biggest barrier to such empathic listening is our self-interest and self-protective mechanisms. We anticipate and fill in the blanks. One of the simple truths of relationships is that often enough, all we need to do to resolve a problem is to listen to our partner, not just passively listen but truly hear what is in the mind and in the heart.

What more often happens is that, when we experience threats to our self-esteem or feel stressed, we resort to styles of communication that usually lead to more of a problem than the problem itself. The styles of communication that we resort to during stress then often prevent real contact from happening. If your partner tends to be a blamer, you will distance yourself. You develop a rational style of relating, but no feelings are ever dealt with. Not only is no love experienced, but at the emotional level nothing can get resolved. (See excerpt in Module 14.)

How, then, can you say what is bothering you, or express what you really need, in a way that your partner can hear it, so that your message can be understood? This is a basic step in building the relationship you want. For this, the Daily Temperature Reading is particularly helpful (see p. 108).

After partners have been heard and understood, they may need to work on forgiveness. Of course, some things are unforgivable, and each partner has to decide if that line has been crossed and the relationship is worth continuing. If it is, there has to be a recognition that you can't change the past. No relationship can recover from past disappointments and mature unless both partners can find a way to let go of grudges. This is one of the most important relationship skills couples can develop.

In a relationship, letting go of grudges is something you do for yourself, not just to make your partner feel better. It is done by making simple statements of facts, not statements of blame. "You took me to your office party and you got so busy with everyone else you didn't introduce me to anyone to talk to me all night. You acted like I didn't matter and that your boss was the most important man in your life."

In the beginning, the course works best in the safety of a group, which prevents the isolation of couples and keeps partners from getting defensive and negative. But once they've practiced this, and it's a simple act of confiding, couples continue it on their own far more easily.

This is not just an exercise of the emotions. There is a cognitive restructuring taking place during these exercises. What is really going on is that one partner is, probably for the first time, learning the meaning of another's experience. That by itself enhances their closeness. All it requires is listening with empathy, and the experience becomes a source of pleasure for both of them. At the same time, there is conceptual understanding of what each is doing that deprives the relationship of pleasure and what they need to do to make it better.

Because the past continually asserts itself in present experience, both partners in a relationship are obligated to explore themselves, their beliefs, needs, and hopes, and even uniqueness of personality through their family's emotional history. Most people operate in the present, using messages and beliefs silently transmitted to them in their family of origin. Or they may be living out invisible loyalties, making decisions based not on the needs of their partner or present relationship, or even their own needs, but on some indebtedness that was incurred sometime in the past.

Particularly at issue are messages we acquire about ourselves, about life and love, trust, confiding, and closeness. Those things we take as truths about love, life, and trust are beliefs we had the chance to learn from specific people and situations in the past. It is on this information that we make the private decision to ourselves: "Nobody cares." "It doesn't matter what I think or say, you're not interested in me." If, for example, you grew up in a family where your mother or father drank or was depressed, or was otherwise emotionally unavailable, you may have drawn the conclusion that no one was really interested in you.

It is vital to know the lineage of our beliefs because we transfer onto our partners what we were dealt in the past. One of the decisions often made unwittingly is, "I don't trust that anybody is really going to be any better to me." It can become a way of saying, "I'm going to get even for the way I was treated." You wind up punishing your partner for what someone else actually did.

When you displace the blame for past hurts onto your present partner, you are activating a dynamic that psychiatrist Ivan Boszormenyi-Nagy, MD, describes as "the revolving ledger." At certain periods in your life important people or even life itself, through events that affected you, ran up a series of debits or credits in terms of what you needed. Time passed. You walked through life's revolving door. And now you hand me the bill. And you hold two hidden expectations. "Prove to me you are not the person who hurt me." In other words, "make up to me for the past." "Pay me back." And, "if you don't, if you do one thing that reminds me of that, I will punish you." The emotional transfer is accomplished.

Freud described this as transference and identified it as a crucial part of the therapeutic relationship. In fact, it is part of our everyday transactions in relationships. It is crucial to understand that this emotional transfer often does not take place early in a relationship. It sets in after a couple has been married for some time when you are disappointed and discover what you expected or hoped to happen isn't happening.

That is the point when we transfer the hidden expectations, especially the negative ones, from our history, from any or all of our previous close relationships, whether to parents, siblings, former spouses, lovers, or friends. It is one of the core emotional transactions of marriage. And making it explicit is one of the psychological tasks of achieving intimacy.

The problem is, the person to whom you hand the bill is unaware of the account books in your head. The result is endless misunderstanding and disturbance. In fact, the attitudes you hold tend to be outside of your own awareness. I believe that they can be found through personal exploration.

Otherwise, you find yourself thinking of your partner as the enemy, someone to hurt, someone to get even with, to punish. And because you don't recognize the ledger as the motivating power behind your behavior, you rationalize. You seek reasons to treat your partner as the enemy. You are really just evening up the balance on someone else's account.

Roger called his wife Jenny at work. She was in the middle of a staff meeting and so she was particularly abrupt with him. When she got home, she found a note from him. He was gone. From somewhere in his past experience he was so sensitized to demonstrations of lack of interest in him that her behavior constituted absolute proof. One misstep one hint that she was anything like whoever ran up the debit was all she was allowed. This is a common pattern in relationships. And the "proof" of disinterest could be anything. Perhaps she didn't look at him. Perhaps she was tired. Perhaps she was sick. One reason men are often intolerant of a wife who gets sick is that she isn't there for them. It is a painful reminder of other accounts from the past.

Not only do couples maintain revolving ledgers, but they also carry over feelings of indebtedness and entitlement from one generation to the next. Invisible loyalties thus accrue in a family over the generations, whether or not we end up acknowledging them. An artistic man buries his creative longing because his family legacy calls for being a success in business. For each of us, behavior is greatly affected by the family ledger of entitlement and indebtedness.

Every couple needs to trace the source of behaviors and attitudes, many of which turn out to have been handed down through their families of origin. Much unhappiness in relationships can be traced to the fact that one partner learned as a family rule never to express anger, or even perhaps happiness. Many people grow up learning to subjugate their own needs and feelings to those of others. Still the feelings influence present relationships, and until they can be brought into awareness and spoken, it is very difficult to improve current relationships.

Once a couple has done this and discovers where their beliefs come from, they can review them together and decide which legacies they want to keep, which they'd rather discard. They each work out their personal history so they do not punish the one who's here now.

At this point I find that couples do well if I introduce an experience in bonding that is usually very emotionally powerful.

For men, these experiences are revelatory. Men, because they are often cut off from the emotional part of themselves, are especially often forced to piggyback their need for intimacy on sex. They have no less need for intimacy than women, but it usually gets suppressed and denied. Or they attempt to satisfy their need for closeness through contact sports and roughhousing. They don't know how to work things out in man-woman intimate relationships. But when they learn, they almost always feel an enormous sense of wholeness and relief.

In growing up men have learned that the only thing they are supposed to need to be close to a woman is sex. They discover that bonding is a valid need in its own right, and needing physical closeness doesn't mean they are going to regress into helplessness and never function again. It doesn't weaken you. it strengthens you.

But this is not learnable merely by cognitive statement. Having the experience illuminates the point and changes the thinking. The exercises are important because they integrate the emotional acceptance, the behavioral change, and the cognitive understanding that occur.

It is no news that sexual problems in a relationship are frequently the by-product of personal and relational conflicts and anxieties. For too many couples. sex has become a substitute for intimacy and a defense against closeness. Most poor sex stems from poor communication, from misunderstandings of what one's mate actually wants   not from unwillingness or inability to give it.

In the realm of sex as in other domains of the relationship, you cannot expect your partner to guess what pleases you. You are obligated to figure out for yourself what stimulates, delights, and satisfies you, and acknowledge it. It is not enough to give and receive, you also have to be able to speak up or reach out on your own behalf and take. Ideally, sexual love will be a flow of this give and take, but it has to go both ways to keep desire alive.

Before sex can be rewarding for both partners, they have to first restore the ability to confide and reestablish emotional openness, to establish a sense of camaraderie. Then physical closeness has meaning, and the meaning serves only to heighten the pleasure of the physical experience even more.

Of course, intercourse is not the only avenue to physical pleasure. There is a whole range of physical closeness couples can learn to offer each other. Being together. Hugging. Holding each other. Caressing each other's face. Massaging your partner's body. In fact, taking pleasure in each other is a habit that some couples actually have to acquire. But taking pleasure in your partner is the very thing your partner needs most from you.

❏ The Daily Temperature Reading

Confiding the ability to reveal yourself fully, honestly, and directly is the lifeblood of intimacy. To live together with satisfaction, couples need clear, regular communication. The great intuitive family therapist Virginia Satir developed a technique for partners and families to maintain an easy flow about the big and little things going on in their lives. I have adapted it. Called the Daily Temperature Reading, it is very simple (and works for many other kinds of relationships as well).

Do it daily, perhaps as you sit down to breakfast. At first it will seem artificial, even hokey. In time you'll evolve your own style.

Couples routinely report it is invaluable for staying close, even if they let it slide for a day or two when they get busy. It teaches partners how to listen nondefensively and to talk as a way to give information rather than to stir a reaction. Here are the basics:

Sit close, perhaps even knee-to-knee, facing your partner, holding each other's hands. This simple touching creates an atmosphere of acceptance for both.

1. APPRECIATION. Take turns expressing appreciation for something your partner has done and thanking each other.

2. NEW INFORMATION. In the absence of information, assumptions--often false ones-- rush in. Tell your partner something ("I'm not looking forward to the monthly planning meeting this morning") to keep contact alive and let your partner in on your mood, your experiences, your life. And then listen to your partner.

3. PUZZLES. Take turns asking each other something you don't understand and your partner can explain: "Why were you so down last night?" Or voice a question about yourself: "I don't know why I got so angry while we were figuring out expenses." You might not find answers, but you will be giving your partner some insight about yourself. Besides, your partner may have insights about your experiences.

4. COMPLAINT WITH REQUEST FOR CHANGE. Without placing blame or being judgmental, cite a specific behavior that bothers you and state the behavior you are asking for instead. "If you're going to be late for dinner tonight, please call me. That way the kids and I can make our own plans and won't be waiting for you."

5. HOPES. Sharing hopes and dreams is integral to a relationship. Hopes can range from the mundane ("I hope you don't have to work this weekend") to the grandiose ("I'd really love to spend a month in Europe with you"). But the more the two of you bring dreams into immediate awareness, the more likely you'll find a way to realize them.

❏ Bonding Exercise

Most people put a lid on the hurts or fears of the past: "It doesn't bother me anymore"; "It isn't that important." But I find that it is essential to lift that lid, in the context of the current relationship, to close the revolving ledger.

Choose a time when you are feeling somewhat edgy. Put on some soft music in the background. Lie down with your partner. Lie on your sides cradled into each other, both facing the same direction.

While your partner is holding you, quietly reveal something he or she does that triggers a full-blown intense emotional reaction in you. It might be that she doesn't listen to you. Or he interrupts you constantly. Or doesn't call when he's away. Or rejects whatever you suggest. "When you do this, I am very upset." As you are speaking, your partner is holding you and listening.

Now tell your partner what experience out of your history your reaction connects to. Perhaps his not calling infuriates you because it arouses the fear you felt when a parent left or died. Or your first husband walked out.

Now comes the remarkable part. Tell your partner what you would have needed to happen in your history that would have helped. What actions would you have preferred to have happen? What words would you have needed to hear?

Now let your partner tell you what you needed to hear, while you take it in. Your partner is free to say it in his or her own way: "I'm sorry that happened to you"; "I wish I had been there."

And now discuss the price you are paying in your current relationship for having this emotional reaction to events of the past. Perhaps it is that you don't talk to your partner, you withdraw, withhold, get even.

What you talk about next is what you can then do to help yourself. "How can I signal you neutrally to let you know when you trigger this response in me?" At this point you are talking about what will help you in the future. You are jointly and consciously outlining useful behaviors, constructing a relationship in which actions and experiences have the same meaning and same effect for both of you. This is essential for happiness to occur in a relationship.☐

-Reprinted with permission from Psychology Today. *Copyright © 1993, Sussex Publishers, Inc.*

DEFINING TERMS

Empathy

Bonding

Trust

WHAT DO YOU THINK?

1. What other ways can you think of to build intimacy?

2. What are your requirements before sexual intimacy can happen?

3. Someone once remarked that nowadays we progress from acquaintances to lovers to friends. Why do you think this is? What does it say about intimacy?

 VIDEO VIEWER:

Rent "The Big Chill" or "Only the Lonely." What different types of intimacy occur between the various characters?

4. What can you do if a partner or friend has fears about intimacy?

 MEDIA WATCHER:

How much emotional intimacy do you see between lovers in sitcoms? How much physical affection? How much sexual innuendo? How might this influence people?

> **Part Four**
> **Marriage Adjustments:**
> **Children and Work**
>
>
> **Module Ten**
>
>
> # Pregnancy and Birth

*T*he decision of whether to have children is probably the most basic that a family can make. Having children is, in many respects, an even greater commitment than the marriage itself. This is true for several reasons: first, financially, the costs of rearing a child have been estimated as high as $200,000 including education; second, the time commitments of raising children is substantial; and third, the emotional commitments entailed by adding members of the family is also great.

If a couple decides to have children, further decisions follow: when to start having them, how many to have, and how far apart. Making these important decisions is called family planning. The implementation of these decisions usually requires the use of some form of contraception. The most effective forms of birth control are: the pill, condom and foam, and diaphragm.

Couples often decide to delay childbearing for several reasons, including: to allow their marriage to stabilize and adjust; to allow their financial resources to grow enough to handle the strain; to finish school or advance in a career. Couples who postpone childbearing may face social pressure from their parents or peers, but nowadays there are no real medical reasons to have children early in the marriage if not desired.

Chapter Preview:

The Decision To Have Children

Pregnancy

Childbirth

Article: "Myths About Pregnancy"

Article: "Sex After the Baby"

Pregnancy

*I*f the woman does become pregnant, how both the man and woman react to the pregnancy depends on a number of factors. The most important is whether the pregnancy is planned or not. If the pregnancy is not planned, the reactions may range from surprise to depression or even anger. A second important factor is the status of the couple's relationship. The more stressful the relationship, the more difficulty the couple will have adjusting to parenthood. Financial stability is a third important factor.

Pregnancy obviously affects the man and woman quite differently. The woman has to carry the child for nine months with a number of physical and emotional changes and reactions. Some women are extremely uncomfortable with the changes, reporting symptoms such as nausea, insomnia, tiredness and so on. Emotionally they may feel extremely sensitive. Many women, however, find pregnancy to be a gratifying and happy period, as they are fulfilling part of their expectation about what it means to be a woman.

By contrast, some fathers find it difficult to get involved with an event that is going on in another's body. They may feel resentful, neglected or worried about the changes a child will bring in the relationship. There may be changes in the couple's sexual activity, particularly in the third trimester. If the pregnancy was not planned, these problems may be accentuated. Not all fathers experience these issues, however, and some report that the period of pregnancy is one of the closest they experience as a couple.

With the advent of pregnancy, a third party becomes affected by the process--the coming child. For that reason, pre-natal care becomes extremely important. Proper pre-natal care includes:

✦ the mother placing herself under a physician's care as soon as she discovers her pregnancy;

✦ proper nutrition, rest and exercise; and

✦ avoidance of drugs of any kind without doctor's approval--including alcohol, tobacco, many medications and even aspirin and coffee, if possible.

Childbirth

The culmination of pregnancy, of course, is childbirth. Nowadays, many couples prepare themselves for childbirth by education about birth, physical conditioning, breathing and relaxation techniques and preparing the husband to give support and help to the wife during labor and delivery. Natural childbirth, such as the Lamaze method, and home delivery are becoming increasingly popular as couples seek to de-intensify the birth experience for both the mother and newborn. If home delivery is chosen, backup medical care should be arranged in case of emergencies or complications.

Often the first indication of labor is the rupture of the amniotic sac, a bag of water surrounding the fetus, or the arrival of rhythmic contractions usually about 15-20 minutes apart. These contractions may decrease to about 3 minutes apart as labor progresses. For first pregnancies, labor will take an average of about 11 hours. The process of labor can be divided into three stages: the first, dilation, during which the uterine muscles push the baby forward, gradually opening the cervix; the second, which involves the passage of the baby through the birth canal, beginning with the completion of dilation and ending with the birth. During this phase, hard contractions occur, and the mother assists by alternately pushing and relaxing; and the third, the afterbirth, which involves the passage of the placenta.

After the birth, because the care and feeding of newborns can be so challenging and tiring, many new adjustments begin for the couple (see second following article). Bonding between both parents and the baby is to be encouraged, because studies show it increases parental "sensitivities" and responsiveness by the baby. ☐

References

Rice, F.P. 1996. *Intimate relationships, marriages and families.* Mountainview, CA: Mayfield.

Shehan, C.L. & K.C. Kammeyer. 1997. *Marriages and families: Reflections of a gendered society.* Boston: Allyn & Bacon.

Wells, J.G. 1991. *Choices in marriage and family.* Alta Loma, CA: Collegiate Press.

☐ Myths About Pregnancy

Sheldon H. Cherry, M.D.

Through the ages, many myths and traditions have become associated with one of life's most basic events, pregnancy. Various bits of folklore, invented to try to make sense of the unknown, have been handed down from generation to generation. Other myths are new to contemporary American culture and arise from recent cultural ideas. All of these myths, however, are inaccurate and counterproductive; following their dictates may actually be physically or emotionally harmful.

Here are a few of the most common myths about pregnancy and motherhood, along with the information to dispel them.

Myth 1: "I'm too old to have a baby." No woman who is ovulating is too old to get pregnant. Although it may be more difficult for you to conceive and to carry a pregnancy as you get older, there is no reason not to try. Pregnancy does not harm a healthy woman. There are increased risks of birth defects as a woman gets older, but there is no cutoff age at which such risks increase dramatically. Prenatal tests, such as amniocentesis, are generally recommended for older mothers-to-be, although many of these tests must be performed after the first trimester.

Myth 2: "I should eat for two during my pregnancy." The generally recommended weight gain during pregnancy is 30 pounds. This includes the weight of the fetus, placenta,

uterus, amniotic fluid, enlarged breasts, and other body changes. If you gain more than 30 pounds, you'll have extra pounds to lose even after you've shed your pregnancy-related weight. This extra weight does not enhance the nourishment of your baby and can make you feel sluggish during and after your pregnancy. Although you needn't eat for two, you may need extra doses of certain vitamins and minerals to meet your baby's need for nourishment. Your obstetrician can prescribe a nutritional plan to meet those needs without requiring you to eat extra portions or exotic foods during your pregnancy.

Myth 3: "I'd exercise, but I'm afraid I'll hurt my baby." Moderate exercise will make your pregnancy more comfortable and can help your body prepare for the physical stress of labor. Daily exercise will also improve your sense of well-being. In a normal, healthy pregnancy, the fetus is well protected in a secure, warm, uterine environment; the amniotic fluid provides a comfortable cushion from the rigors of exercise. Overexertion to the point of pain or exhaustion is not good for you and may momentarily reduce the oxygen supply to the fetus. Common sense dictates that such strenuous exercise be avoided.

Myth 4: "Labor will be more pain than I can endure." Labor, a natural occurrence, has become associated with a lot of fear and anxiety. No one can predict how your labor will feel. Horror stories do nothing but frighten first-time mothers, and tales about breezy labors are usually too glowing to be credible. The best advice is to ignore the sagas of well-meaning friends and relatives and to learn as much about the scientific aspects of giving birth as possible. Such knowledge is the key to having a relaxed birth. The discomfort of labor can also be eased considerably by using the natural conditioning methods of prepared childbirth, such as Lamaze, or by using modem anesthetic techniques. Investigate these options so you are prepared by your due date.

Myth 5: "Mothering is a natural instinct." Many women think they should instinctively know how to care for an infant. This is not true. Just as with any other skill, new mothers need to learn how to care for a newborn. It takes time, patience, and love to become comfortable with mothering. It involves observing other mothers, reading books, and asking professionals, such as your pediatrician, for advice. With time and practice, your confidence and competence will grow. Be realistic about motherhood. The more a woman idealizes it, the more likely she is to feel disappointed and depressed as she faces the day-to-day realities of mothering.

Myth 6: "I will automatically love my baby." "Mother love" is not automatic. Some women at first feel very little toward their newborns and are troubled if they aren't swept off their feet by motherhood. And many mothers feel guilty when they are overwhelmed by trying to master the art of baby care. It may help to remember that caring for your child is a lifelong learning process, and it may take days or weeks to form the initial bond with your newborn. Eventually, the special maternal feelings of warmth, tenderness, protectiveness, and delight will begin to emerge. As you get to know your baby, complete with likes, dislikes, and even a sense of humor, your maternal feelings will grow.

Myth 7: "My breasts are too small for me to breastfeed." Almost every woman can produce milk after her baby is born and can successfully breastfeed, regardless of the size of her breasts. Breastfeeding works on a perfect supply-and-demand system in which the more your baby nurses, the more milk your body produces, regardless of the size or shape of your breasts. Even retracted nipples can be prepared before delivery so that breastfeeding is possible.

Myth 8: "I can't get pregnant while I'm breastfeeding." Many women will occasionally ovulate while breastfeeding, even if they have not yet had a period. This is especially true during the first three months after delivery. Therefore, breastfeeding should not be viewed as a method of contraception. □

-- Reprinted by permission from Parents *Magazine, August 1991. Copyright © 1991 Gruner + Jahr USA Publishing.*

☐ Sex After the Baby

Leslie Bennetts

The books make it sound so easy. Just wait six weeks after delivery, they assure you brightly, and then you can resume your normal sexual relationship as if nothing had ever happened. All those cheerful childbirth manuals give you the impression that everyone waits the prescribed month and a half, heals neatly on schedule, then resumes an active sex life with her eager husband. There may be people for whom this is the case, but you could look a long time before you met any.

The reality is far more complicated and tends to be obscured by embarrassed secrecy. Giving birth may be the most transcendent experience a woman can ever have, but joy and elation are only part of the picture. Some women manage to be quite chipper within a couple of days, but others feel more like victims of a train wreck: weepy, overwhelmed by powerful emotions, and bruised and battered in parts of their bodies they didn't even know existed. A difficult labor can be emotionally traumatic, and women whose pregnancy ended in a cesarean section are recuperating from major surgery; it can be weeks before they can even imagine feeling normal again. Then there's sleep deprivation: Every night, that angelic little bundle seems to howl for hours, demanding to be fed with a frequency you didn't think possible. Who knew such a tiny creature could eat so much, not to mention so often? Between the feeding and the burping and the changing, it can easily get to be four o'clock in the afternoon before you realize you're still in your flannel nightgown because you haven't yet had a chance to grab a shower and brush your hair, which is glued together with baby spit-up. This is a sex object?

Conflicting emotions

For many women, the prospect of making love again is initially horrifying. "A friend had warned me that the doctor would come sidling up after I had my baby and want to talk about sex," says Stephanie, a Texas writer and mother of two. "I remember lying there in my hospital bed. Every erogenous zone in my body hurt." When the doctor told her she could resume sexual relations after six weeks, she was appalled. "I said, 'you don't understand--no one is going to touch me for the rest of my life!' After I got out of the hospital, I felt as if my husband were following me around clicking off the days, which to my mind were going all too quickly. Just the thought of sex was absolutely traumatic."

Needless to say, Stephanie's second child is proof that such feelings don't last forever. Still, even after a woman heals physically, the psychological adjustments can take time. Some women feel a certain distance from their partners because of what they've been through. "I felt my husband just didn't understand that no matter how much a man and woman go into this together, certain things had happened to me alone," says Stephanie. "A baby changes everything. Pregnancy and childbirth give you a redefinition of your body; all those sexual

parts of your body are being used in a very different way, first to give birth, and then to breast feed. It makes you think very differently about sex for a while."

Even the method of giving birth can have long-term repercussions. "Having a Caesarean made me feel like less of a woman on some level," admits Susan, a psychologist who lives in Chicago. "It confirmed all my negative feelings about myself as a woman, and I'm sure it made me feel less desirable." A stunning, auburn haired woman with the figure of an eighteen-year-old, Susan might seem an unlikely candidate for such doubts, but they affected her for months after the birth of each of her two children. The fact that she was breastfeeding also had a major impact. "It made me feel more married, more connected in a physical way, to my baby than to my husband," she confesses. "I fell in love with both my babies in a way I never dreamed was possible, and I'm sure the fact that they're both boys had significance, in terms of feeling less sexual toward my husband. I got a tremendous amount of gratification and intimacy from breastfeeding, and in some ways that replaced sex."

Although many women are ashamed to talk about such conflicts, they are quite common. "I feel very torn between my loyalty to my husband and my loyalty to the baby" says Alice, a Florida social worker who is currently nursing her second child. "I feel very drawn to the baby and it's as though anything sexual is a violation of trust. Once the breast feeding stops it gets easier; but for a while you feel like your body's being used and used and used and you just want a little private time. It's a wonderful luxury just to be left alone."

For a new mother feeling overwhelmed by her baby's demands, the additional pressure of her partner's needs may breed resentment and anger. And a man who is used to being his wife's first priority may find her attachment to the baby a rude shock. "The husband has to take second place for a while," says Roy Whitman, M.D., a psychiatrist who specializes in sex therapy at the University of Cincinnati College of Medicine. "The woman may try to satisfy her husband, but it can seem more like she's placating him; I think her heart tends to be with the baby at this point. Bonding with the infant is uppermost for the mother, and the father may be seen as an intruder," Whitman says.

Some fathers are jealous of the baby, and if they start to interfere with the mother-child bonding in an envious, intrusive way, the mother will push them away. Bottle-feeding mothers may be more receptive because the breast becomes an erotic source again rather than a nurturant source--but if you're breastfeeding, the breast belongs to the baby."

Such changes have been known to cause enormous stress. "This is a dangerous time for a marriage," warns Domeena Renshaw, M.D., a professor of psychiatry and director of the Sexual Dysfunction Clinic at Loyola University Medical Center, in Maywood, Illinois. "There are some husbands who cheat during pregnancy and afterward because the mother has a romance with the baby and they feel left out."

New fathers may be just as exhausted as mothers, which doesn't enhance their interest in sex either. My baby has never been a good sleeper. My husband clocked her one night when she was about eight months old; the longest she slept without calling us was 40 minutes, so we were up approximately every half hour all through the night. Sleep deprivation can definitely alter your sense of priorities. "For me the most erotic, pleasurable thing I can think of for the first six months after a baby is born is ten hours of sleep," says Elaine, a computer programmer with four small children.

What fathers feel

Although new mothers get most of the attention, husbands have to make their own psychological adjustments. Many men have a hard enough time with their wives' pregnancies, and when the baby arrives, any sexual problems can be compounded; the fact that a man's partner has just become a mother may present a real sexual hurdle that experts generally attribute to subconscious incest taboos.

"My husband basically doesn't like to have sex with a pregnant woman," confides Elaine, who lives in San Jose, California. "He's not crazy about breastfeeding from a sexual point of view, either. He thinks breastfeeding is the greatest for the baby, and he would feel very put out if I didn't nurse, but at the same time, I think he finds it a turnoff. Breastfeeding keeps me tied to the baby longer, and it keeps me more mother than wife--and with four kids, I'm often more mother than wife."

People vary tremendously, of course. One man may find his wife's swollen breasts tremendously sexy while another is turned off by the leaking and spraying a nursing mother may experience when she is sexually aroused. Women's reactions run the gamut as well, and some feel a strong need to reassert their own sexuality after a baby is born. "The classic scenario is, Dad's howling at the door of the cage and Mom's not in the mood for months, but sometimes it's the opposite," observes one mother. "Afer I had my baby it was very important for me to feel I wasn't just this lactating mommy." However, her husband seemed to feel that if he touched her, she might break. "I felt as if he was treating me like some giant egg," she says.

When both partners are ready and willing, sometimes they can resume an active sex life with little delay, particularly if they have a cooperative baby. "I was very interested in sex during pregnancy and I didn't wait for six weeks after either of my children were born," says Marcy, a Philadelphia mother of two. "I found childbirth very exciting and sexy, and I thought nursing was absolutely sexual. My first kid slept through the night ridiculously early so I wasn't having the kind of fatigue a lot of people have. There was no reason not to have sex."

Some new fathers find that parenthood strengthens their feelings of love for and sexual attraction to their mates. "Having a child deepened my love for my wife and made her special in a new way," says Steven, a New York City lawyer. "Our sex was made better by the baby, not worse."

Easing physical discomfort

This situation is the ideal, of course, but you can enhance your prospects by taking note of some practical advice. If you're experiencing acute pain, you should consult your doctor to make sure you're healing properly and that there's no infection. If you receive a clean bill of health but find that sex remains difficult, don't worry--it's quite normal. Women who are postpartum have diminished estrogen levels, resulting in lessened lubrication and a thinning of the vaginal walls, both of which are exacerbated by nursing and can cause discomfort during intercourse. Simply using additional lubrication for a while can improve the situation significantly. "Sex was not pleasurable for me after I had my first child, and I didn't know how to make it feel better," one mother admits. "If someone had just said to me, 'It's going to be painful and dry now, so just use a lot of K-Y Jelly,' things would have been much easier. As it was, I took my non-lubricated status as a statement about my womanliness."

When his wife is in such a tender state, a man can help matters immeasurably by being sensitive to her discomfort. Doctors and sex therapists say that longer periods of foreplay may make intercourse more pleasurable, and they also recommend experimenting with different positions. For example, although penetration can be deeper with the woman on top, she also may be able to control contact better and avoid any pain.

If it seems for a while that no position is comfortable, consider other ways of satisfying one another and maintaining a sense of emotional and sexual intimacy.

The experts offer a variety of additional suggestions to new parents who may be having trouble with their sex lives. "Some people keep the baby in their room, so there's a third person there, which may be a factor," observes Renshaw.

If you find yourself listening for every rustle of the baby's bed covers rather than thinking sexy thoughts, it might be a good idea to reclaim your bedroom for yourselves.

Realizing you're not alone in this can also help; having the mistaken notion that other people aren't troubled by any of these problems can make you feel even worse. "It's like some kind of dirty little secret. You assume you're the only one on earth who feels this way," says one woman. Indeed, it sometimes seems as if there's a conspiracy to keep new parents in the dark. "Why doesn't anybody level with you about this?" asks writer Dan Greenburg in his book *Confessions of a Pregnant Father* (Fawcett). "Why do the obstetricians and the guidebooks imply that you'll be having sex right up to the time you're fully dilated, and that the longest it ever takes any normal couple to get back to regular sex is six weeks? If there could be a bit more candor in this area, new parents might feel they were within the mainstream of human experience rather than candidates for the Masters and Johnson clinic."

Maintain an open dialogue

Whatever you're feeling, talking about it with your mate will help. Even without sex, sharing your thoughts will make you feel closer and may clear up any misunderstandings. Don't wait for them to make the first move; tell them what you're going through, and ask them how they feel about it all. Sometimes people act as if their spouses can read their minds, which isn't fair no matter how long a couple has been married. Not communicating directly leaves room for all kinds of missed signals. One woman was eager to resume a lusty sex life, but her husband kept acting as if she were some kind of invalid. When they finally talked about it, she learned that he had been preoccupied with her episiotomy and had been terrified of hurting her.

Other than communication, the best therapy is simply time. As the weeks pass, you will start feeling better, life will seem more manageable, and eventually you will find yourself thinking that making love sounds like a fun idea instead of the worst idea anyone ever had. How long this takes may vary widely, and just because you have a friend who felt great three weeks after delivery, or you read in some book that everything should be fine in six weeks, doesn't mean you need to feel bad if it takes you as much as a year to adjust.

No matter how long it takes, don't panic. "Women put so much pressure on themselves," Elaine observes. "They say, 'So I haven't gotten a decent night's sleep in six months, I'm stressed out, I'm fifteen pounds overweight, my body organs still haven't gone back to where they're supposed to be, and my hormones are all over the map. So what's the problem with me?' There are so many pressures. I think that a good sex life is really cyclical, anyway. There can be dry periods, and then things will get real hot and heavy again. I think we tend not to be patient enough with ourselves." □

-*Reprinted by permission from* Parents *Magazine, July 1990. Copyright © 1990 Gruner + Jahr USA Publishing.*

DEFINING TERMS

Family Planning

Pre-Natal Care

Post-Partum

WHAT DO YOU THINK?

1. Why does the arrival of a baby often cause increased conflict?

2. How much of the conflict is the husband's fault and how much the wife's? What can husbands do to minimize conflict? What can wives do?

4. If you/your spouse had an unplanned pregnancy, would you consider an abortion? Why or why not?

3. Which of the myths about pregnancy did you believe? Where did your beliefs come from?

5. How large a family would you like to have? Explain why.

☺ **MEDIA WATCHER:**

What do TV programs show about pregnancy and birth? What parts don't they show? Why?

🛆 **VIDEO VIEWER:**

Rent "She's Having a Baby." What are the adjustments the couple have to make for conception and pregnancy?

> **Module Eleven**
>
> # Raising Children

*R*aising children is the recapitulation of the process by which we were raised, the socialization of a new generation, just as we were socialized. It is interesting to look at history, and the evolution of society as a process of repeated socialization--of generation after generation, learning from its parents' mistakes, making new ones and learning from those.

Of course, that is not the way most people look at having children. Most see children in a series of happy images; as an expression of the love between themselves and their partner; as someone to cuddle and love and be loved back; as a chance to live out opportunities one never had the chance to explore. Of course, we also know from our parents' comments that parenting can be a frustrating, even exasperating experience, but we think perhaps, that we can easily avoid the pitfalls.

*O*nce children are born, however, we quickly become aware of the challenges. From the infant that cries all night to the teenager who wants to stay out all night, each age brings different problems to consider. Most parents come to the marriage with idealized notions and theories of childrearing, often developed as a critique of their own upbringing. Experts' childrearing philosophies seem to change from generation to generation, too, so that parents often need to sort out conflicting advice from parents, friends, books, etc. Other differences can occur between ethnic groupings, regions and social classes. For example, middle class families tend to stress values like independence and creativity, while lower class families stress obedience and hard work. Immigrant families tend to stress fitting in. Because of these differences, and the differences between individual families, husbands and wives may differ on a number of questions including values, discipline and the like. These differences can be the source of conflicts between parents.

Providing for children's needs

Perhaps the simplest way to view parenting is as the provision for the child's basic needs. For most families these needs fall into four

> **Chapter Preview:**
>
> **Overview of Childrearing**
>
> **Providing for Children's Needs**
>
> **Discipline**
>
> **Article: "The Parent Trap"**
>
> **Article: "Ethical Parenting"**

categories: physical, emotional, intellectual, and moral/spiritual.

- **physical** -- parents need to provide adequate nutrition, clothing, shelter and medical care for children to grow up healthily.

- **emotional** -- children need love, attention, approval and security to be happy. If they are deprived of these, they become insecure, and may take these insecurities into later life. In later life, they will depend on others for emotional fulfillment, so parents must allow social opportunities to develop, and teach social skills. Providing for emotional needs is not "spoiling the child." Excessive demands for attention are just as likely caused by lack of support and attention as from overindulgence.

- **intellectual** -- children are naturally curious. Parents can encourage this curiosity by providing stimulation and change, a variety of learning environments, and by rewarding children for asking questions.

- **moral/spiritual** -- children are also naturally trusting. They have a strong potential for moral behavior. If they are mistreated, they become mistrustful, however. They must also be taught how to handle conflicting impulses of selflessness and selfishness. In this area more than any other, children learn by example. How the parents behave will be noticed and accepted or rejected by the child. Spiritual and religious values must also be lived as well as taught. Children are curious about life and death and wish to know about such things.

Discipline

Probably the most difficult and even controversial aspect of parenting is discipline. It may be helpful to realize that the word stems from a Latin root meaning "to learn," which indicates that discipline is not necessarily an end in itself, but a means to learning, i.e. being

socialized. Rulers of countries know that the most effective form of social control is not accomplished with laws and armies or police, but by "winning the hearts and minds" of their citizens. Similarly, the goal of discipline is not to control behavior by fear, but to develop the conscience and self-control necessary to fit in and succeed in life. Parental exercise of external control is necessary until children develop sufficient internal controls of their own. How can discipline best be developed? Rice (1996) has summarized the research with ten principles which are reviewed here:

1. Children respond more readily to parents in a loving environment.

2. Discipline is more effective when it is consistent.

3. Learning is enhanced if both rewards and punishments are used.

4. Discipline is more effective if applied as soon after the offense as possible

5. Severe punishment, particularly if cruel or abusive, is counter-productive because it stimulates resentment and rejection as a response.

6. Discipline becomes less effective if it is too strictly or frequently applied.

7. Extremes of permissiveness or authoritarianism are counterproductive.

8. Avoid threatening the child's security or self-esteem. Threats like "we won't love you anymore" may work temporarily, but they may undermine children's esteem and can cause later problems.

9. Giving children choices usually works better than "laying down the law." Of course, the choices given can be limited by the parents' needs.

10. Children who show excessive aggression may need therapeutic help.□

References

Rice, F.P. 1996. *Intimate relationships, marriages and families.* Mountainview, CA: Mayfield.

Shehan, C.L. & K.C. Kammeyer. 1997. *Marriages and families: Reflections of a gendered society.* Boston: Allyn & Bacon.

Wells, J.G. 1991. *Choices in marriage and family.* Alta Loma, CA: Collegiate Press.

❑ The Parent Trap: Breaking Free from Cycles of Anger and Guilt

Nancy Marriott

We've all seen it the over-stressed mother at the supermarket check-out line, trying to discipline an unruly child with angry words and sharp yanks, obviously out of control to everyone but the distraught parent herself. It's easy to look down our noses at such a shameful scene, until it's our turn, and we find ourselves trapped in the same sad struggle, yelling, threatening, trying to control our child and eventually blowing our tops.

None of us feels good after a parental temper tantrum, whether it's on public display or in the privacy of our own homes. In the aftermath, we cringe with self-recrimination over what we did and said at the time, telling ourselves that somehow, it all means we are inadequate as parents. We vow we're not going to ever do that again . . .

It's a familiar and timeworn cycle, first the flaring temper and then the guilt, repeated so often that it becomes second nature and we lose all ability to stop ourselves. Why are parents so easily trapped in this vicious cycle, and how can we avoid being endlessly caught up in it?

Understanding Anger

Most of us were taught that anger is an unacceptable emotion. We learned early from our parents' modeling that anger is not only impolite, but worse, can do grave harm to others and earn us justified condemnation. But the real problems with anger arise more from a lack of understanding and accepting this troublesome emotion than from it's actual expression.

The first step for parents wanting to get free from the trap of anger and guilt is to understand that anger comes in two distinct varieties. The first is the normal, healthy emotion we feel in response to a dangerous situation. The second is the less direct, often harmful kind of anger that erupts unpredictably when we're frustrated and stressed. Recognizing the difference between these two kinds of anger allows us to accept the healthy expression while safe-guarding against the harmful kind. The expression of these two kinds of anger may appear to be the same loud, sudden verbal or physical outbursts that shatter the air and startle everyone around us. But the healthy, authentic variety has a pure, raw quality to it, one which gives notice that boundaries have been overstepped and a clear threat is at hand. The mother who lets out a shriek when her nursing infant cuts a new tooth at her breast is expressing this kind of anger, as is the father yelling abruptly at the three-year-old who has wandered into the street. This kind of emotion is useful for our continued survival, and, scientists tell us, has been hardwired into our biochemistry since our early, single-celled existence.

The second kind of anger has none of the protective immediacy of the healthier expression. Instead, it seems to spill over from a reservoir of unexpressed resentments we may be harboring from previous experiences.

Similar to the old "kick-the-dog" syndrome, it lands on whomever might get in our way and finds its mark at the first convenient provocation. This "spill-over" anger is in effect when we lose our temper and rain down insults, sarcasm and threats upon our children's heads, terrifying them and destroying trust and goodwill. Over time, it becomes a default mechanism for dealing with all frustrating behaviors, a knee-jerk reaction we later regret.

When anger is authentic, it cuts to the chase and swiftly passes like a storm, leaving a clearing in which parents and children are better off for the experience. Kids understand when we are legitimately angry at their behavior. It's that other stuff, the manipulation and punishing intent that confuses them and teaches them to react to problems in the same destructive ways. And they learn fast.

As parents, we need to be authentic with our children, not phony. The healthy expression of real emotions can teach them more than a million lectures or punishments. At the same time, we want to be careful to not target our children with spill-over anger that so devastatingly diminishes their self-esteem and leaves us helplessly wallowing in guilt.

Breaking the Cycle

Once we clearly distinguish the two kinds of anger, we can save our healthy anger for only the most necessary situations and begin to replace the spill-over variety with more effective and beneficial responses. Following are some short- and long-term suggestions for doing this.

Brian returned home after a long and frustrating day at the office to hear the complaints of his ten-year-old son, Sam. "I don't want to do my homework, I want to go out and play baseball with my friends." The whining escalated as Brian's wife tried to reason

with Sam. Intending to intervene in a friendly way, Brian offered: "Hey sport, I've been looking forward to seeing you all day. How about we play a quick game of toss and then I'll help you with your math?" "No!" shouted Sam. "I want to play with my friends, not you!" The rejection, heaped upon the day's stresses, hurt Brian deeply. Before he could stop himself, he grabbed his son by the back of the neck and began a familiar tirade. "You spoiled brat, I'll show you what happens to selfish kids like you! You won't be able to watch any videos for a whole month and you can forget about dinner! Now get yourself upstairs and do your homework alone!"

Brian fell right into the parent trap and, blaming himself for "losing it," felt guilty long after his son had gone to bed hungry. By yelling and grabbing Sam by the neck, he modeled that force and violence are the ways to resolve conflicts. By insulting and threatening Sam, he gained the desired submission, but at the price of his son's resentment and his own feelings of inadequacy.

An alternative way of dealing with this situation would be for Brian to diffuse his anger by simply withdrawing from the situation before it got confrontational. Instead of unleashing a verbal attack, he could leave the room, prefacing his exit with a statement like: "When I hear you talking that way, I get furious. As soon as I calm down, we can discuss this." In this way, Brian could the time to own up to his feelings of hurt and rejection, and give himself some emotional space to recognize this. Handling Sam's disrespectful outburst could come later, after a cooling off period.

A danger in this strategy is to use silence as a punitive measure and shun the child. Parental time-out shouldn't be confused with resentful ignoring, the "silent treatment." The latter sends the message that your child is so awful you can't stand to be around him.

Once your own anger is diffused, you're in a better position to help children diffuse theirs. You can do this by verbally mirroring a child's own feelings in a way that lets him know he's been heard.

A calmer Brian could have said to Sam: "Son, I hear that you want to be with your friends and are frustrated you can't play ball right now." A brief pause might elicit a response by Sam: "That's right, and I don't want to do my homework anyway!" More mirroring by Dad: "I understand that doing homework isn't as much fun as playing ball." Another pause and then some problem solving: "What do you think you could do to make it easier?" Or: "How could you play ball and also get your homework done?" After listening respectfully to the child's ideas, however off the mark, Brian could coach: "Do you think not watching TV when you come home from school would give you more time to play ball?" Kids will surprise you and often come up with their own solutions if given the chance, and if they know they've been listened to.

Another short-term strategy for diffusing anger is to greet misbehavior with a simple explanatory statement and then request an agreement. Four-year-old Michelle often got into her mother's cosmetics to play "make up," a messy game that always resulted in red eyebrows and stained bathroom towels. When discovered, Michelle was treated to her mom's explosive comments: "You're always ruining my things!" Or: "Why can't you ever learn?"

When rules have been broken, a more effective response is to deliver the message simply and leave out the ancient history and gloomy predictions. Instead of telling your child how impossible she is, briefly describe the behavior that has upset you, including your feeling about it and the reason your feel the way you do. Michelle's mom might have said: "When you play with my lipstick, I get upset because I have to clean up after you." Then she could make a simple order: "Next time, ask my permission first." If she had the time and inclination, Michelle's mom might supply some old lipsticks and monitor the creative play more closely. Or if the behavior were strictly verboten, she could calmly state the rule and make a simple request for agreement. "The rule is no playing with Mommy's lipstick. I need your agreement that you'll obey the rule."

Children, especially younger ones, may have to restate their agreements several times, a process best aided by patience and understanding of a four-year-old's memory limits. But it's worth the extra effort to enroll your child in making a choice for better behavior. An angry reaction is more likely to erupt when we take the child's forgetfulness personally, as if the misbehavior were intentional. Also, beware of overdoing "please," in your requests, which can express tentativeness and give your child the idea that the outcome is still an open-ended matter.

Sometimes avoiding spill-over anger takes more forethought and planning. Two strategies that are especially effective are examining your rules to determine which ones are worth risking potential conflicts, and creating reasonable consequences in advance for repeated misbehaviors.

Simplify Your Rules

Having too many rules can be an invitation for children to rebel. It works better to limit your rules to a half dozen or so that are the most crucial to the harmony of your household. You can decide what these are by reviewing the most recent confrontations and noting which ones made you the angriest. It will also help to examine what is most important to you and your family. For example, if weekday mornings are stressful, you could relax the rule about tidying bedrooms before leaving for school. But the rule that homework must be finished before TV remains on the books. A limited number of clear rules that children can keep track of will help you to prevent frustrating incidents that tempt you to spin out of control.

Creating Careful Consequences

Giving children consequences works particularly well when you are frustrated by your child's irresponsible behavior. But this method easily backfires if not done carefully and with some advance planning. Fred was frustrated that 8-year-old Sara repeatedly left her bike in the driveway, creating a hazard and an extra chore for him whenever he tried to put the car in the garage. Fully exasperated by her lack of response to his frequent reprimands, Fred finally threatened his daughter: "If you leave that bike out one more time, you won't go with the family to Disneyland next summer!" Somehow, these threats never worked. The summer was too far away to worry Sara, and she knew her parents would never leave her home alone while the family went on vacation. She had become deaf to the consequences her parents so often announced but never kept.

Fred would have been more effective if he'd used a consequence that could be carried out closer in time to the offense, and designed results he and the family could live with. Instead of threatening Sara with what they both knew would never come to pass, Fred could have said: "If the bike isn't put away, I'm going to store it up in the garage rafters where it will remain for two weeks. The next time you leave out your bike, I'll take it to mean this is what you want." For this to work, of course, Fred would need to make sure he follows through. When the surprised and angry Sara pleads to have her bike back, he would respectfully remind her that the situation was her own choice.

The important thing is that the consequences be given calmly and with the attitude of a traffic cop giving a ticket to a speeding motorist. Rubbing the offending child's nose in the penalty, either by voice tone or further insults, will spoil the chance for an opportunity to teach responsibility and bring about a change in behavior.

It's Never Too Late

No matter how hard we try to avoid falling into the parent trap by safe-guarding against nasty flare ups and confrontations, there will always be times when we blow a gasket and say and do things we later regret. To expect to be rational and in control all the time is a set up for failure, as we can't possibly meet such an unrealistic goal. When we "lose it" on occasion, we should do what we'd do in any other relationship, apologize. A sincere expression of regret, done after we've calmed down and not before (kids can tell the difference) goes a long way to mend and rebuild the shattered trust. "You must have felt really awful when I called you those names. I'm sorry. I don't really think you're stupid (or lazy, or spoiled)."

And most important, you can reaffirm the love that was lost in the fray by reassuring your child: "I love you very much and I'm sorry I hurt you." Children will respect an honest admission that you made a mistake, and a sincere apology will take the burden off you to be the perfect parent who is somehow inadequate when tempers flare. Instead, you'll be able to discipline your children more effectively and provide them with an cool-headed, exemplary role model no longer caught in the parent trap.□

–Used with permission.

❑ Ethical Parenting: A Promethean Reply to an Age-Old Problem

Chris Kuchuris

Chris Kuchuris is a Philosophy Instructor at the Community College of Southern Nevada

Heard one of these phrases lately?

"You need a license to drive, but not to have a child," or "Children, unlike their toys, do not come with instructions."

Everyday attitudes relating to parenting, reflected in catch phrases such as these seem to indicate the difficulty or lack of direction parents face with the overwhelming responsibility for raising a moral adult. Over the course of human history, in every culture and in every era, questions have been raised, debated, settled, and re-examined with respect to the riddle of becoming a "good" parent. And the amount of concern we express over raising our children is exceeded only by the variety of parenting models currently being advocated. Everyone seems to have an opinion on how to raise children.

The recent pandemonium concerning teen violence has launched an explosion of explanations from so-called experts in the field who are attempting to account for what went wrong with these kids.   The conventional wisdom, espoused on recent TV new magazines such as *60 Minutes, 20/20, 48 Hours,* and *Dateline,* runs the gamut from claiming that violent kids should have been spanked more, to the fact that they were spanked too much, and from claiming that video games promote violence, to the conclusion that they provide a release from violent outbursts.

Many of these experts have offered to place the blame, or at least the liability, squarely on the parents of the children who have run afoul of society's standards. Lots of us seem to agree. For example, during an interview on *Dateline,* a family closely linked to the Columbine High massacre questioned the lack of awareness on the part of the parents of the two students involved in the killings. The outraged father exclaimed, "How is it possible for your child to be making pipe bombs in the basement and the parents claim they had no clue as to their activities. Where were they? Why didn't they know what their children were up to? I'll tell you why. They had long since given up the responsibility of raising their kids and they let them run wild. Now they should pay for the crimes their monsters have committed."

The more traditional psychologists attempt to account for the cause of teen behavior by looking to genetic or environmental factors. Still others attempt to solve the mystery of the teen "mentality" by claiming that its just a "phase" they are going through, or by claiming that these children are infected with evil and need religious salvation. From the Bible Belt to the coastlines and all points in between, a resurgence of religious training has taken our country by storm. Sunday morning evangelists are cramming the airwaves with advice to parents to protect their children from the evils of our materialistic culture by making sure they are taught "family values" and "brotherhood." This, they claim, is their only protection from the seductions of secular society.

In the face of all this conflicting advice, many parents seem to be throwing their hands in the air simply hoping that everything will turn out OK for their kids. Parenting, for many, has become the ultimate game of Russian Roulette. You close your eyes, cover your ears, and hope to God that when the gun is fired, your child is not the one who pulled the trigger or is struck by the bullet. When the last child turns 18, the parent can finally let go a big sigh of relief, providing they don't return home any time soon. Margaret W., a former student of mine and a single mother living in Las Vegas put it this way:

"I get home at 6:30 or so and I've been busting my butt all day. I'm tired and miserable but I try to find time for my kids: 2 boys, 8 & 11 years old. Thing is, I feel like I'm losing 'em to the neighborhood punks because they get out of school at about 3:15 and I don't know what they do with the time before I get home. I worry about them but feel helpless, I mean, I have to work or the State will take them away, right? I hope God is watching them when I can't."

The one thing that all of us, both layperson and expert, seem to agree on is that the cause of teen violence can be found in influential factors external to the psyche of the "offender." For it is correcting the behavior of the child that concerns us most, rather than discovering any essential cause. The dilemma we face in placing responsibility on the parents seems to be clearly defined as a question of quantity, of how much or to what degree a parent can, should, or did influence, control, shape, or mold their child. Surely this will be the bone of contention in any liability case brought forth by the victims.

Despite the fervor, the real dilemma, perhaps, is not found in how much or how well a parent can author the identity of a child, but rather in how judiciously a parent can teach a child to be the author of, and therefore responsible for, their own actions, and consequently their own identity.

Still, few doubt the right or the potential power and scope of a parent's ability to form a child's awareness of himself or his worldview. Indeed we hear much talk from educators about the "formative years" and the importance of learning by example and role modeling. An illustration from a recent episode of the Geraldo Rivera Show adds powerful testimony to this fact. A segment featured guests that had shaped their children into good neo-Nazis. The children were paraded for the entire world to see in their uniforms and with the gestures and the mantra of the cause perfectly memorized and efficiently demonstrated. The zombie-like children appeared robotic in their actions, and many of us may feel outraged or saddened by the depth that their ability to think for themselves has been overlaid by the dogma of their parent's beliefs.

And while we may be horrified by this form of "education" it raises a question that cuts to the heart of the national debate about ethical parenting, namely: Is there a difference between teaching and brainwashing, and how or where do we draw the line?

At least two extremes have emerged in response to this emotionally charged question. One camp, promoted by the famous child psychologist Dr. Spock, argues that the inculcation of a child's mind to any degree can stifle the development of the child's ego personality, creating automatons or puppets incapable of acting except in prescribed behavioral patterns. Spock's anything goes mentality was led by his belief in self-expression. And kids have been coloring outside the lines ever since. These people would be outraged not by what the parents of the neo-Nazi's have taught their children, but rather by the fact that they taught them at all. They call for the least restrictive or intrusive forms of parenting.

Another camp, spurred on by religious fundamentalists like Oral Roberts and Pat Robertson, claims that it is ridiculous and dangerous to let children grow up "wild," and so they call for the rigid formation of the child's mind based on scripture. It is thought that children will grow to know right from wrong and be saved only if the doctrine is implanted in their minds through rigorous religious training.

And as with the Jesuit tradition, they need only have access of the child's mind up to age 7. This camp would agree with the neo-Nazis that the children should be indoctrinated, but they would, of course, disagree with the content of this training.

While these two camps remain the most popular schools of child rearing in western culture today, it must be obvious that neither pays much attention to the individual spirit of the child. For, by placing emphasis on the behavior of the child, both these views account for a child's actions by appealing only to external influences. On the one hand, the so-called self-expressionists see the value of developing the freedom of the child, yet their solution is empty since they assume that the child will spontaneously develop his capacity of choice if he is allowed to simply express his natural instincts. But acting on one's instincts alone does little to prepare the child for making decisions and enhancing his spirit.

In a complex society filled with arbitrary rules, laws, and norms which seek to stop us from acting willy-nilly on our instinctual impulses, a child's ability to initiate or author action on his own can also be limited. Frustration is only increased as the self-expressive child confronts modern society's controls and is forced to repress his impulses, leading to all kinds of neurotic, and often savage, behavior. More importantly, a child who has no self-control can never be expected to attain the full potential of human freedom, and thus remains unfulfilled and incomplete, moved on not by his spiritual power to create meaning through choice, but by his biological urges.

On the other hand, the fundamentalist camp views the child's soul or spirit not as an individual entity with the right or even the capacity for free choice, but rather the soul as the property of God, and so it must be trained to act in accord with the maker's plan. Indeed, we have heard many people account for teen violence by laying responsibility on fate, chance, or God's will. But acting in accord with the will of God also seems to corrupt the child's spirit, and the force of early religious training has the same effect as the training of the neo-Nazis; the child is turned into a robot, capable of repeating the dogma while remaining unaware of why the dogma ought to be obeyed.

We see this concept in action in our culture expressed in pop moral imperatives like "Just do it" or "Just say no" which suggest that we need to act before we think or without any thought at all. Here a child's freedom is not promoted, but stolen by demanding conformity and blind faith. Moreover, the ability to act as a moral agent is also eliminated, for acting according to a creed or in obedience to an arbitrary authority is in no way conducive to moral action because the action is not done by reason of its being the right thing to do, in and of itself but, rather, because it will produce pleasure or prevent pain in the agent, and morality is then reduced to "what pays."

So, it is becoming clear to those of us bothering to look that in either of these two forms of child rearing the highest function of being human, namely the capacity for free choice, is ignored while the more base aspects of our identity, our instincts and our capacity for unconscious habituation are promoted. The consequences for the child are dire for with either of these two assessments, and many others as well (remember Russian Roulette parenting); the child develops an ill defined impetus and is incapable of forming judgments and making decisions that will promote his humanity, let alone the humanity of others. What we now need is to develop is a concept of parenting which balances these two extremes and tames the wild, overly self-expressive side of us and tempers the side of us that would brainwash, or erase from us, that which makes us most human.

Parents of violent teens, or of any children for that matter, can now be judged in the light of how well the parent has nourished, nurtured, and prepared the child to make free choices based on the spirit of the child himself. Maybe we can judge the parents of violent teens not so much by what the parents did to them, but more so by what they did not do. Ethical parenting may generally be defined as that which develops not only the lower order functions such as health and socialization, but the highest functions of being human which have to do with reflective, critical thought, in order to make responsible choices. And individual responsibility is only possible if the person is free to choose.   This broad freedom is impossible for the child of either the self-expressive parent or the religious fanatic because the perspective of the child is so narrow in scope that the child's choices are severely restricted and reduced to simple behavior.

While this is by no means an exhaustive accounting of an ethics of parenting, my goal was to raise an issue and evoke some new thinking on an old subject sorely in need of an injection of fresh ideas. One hasty response then to the question, "What can one do to become an ethical parent?" is to develop the child's capacity to make responsible choices by allowing the child a variety of experiences in an effort to expand their perspective of themselves and their world, and then holding the child, and the child alone, responsible for their choices. And this in turn assumes that the parent has the capacity of choice fully developed in their own character which, as we are all to well aware, is the rare exception rather than the rule.

We might further ask how parents who have themselves been brainwashed and indoctrinated or allowed to run wild are supposed to do a good job raising children who are free from these psychic infections. And we sink deeper into the parenting quagmire. But like any good mystery we must first get to the bottom of things before we can flush out the truth.□

—Used with permission.

DEFINING TERMS

Permissiveness

Authoritarian

Discipiine

Self-Expressive

WHAT DO YOU THINK?

1. What did you like most about your parents' relationship? What did you like least?

2. Why would you like (or not like) to be like your parents?

3. Do you feel that spanking or other physical punishment is appropriate? If so, why and when? If not, why not?

4. Can even good parents "screw up" their kids? Why or why not?

5. What do you think the hardest thing about parenting would be? What do you think the best thing would be?

View some reruns of "Roseanne" or "Family Ties." What are some parenting problems portrayed in those shows?

6. Who was Prometheus, and why does the second author call his approach Promethean? Do you agree with him? Why or why not?

⊗ VIDEO VIEWER:

Rent "Parenthood." List the problems of parenting depicted. Pick one, and tell how you might try to solve it differently.

Module Twelve

Work and Marriage

Women and Work

*O*ne of the biggest social changes in the last fifty years, according to many, has been the movement of women into the paid labor force. This notion is only partially correct, however. Women have always worked, and usually contributed to the economic well-being of the family as well as its physical well-being. In native societies, women's gatherings and/or horticulture provided the staples of a family's diet. In rural societies, women both worked alongside men producing cash crops in addition to producing goods for the family. As western societies industrialized, both men and women moved into the labor force, but women did so less, mainly working before marriage. After marrying, women often split household and childcare duties with tasks designed to produce goods needed for the household, such as gardening or clothes-making, or part-time activities that could be performed for money at home such as laundering, room-renting, etc.

*I*t was not until after WWII, that the notion of full-time housekeeping became promoted as an ideal, ironically at the same time that food distribution and labor-saving advances made those activities far less time consuming. During WWII, many women had entered the workforce to replace men in

---

Chapter Preview:

Women and Work

Consequences of Both Parents Working

Article: "America's Family Time Famine"

Article: "Is There a Second Shift?"

---

service, and when the war ended there was concern that the unemployment of the depression might return, unless the size of the labor force was decreased. Notions like college education, forty-hour work weeks, and returning women to the home were promoted.

There are a number of reasons for the entry (or re-entry) of great numbers of women into the workforce starting in the early seventies: [1] the growth of the service economy where women were already present, [2] the effects of the women's movement which pressured businesses to open opportunities to women, [3] changes in the economy which saw men's real (after inflation) wages decline to a level where most families required two incomes, and [4] rising divorce rates, which forced women to become financially more independent. So the actual changes in women's participation in the work force are the entry of married women and the fact of life-long employment for most women.

Consequences of Both Parents Working

What are the consequences of having both parents work to a family and a marriage? Sociologists have examined quite a number of factors. One early concern was the effects of mothers working on delinquency. While the results have been mixed, and other factors are more important, decreased supervision particularly when families are divorced or working during evenings has been found to increase the likelihood of delinquency. The effects of women working upon the marriage itself is also unclear. Although a certain amount of guilt has been found to occur among working women, it was less among women who enjoyed their careers. Men's self-esteem may be threatened if the wife makes more money, but generally there is little effect on their emotional well-being. The employment of women may have had an effect on the increased divorce rate, however, as women are less likely to see finances as a barrier to leaving unhappy marriages.

One thing has clearly happened in the last twenty years, with both sexes working harder, the pressures on families have increased. The following two articles explore some of the results. □

References

Bradley, Harriet. 1989. *Men's work, women's work.* Minneapolis: University of Minnesota Press.

Rice, F.P. 1996. *Intimate relationships, marriages and families.* Mountainview, CA: Mayfield.

Shehan, C.L. & K.C. Kammeyer. 1997. *Marriages and families: Reflections of a gendered society.* Boston: Allyn & Bacon.

Tilly, Louise & Joan Scott. 1978. *Women, work and the family.* New York: Holt & Rhinehart.

Wells, J.G. 1991. *Choices in marriage and family.* Alta Loma, CA: Collegiate Press.

❏ America's Family Time Famine

William R. Mattox, Jr.

Many parents in America today are out of time. Out of gas. Running on empty. "On the fast track of two-career families in the go-go society of modern life, the most rationed commodity in the home is time," observes syndicated columnist Suzanne Fields. And the children of today's overextended parents are starving, starving from a lack of parental time, attention and affection.

Parents today spend 40 percent less time with their children than did parents in 1965, according to data collected from personal time diaries by sociologist John Robinson of the University of Maryland. In 1965, parents spent approximately 30 hours a week with their kids. By 1985, parent-child interaction had dropped to just 17 hours a week.

These changes are presenting significant challenges to American family life. Parents today employ a variety of time management strategies to meet their work and family responsibilities. In roughly one-third of all two-income families today (one-half of those with preschoolers) spouses work complementary shifts to maximize the amount of time children are cared for by at least one parent. The most common "tag-team" arrangement is one in which the father works a standard 9-to-5 job and the mother works part-time in the evenings or on weekends.

Other two-income households work concurrent shifts. Families in which the youngest child is of school age often choose this strategy to minimize the amount of time parents are unavailable to children during non-school hours. Same-shift arrangements are also common among families in which both parents have a high attachment to their careers and in those in which limited employment opportunities leave few alternatives.

Whether couples adopt a tag-team arrangement or a same-shift strategy, two income households spend considerably less time with their children than do breadwinner-homemaker households. (Although there are certainly some traditional families that suffer from father absence due to the time-demanding nature of the sole breadwinner's work.) This discrepancy is most pronounced in maternal time with children. In fact, research by University of Virginia sociologists Steven Nock and Paul William Kingston shows that employed mothers of preschool children on average spend less than half as much time with their children as full-time mothers at home. Moreover, Nock and Kingston show that employed mothers do not compensate for this shortage in quantity of time by devoting a higher proportion of the time they do spend with children to "high quality" child-centered activities such as playing with dolls, going to the park, or reading.

Time pressures can be especially daunting for single parents and especially harmful to their children. Children in single-parent homes usually receive less parental attention and supervision than other children. Not only is one parent absent from the home (and research by sociologist Frank Furstenberg shows that three-fourths of all children of divorce have contact with their fathers less than two days a month), but the other parent is overloaded with money-making and household tasks. Indeed, Robinson's data show that, on average, single mothers spend 33 percent less time each week than married mothers in primary child-care activities such as dressing, feeding, chauffeuring, talking, playing, or helping with homework.

Moreover, children in single-parent families often have very irregular schedules. One study found that preschool children of single mothers sleep two fewer hours a night on average than their counterparts in two-parent homes, in part because harried mothers find it difficult to maintain a consistent bedtime routine.

Sibling Revelry

Kids aren't just missing out on time with their parents. Thanks to the "birth dearth," they are also missing out on interaction with siblings.

In 1975, 62 percent of all women aged 40-44 had given birth to three or more children over the course of their lifetimes. In 1988, only 38 percent had done so. The percentage of those giving birth to just one child rose from 9 to 15 percent during this same time period.

Some regard the decline in family size as a positive development because it means children today receive more individualized attention from their parents than did children a generation ago.

Even if this were true--and sociologist Harriet Presser reports "not only are Americans having fewer children than ever before, they are spending less time with the children they have"--it can hardly be argued that a one-child family generally has as rich a family experience as a larger family. Even if an only child receives more individualized parental attention, he still misses out on the intimate joys of having brothers and sisters, playing wiffle ball in the backyard, exchanging gifts at Christmas time, double teaming Dad in a wrestling match on the family room floor, attending a sibling's ballet recital, and (later in life) reminiscing about old times at family reunions.

Today's fast-paced family life is also eroding the development of other aspects of what sociologist David Popenoe of Rutgers University says "is arguably the ideal child-rearing environment": a relatively large family that does a lot of things together, has many routines and traditions, and provides a great deal of quality contact time between adults and children; regular contact with relatives, active neighboring in a supportive neighborhood, and contact with the world of work; little concern on the part of children that their parents will break up; and the coming together of all these ingredients in the development of a rich family subculture that has lasting meaning and strongly promulgates such family values as cooperation and sharing.

Eating dinner together is one time honored family tradition some believe is on its way out. "The family meal is dead," columnist Jonathan Yardley has written. "Except on the rarest occasions, Christmas, Thanksgiving, certain religious holidays when we reach down to the innermost depths of the tribal memory and summon up turkeys and pies, roasts and casseroles, we have given up on what was once a central element in American domestic life."

Research on the prevalence of regular family mealtimes is mixed. Some reports claim as many as 75 percent of all families regularly dine together, while others suggest less than 35 percent do so. Whatever the case, polls taken by the Roper organization show that the proportion of families that dine together regularly declined 10 percent between 1976 and 1986. This helps explain why heat-and-eat microwavable dinners for children to prepare alone are "the hottest new category in food products," according to a food industry spokesperson.

Whatever the virtues of microwavable meals and other convenience foods, there is reason to be concerned about children routinely feeding themselves. As Suzanne Fields observes, "The child who grazes, standing in front of a microwave eating his fried chicken, biscuits, or refried beans, won't starve, but he may suffer from an emotional hunger that would be better satisfied if only Mom and Dad were there to yell at him for every pea he slips onto the knife."

So Many Bills, So Little Time

So how did American families run out of time? Growing economic pressures have a lot to do with the American family time crisis.

One of the supreme ironies of recent economic developments is that while America has experienced steady growth in its gross national product, the economic pressures on families with children have risen significantly. How can it be that at the same time we hear so much about the longest peacetime economic expansion in our nation's history, we also hear talk that economic pressures have grown so much that many families today must have two incomes?

Wage stagnation is one big reason. During the 1970s and 80s, constant dollar earnings of American husbands grew at less than 1 percent per year compared to a real growth rate of 3 percent per year in the 1950s and 60s. Moreover, for some occupational and demographic groups--particularly non-supervisory workers and males under age 25--real wages have actually fallen since 1973.

While wages have stagnated, taxes have risen dramatically. In 1950, a median-income family of four paid 2 percent of its annual gross earnings to the federal government in income and payroll taxes. Today, it pays 24 percent. In addition, state and local taxes, on average, take another 8 percent from the family's gross income.

Moreover, the erosion in the value of the personal exemption (the tax code's chief mechanism for adjusting tax liability to reflect differences in family size) has shifted more of the federal income tax burden onto the backs of families with dependents. Had the exemption kept pace with inflation since 1950, it would now be worth close to $7,000. Instead, it stands at $2,050.

On top of this, families are finding their take-home pay does not go as far as it once did. As economist Sylvia Ann Hewlett puts it, families today are "like hamsters on a wheel," running hard just to keep up.

Over the past 25 years, increases in the cost of several major family expenses-- housing, health care, transportation, and higher education--have significantly outpaced the general inflation rate. For example, Joseph Minarik of the Congressional Joint Economic Committee has calculated that the typical 30-year-old man could get a mortgage on a median-priced home in 1973 with 21 percent of his income. By 1987, a median-priced home mortgage would take 40 percent of a typical 30-year-old's gross income.

The cost of housing, which is typically a family's single greatest expense, is tied directly to crime rates and school districts. As crime rates have risen and school performance has declined, an under-supply of housing in good school districts with low crime rates has driven the price of housing in such neighborhoods way up. Thus, parents who value safety, education, and time with children must either live in areas with poorer schools and higher crime or divert time from children to market their labor in order to purchase a home in a safe neighborhood with good schools. That is a quintessential Hobson's choice.

Perrier and Teddy Bears

Growing economic pressures aren't the only reason families have less time together. A number of cultural factors have also played a major role.

"Unbridled careerism" is partly responsible for the decline in family time, says Karl Zinsmeister of the American Enterprise Institute. "For years, one of the most cogent criticisms of American sex roles and economic arrangements has been the argument that many fathers get so wrapped up in earning and doing at the workplace that they become dehumanized, losing interest in the intimate joys of family life and failing to participate fairly in domestic responsibilities," he writes. "Now it appears workaholism and family dereliction have become equal opportunity diseases, striking mothers as much as fathers."

The devaluation of motherhood stands behind such trends. As Zinsmeister notes, "Today, women are more likely to be admired and appreciated for launching a catchy new ad campaign for toothpaste than they are for nurturing and shaping an original personality." Ironically, this has a detrimental impact on fatherhood as well. So long as childrearing is viewed as a low calling for women, it is unlikely that it will take on increased significance for men.

Apart from unbridled careerism, some of the reduction in family time has been driven by a rampant materialism that places a higher premium on obtaining or retaining a "Perrier and Rolex life-style" than on investing time in a larger kin group.

"Increasingly, Americans are pursuing a selfish individualism that is inconsistent with strong families and strong communities," writes University of North Carolina sociologist Peter Uhlenberg. "This movement is fueled by the media, most especially television (both in its programming and advertising), which suggests that personal happiness is the highest good and that it can be achieved by pursuing pleasure and material goods."

Indeed, it has become all too common for parents to buy material goods for their children in an attempt to compensate for their frequent absence from the home. Harvard University child psychiatrist Robert Coles calls this the "teddy bear syndrome":

> Some of the frenzied need of children to have possessions isn't only a function of the ads they see on TV. It's a function of their hunger for what they aren't getting: their parents' time. The biggest change I have seen in 30 years of interviewing families is that children are no longer being cared for by their parents the way they once were. Parents are too busy spending their most precious capital--their time and their energy--struggling to keep up with MasterCard payments. They're depleted. They work long hours to barely keep up, and when they get home at the end of the day they're tired. And their kids are left with a Nintendo or a pair of Nikes or some other piece of crap. Big deal.

Swimming Upstream

Of course, not all parents are trying to "buy off" their children with Teenage Mutant Ninja Turtles gear or overpriced sneakers. Many are struggling to raise responsible children and to transmit family values such as sharing, responsibility, commitment, and self-control. But these families are finding themselves swimming upstream against an increasingly unfriendly culture that instead promotes casual sex, instant gratification and selfish individualism.

Whereas once institutions outside the family, such as schools, churches. the mass media, and businesses, formerly reinforced the inculcation of traditional values, today they are often indifferent or downright hostile to family values and the rights of parents to pass on such values to their children. Many parents sense that they are being undercut by larger institutional forces. And they recognize that children who lack the self-esteem that comes from parental attention and affection are especially vulnerable to negative peer and cultural influences.

Doing things together . . .

Some opinion leaders in government, academia, and the mass media view initiatives designed to increase family time, especially those that recognize the legitimacy and strengths of the breadwinner-homemaker family model, as an attempt to "turn back the clock" rather than "facing the realities" of modern family life. These leaders overlook the fact that concerns about family time are not limited to those who believe the traditional family model is ideal.

A 1989 Cornell University study found that two-thirds of all mothers employed full-time would like to work fewer hours so that they could devote more time to their families. And when respondents to a 1989 survey commissioned by the Mass Mutual Insurance Company were asked to identify "extremely effective" ways to strengthen the family, nearly twice as many opted for "spending more time together" than listed "full-time parent raising kids."

Moreover, most Americans do not sneer at the past the way elitists do. As Whitehead observes:

> In the official debate (on family issues), the remembered past is almost always considered a suspect, even unhealthy, guide for the present or future . . . . But for the parents I met, the remembered past is not a dusty artifact of the good old days; it is an important and vital

social resource. Parents take instruction from their own family 's past, rummaging through it for usable truths and adopting, or modifying or occasionally rejecting, its values . . . . In the official language, the family isn't getting weaker, it's just "changing." Most parents I met believe otherwise.

Americans believe "parents having less time to spend with their families" is the most important reason for the family's decline in our society, according to a recent survey. And most parents would like to see the work-family pendulum swing back in the direction of home.

To be sure, most children would not object to spending more unhurried time with their parents. Indeed, when 1,500 schoolchildren were asked, "What do you think makes a happy family?" social scientists Nick Stinnett and John DeFrain report that children "did not list money, cars, fine homes, or televisions." Instead the answer most frequently offered was "doing things together." □

– *This article appeared · in* Children Today, *Volume 19, number 6, 1990. A government publication.*

□ Is There a Second Shift?

Randall Prebinski

Many changes have rocked the American family since the 1960s. The sexual revolution, divorce, women's liberation, single parents, but perhaps the largest of these was the great expansion of women into the workforce. Previously, women indeed worked, at least some did all the time, and nearly all at least some of the time. Lower and lower-middle class women did work consistently, mostly at low-paying jobs, and middle class women worked during school or for a few years until they married or had children. A few noble souls continued to support their husbands through graduate degrees and were hopefully rewarded by a better lifestyle afterwards, though there were many horror stories about new M.D.s and lawyers dropping their long-suffering spouses for the more glamorous types they felt their new degrees entitled. But mostly, women were supposed to stay home.

All this began to change in the 1970s. Motivated partially by new opportunities to "have it all"--career and family--and perhaps by fear at the rising divorce rate, women entered the workforce in record numbers. The overall effect on society and the economy is still to be determined, but there is no doubt that it was fabulous for U.S. corporations. The increase in the supply of workers kept wages low despite an expanding economy, to such an extent that two wage earners are now required to support a family in a lifestyle similar to that provided earlier by a single wage· earner--and this despite nearly 20 years of exceptionally low inflation.

Women's entry into careers also proved somewhat less than fantasized. Though an historic number of women became judges, politicians, university professors, and lawyers, many women discovered a "glass ceiling" that allowed them to be promoted just so far as middle management, but not into the uppermost echelons.

Likewise, the movement away from home was not without drawbacks. Many women found that adding responsibilities away from home did not cause a decrease in work to do around the house. And far from welcoming them into their new careers by volunteering for extra housework, many men resented the demand that they suddenly take up some of the slack. Other men attempted to do so, but were they making the grade? This was the question raised in the late 1980s by Berkeley sociologist Arlie Hochschild.

Dr. Hochschild garnered much attention by asserting a new "double standard" was evolving in the modern family, not in the bedroom where sexual mores were now becoming equalized, but in the whole house, so to speak--in that whereas the family contract once stated that men worked and women cleaned, now that women were working more, men weren't cleaning. As she put it, the exodus of women from the home to work "has not been accompanied by a new view of marriage and work that would make this transition smooth." Workplaces were not flexible to the new needs of working families, and most men had yet to adapt to the new roles at home. She explained this phenomenon as being a "stalled revolution." In fact, she called the additional work women were now doing a "Second Shift."

Hochschild studied 52 families over an eight year period. She found that, counting housework, women worked roughly fifteen hours a week more than men. This would be the equivalent of the typical moonlighting second job. Hence the term "second shift." Over time, that adds up to an extra month per year of work.

Many men did pitch in to help. Twenty percent of Hochschild's study shared household duties equally. Seventy percent did a substantial amount (less than half, but more than a third.) Only ten percent did less than a third. But even when couples shared equally, women did 2/3 of the daily jobs like cooking and cleaning up. Men did a disproportionate share of maintenance type tasks, like changing the oil in the car, yard work or fixing an appliance. These tasks are often time-consuming, but can be postponed until "I have time." Men thus have more control over when they make their contributions than women do.

One result of this discrepancy is women's greater stress. Women talked much more, according to Hochschild, about being sick, overtired or emotionally drained. A number were fixated on the topic of sleep: how much they could "get by on," who they knew who needed less. Women also talked about trying to do two jobs at once: writing checks and returning phone calls, vacuuming and watching the kids.

The result of all this was clear. Hochschild cited research by George Levenger finding "neglect of family or home" the number two common reason given by women for divorce, right after "mental cruelty," in the 600 couples he studied.

Some limitations do need to be pointed out. Her study was of only 52 couples, small by any standard, and geographically limited to the San Francisco Bay area. Additionally, some critics have pointed to studies showing men commuting over half an hour longer per day, and men working more overtime than women. Put together, this may account for nearly the entire two hour a day difference in workloads. Men put in greater amounts of time at work or in their car before they get home.

Nevertheless, it's still clear that women are working harder at home, right? Maybe so, but maybe they don't need to, say these critics. They point to Hochschild's own findings that women take the primary reponsibility for many household tasks. "Women often don't want to give up tasks if they feel men won't do as 'good' a job," said one female marriage counselor. "They often have higher standards of cleanliness, neatness, etc., than do their men. Especially with small children, women may have an irrational fear that men can't handle them or may let them hurt themselves. In essence, they feel they have to be Supermoms."

Elissa is one example of this syndrome. She has been married thirteen years to an Air Force officer, and worked full-time since she was eighteen. After four years of marriage they had their first child. She continued working, moving into higher paying positions to help pay for child-care. The daycare providers she utilised frequently told her that "good mothers would not want to work and let someone else take care of their child." She felt torn in many directions, dissatisfied and turned to magazine articles to see what she was doing wrong . "There were all sorts of articles on how to clean faster, spend quality time, spend less time on make-up and still be the perfect mom. There were endless articles about moms who were perfect in their job, had the perfect marriage, perfect children and the perfect home."

After a year of marriage counseling, her husband finally got the message and now does all the dishes, laundry and four hours of childcare per weekend. Since he's traveling a lot during the week, this is a substantial investment of his time at home. But Elissa had to lower her standards, too.

"I lowered my expectations about the cleanliness of the home, the extra-curricular activities of the kids, and I no longer cook extraordinary meals. But it wasn't worth it anyway."

"I had to let go of the feeling that others would judge me by the cleanliness of my house," said another working wife and mother. "The only opinions that really count is that of my family."

Another issue is how women raise the issue of work. Too often, say some experts, women end up being like bosses at home, assigning tasks to their husbands and checking up on them. This makes men feel like unpaid employees, a feeling women might recognize, but which works even worse without the motivation of the traditional sex role expectations.

"Men need to be shown that participating in housework is participating in family life," says one counselor who leads workshops for couples. "But women need to be careful about demanding changes. Men don't respond to that, and if they do it's resentfully. After all, men didn't ask for women to join the workforce, though they're probably grateful for the extra income."

"There needs to be real communication about tasks and standards, and real negotiation. Women shouldn't assume they're automatically right about things like housework, but set up an agreement that is satisfactory to both parties."

One good note in Hochschild's research is that men are starting to take up more of the childrearing duties. "Absent fathers will hopefully become a thing of the past, at least in two-parent families," says one therapist in the San Francisco Bay Area.

Still, there is much to be done. Hochschild goes beyond just individual solutions to recommend tax breaks for companies that offer job-sharing, flex time, and part-time work. This means putting our money where our mouths are. It also means changing the way we look at families and work.□

– Used by permission.

DEFINING TERMS

Inflation

Careerism

Family Leave/Paternity Leave

Dual Career Families

WHAT DO YOU THINK?

1. List several factors that have contributed to increasing numbers of women working outside the home. Which is (are) most significant for the future? Why?

2. What are the advantages and disadvantages of dual-career marriages? What will you choose and why?

3. What can be done about the fact that working women still bear the largest part of the household and childrearing burden?

4. Men often believe, though research shows otherwise, that they are contributing equally to the housework. How can this be so?

VIDEO VIEWER:

Rent "Mr. Mom" and "9 to 5." What do these comedies tell us about real tensions between males and females at home and work?

MEDIA WATCHER:

What sitcoms deal with problems of balancing work and home lives? Housework issues? How realistic are they?

Part Five
Communication and Conflict

Module Thirteen

Communication

Seldom is anything proposed as a relationship panacea so often as communication. When students hear of couples' problems, their immediate advice is nearly always . . . more communication. Few people think of themselves as poor communicators, but the divorce and breakup statistics give lie to that idea. Most people do fairly well at expressing their ideas in ordinary situations, but under the stresses and strains of daily life and long-term relationships, many pitfalls emerge. Communication is a much more complex process than one might think. There are a number of factors which account for this complexity.

Communication complexities

♦ Multiple word meanings: Many words have a number of meanings, for example, "it's my turn," versus "turn around." Listeners sometimes must hear an entire sentence to understand a meaning.

♦ Inflection meanings: Some experts believe that sometimes as little as 10% of a phrase's meaning may be contained in its words alone. Often a larger percentage is determined by the intonations the speaker uses. Such inflections indicate whether the person is stating a fact, questioning, being humorous, sarcastic, or other possibilities.

♦ Non-verbal communications: Meanings are also given through facial expressions and gestures. Both speakers and listeners must pay attention to the cues given by these means.

♦Connotations: Besides having an official meaning, most words have connotations-- unofficial meanings, associations and images that come to mind when the word is thought of --and people's connotations often differ. For example, plump to one person may mean heavier than average but not fat, but to another may have the connotation of "being like Aunt Mary" who was "gross."

♦ What isn't said: Sometimes what is said can be less important than what is left unsaid. Particularly when there are expectations or situations that call for a typical response, not

Chapter Preview:

Communication Complexities

The Communication Process

Article: "What Makes Love Last?"

Note: On Communication Styles

saying something could be an act of hostility, or conversely could be an expression of politeness. And it could be difficult to tell which.

The communication process

The process of communication itself is complex. It is not simply a process of one person sending a communication and the other receiving, but a much more complicated one that includes several steps: thinking, censoring, expressing, monitoring, and adjusting on the part of the sender, and simultaneous listening, reacting, and understanding on the part of the receiver.

For example, suppose a wife is upset because her husband was talking too loudly at a party. She might think he was "being a jerk," but might censor that as too extreme; instead she might express the words, "Don't you think you were talking a little loudly?" while unconsciously frowning, and clenching her hand.

The husband might see her frown and think, "Oh no, now she's going to get on my case," and react with a scowl which the wife would monitor and adjust her communication -- probably without knowing what caused his reaction. She might get angry, feeling that he wasn't interested in listening, or alternatively soften her tone, fearing she'd hurt his feelings. His response when finally uttered, would go through a similar complex process.

Because of these complications, communications can be highly unpredictable-- and even more so when we consider two other factors:

♦ Emotions: Communication becomes especially difficult when people are upset. This is unfortunate, because it is probably the precise moment when we need communication to be clearest. But under stress, we may miss subtle cues, say things we don't really mean, say them too loudly and react to unintentional connotations.

♦ Ego defenses: In order to feel happy about themselves, people need to maintain a positive self image. This self-concept is based on how we view ourselves. We like to think of ourselves as good people, as kind or strong or smart or whatever. Depressed people tend to have a negative self-image. We protect ourselves against depression and other complexes by maintaining an ego defense that protects our self-esteem from being too easily lowered. Comments seen as criticism can be felt as threatening to the ego, since it seems to attack the basis of our self-esteem. This particularly seems true if we have been heavily criticized as children, or the criticism strikes at an important foundation of our self-concept, or it hits at a weak or sensitive point. When their self-concept is threatened, people often respond with anger or defensiveness even if no threat was intended.

Given the many hurdles faced in communications, it is no wonder many communication attempts founder, particularly in couples going through difficulties. There is good news, though. Social scientists have begun to study communication, and are beginning to understand what works. Communication counselors at the University of Denver have found that they can reduce the likelihood of divorce by almost 50%, through a course teaching basic communications skills over a few weeks, and other innovative programs also offer significant benefits. The following article shows one such program.□

References

Brinkman, Rick & Rick Kirschner. 1995. *Dealing with people you can't stand.* New York: McGraw-Hill.

Hybels, Saundra & R.L. Weaver. 1986. *Communicating effectively.* New York: Random House.

Giblin, Les. 1956. *How you can have confidence and power.* Englewood Cliffs, NJ: Prentice-Hall.

Wells, J.G. 1991. *Choices in marriage and family.* Alta Loma, CA: Collegiate Press.

◻ What Makes Love Last?

Alan AtKisson

My old friends Karen and Bill, married since 1955, recently celebrated another anniversary. "I wore the same nightgown I wore on our wedding night," confessed Karen to me over the phone. "Just as I have every anniversary for thirty-nine years."

"I wore pajamas on our wedding night," offered Bill. "But last night I didn't wear nothin'." They laughed, and even over three thousand miles of telephone wire I felt the strength of their love for one another.

Long-lasting marriages like Bill's and Karen's are becoming increasingly rare. Not only do more than 50 percent of all first marriages in the United States end in divorce (make that 60 percent for repeat attempts), but fewer people are even bothering to tie the slippery knot in the first place. One fourth of Americans eighteen or older--about 41 million people--have never married at all. In I970, that figure was only one sixth.

But even while millions of couples march down the aisle only to pass through the therapist's office and into divorce court, a quiet revolution is taking place when it comes to understanding how long-term love really works. Inside the laboratories of the Family Formation Project at the University of Washington in Seattle, affectionately dubbed the Love Lab, research psychologists are putting our most cherished relationship theories under the scientific microscope. What they're discovering is that much of what we regard as conventional wisdom is simply wrong.

"Almost none of our theory and practice [in marital therapy] is founded on empirical scientific research," contends the Love Lab's head, John Gottman, an award-winning research psychologist trained both as a therapist and a mathematician. Indeed, it is this lack of solid research, Gottman believes, that contributes to a discouraging statistic: for 50 percent of married couples who enter therapy, divorce is still the end result.

Gottman believes that, although relationship counseling has helped many people, much of it just doesn't work. Not satisfied with warm and fuzzy ideas about how to "get the love you want," Gottman is scouting for numbers, data, proof, and he's finding it.

For the past twenty years, in a laboratory equipped with video cameras, EKGs, and an array of custom-designed instruments, Gottman and his colleagues have been intensely observing what happens when couples interact. He watches them talk. He watches them fight. He watches them hash out problems and reaffirm their love. He records facial expressions and self-reported emotions, heart rhythms and blood chemistry. He tests urine, memories, and couples' ability to interpret each other's emotional cues. Then he pours his data, like so many puzzle pieces, into a computer. The resulting picture, he says, is so clear and detailed it's like "a CAT scan of a living relationship."

What Gottman and his colleagues have discovered and summarized for popular audiences in a new book, *Why Marriages Succeed or Fail* (Simon & Schuster), is mind-boggling in its very simplicity. His conclusion: Couples who stay together are . . . well . . . nice to each other more often than not. "Satisfied couples," claims Gottman, "maintained a five-to-one ratio of positive to negative moments" in their relationship. Couples heading for divorce, on the other hand, allow that ratio to slip below one-to-one.

If it ended there, Gottman's research might remain just an interesting footnote. But for him and his colleagues, this discovery is just the beginning. In fact, Gottman's novel and methodical approach to marriage research is threatening to turn much of current relationship therapy on its head. He contends that many aspects of wedded life often considered critical to long-term success--how intensely people fight; whether they face conflict or avoid it; how well they solve problems; how compatible they are socially, financially, even sexually--are less important than people (including therapists) tend to think. In fact, Gottman believes, none of these things matter to a marriage's longevity as much as maintaining that crucial ratio of five to one.

If it's hard to believe that the longevity of your relationship depends primarily on your being five times as nice as you are nasty to each other, some of Gottman's other conclusions may be even more surprising. For example:

♦ Wildly explosive relationships that vacillate between heated arguments and passionate reconciliations can be as happy--and long-lasting--as those that seem more emotionally stable. They may even be more exciting and intimate.

♦ Emotionally inexpressive marriages, which may seem like repressed volcanoes destined to explode, are actually very successful--so long as the couple maintains that five-to-one ratio in what they do express to each other. In fact, too much emotional catharsis among such couples can "scare the hell out of them," says Gottman.

♦ Couples who start out complaining about each other have some of the most stable marriages over time, while those who don't fight early on are more likely to hit the rocky shoals of divorce.

♦ Fighting, whether rare or frequent, is sometimes the healthiest thing a couple can do for their relationship. In fact, blunt anger, appropriately expressed, "seems to immunize marriages against deterioration."

♦ In happy marriages, there are no discernible gender differences in terms of the quantity and quality of emotional expression. In fact, men in happy marriages are more likely to reveal intimate personal information about themselves than women. (When conflict erupts, however, profound gender differences emerge.)

♦ Men who do housework are likely to have happier marriages, greater physical health, even better sex lives than men who don't. (This piece of news alone could cause a run on aprons.)

♦ Women are made physically sick by a relentlessly unresponsive or emotionally contemptuous husband. Gottman's researchers can even tell just how sick: They can predict the number of infectious diseases women in such marriages will suffer over a four-year period.

♦ How warmly you remember the story of your relationship foretells your chances for staying together. In one study that involved taking oral histories from couples about the unfolding of their relationship, psychologists were able to predict--with an astonishing 94 percent accuracy--which couples would be divorced within three years.

Three Varieties of Marriage

In person, Gottman is a fast-talking, restless intellect, clearly in love with his work. Now in his late forties and seven years into a second marriage (to clinical psychologist Julie Schwartz), he seems very satisfied. Yet, in his book, he sheds the mantle of guru in the first sentence: "My personal life has not been a trail of great wisdom in understanding relationships," he says. "My expertise is in the scientific observation of couples."

Gottman began developing this expertise some twenty years ago, when a troubled couple who came to him for help didn't respond well to conventional therapy. In frustration, Gottman suggested that they try videotaping the sessions. "Both the couple and I were astonished by the vividness and clarity on the tape of the pattern of criticism, contempt, and defensiveness they repeatedly fell into," he recalls. "It shocked them into working harder . . . [and] it gave me my life's work."

Struck by the power of impartial observation, Gottman became fascinated with research. His goal: to systematically describe the differences between happy and unhappy couples, and from those observations develop a scientific theory capable of predicting marital success. This seemed a daunting task, both because "marriage is so subjective" and because "personality theory, in psychology, has been a failure at predicting anything."

The result of Gottman's passion is a veritable mountain of data: tens of thousands of observations involving thousands of couples, gathered by the Love Lab's researchers and stored in its computer data-bases. The geography of that mountain reveals a surprising pattern: Successful marriages come in not one but three different varieties, largely determined by how a couple handles their inevitable disagreements. Gottman calls these three types of stable marriages validating, volatile, and conflict-avoiding.

Validating couples are what most people (including most therapists) have in mind when they think of a "good marriage." Even when these couples don't agree, they "still let their partner know that they consider his or her opinions and emotions valid." They

"compromise often and calmly work out their problems to mutual satisfaction as they arise." And when they fight, they know how to listen, acknowledge their differences, and negotiate agreement without screaming at each other. "These couples," Gottman notes, "look and sound a lot like two psychotherapists engaging in a dialogue."

But where modern therapy often goes wrong, says Gottman, is in assuming that this is the only way a marriage can work--and trying to force all couples into the validating mold. While "viewing this style of marriage as the ideal has simplified the careers of marital therapists," it hasn't necessarily helped their clients, he says, who may fall into the other two types of stable pattern.

Volatile couples, in contrast to validating ones, thrive on unfiltered emotional intensity. Their relationships are full of angry growls and passionate sighs, sudden ruptures and romantic reconciliations. They may fight bitterly (and even unfairly), and they may seem destined for divorce to anyone watching them squabble. But Gottman's data indicate that this pessimism is often misplaced: These couples will stay together if "for every nasty swipe, there are five caresses." In fact, "the passion and relish with which they fight seems to fuel their positive interactions even more." Such couples are more romantic and affectionate than most--but they are also more vulnerable to a decay in that all-important five-to-one ratio (and at their worst, to violence). Trying to change the style of their relationship not only isn't necessary, Gottman says, it probably won't work.

Nor will conflict-avoiding couples, the third type of stable marriage, necessarily benefit from an increase in their emotional expression, he says. Gottman likens such unions to "the placid waters of a summer lake," where neither partner wants to make waves. They keep the peace and minimize argument by constantly agreeing to disagree. "In these relationships, solving a problem usually means ignoring the difference, one partner agreeing to act more like the other . . . or most often just letting time take its course." The universal five-to-one ratio must still be present for the couple to stay together, but it gets translated into a much smaller number of swipes and caresses (which are also less intensely expressed). This restrained style may seem stifling to some, but the couple themselves can experience it as a peaceful contentment.

Things get more complicated when the marriage is "mixed"--when, say, a volatile person marries someone who prefers to minimize conflict. But Gottman suggests that, even in these cases, "it may be possible to borrow from each marital style and create a viable mixed style." The most difficult hurdle faced by couples with incompatible fighting styles lies in confronting that core difference and negotiating which style (or combination of styles) they will use. If they can't resolve that primary conflict, it may be impossible to tip the overall balance of their relational life in the direction of five-to-one.

The important thing here is to find a compatible fighting style--not to stop fighting altogether. Gottman is convinced that the "one" in that ratio is just as important as the "five": "What may lead to temporary misery in a marriage--disagreement and anger--may be healthy for it in the long run." Negativity acts as the predator in the ecosystem of marriage, says Gottman. It's the lion that feeds on the weakest antelopes and makes the herd stronger. Couples who never disagree at all may start out happier than others, but without some conflict to resolve their differences, their marriages may soon veer toward divorce because their "ecosystem" is out of balance.

The Four Horsemen of the Apocalypse

Even the most stable marriages of any style can fall apart, and Gottman and company have observed an all-too-predictable pattern in their decline and fall. He likens the process to a cascade--a tumble down the rapids--that starts with the arrival of a dangerous quartet of behaviors. So destructive is their effect on marital happiness, in fact, that he calls these behaviors "The Four Horsemen of the Apocalypse."

The first horseman is criticism: "attacking someone's personality or character" rather than making some specific complaint about his or her behavior. The difference between saying, say, "I wish you had taken care of that bill" (a healthy and specific complaint) and "You never get the bills paid on time!" (a generalizing and blaming attack) is very significant to the listener. Criticism often engenders criticism in return and sets the stage for the second horseman: contempt.

"What separates contempt from criticism," explains Gottman, "is the intention to insult and psychologically abuse your partner." Negative thoughts about the other come out in subtle put-downs, hostile jokes, mocking facial expressions, and name-calling ("You are such an idiot around money"). By now the positive qualities that attracted you to this person seem long ago and far away, and instead of trying to build intimacy, you're ushering in the third horseman.

Defensiveness comes on the heels of contempt as a seemingly reasonable response to attack--but it only makes things worse. By denying responsibility, making excuses, whining, tossing back counter-attacks, and other strategies ("How come I'm the one who always pays the bills?!"), you just accelerate your speed down river. Gottman also warns that it's possible to skip straight to the third horseman by being oversensitive about legitimate complaints.

Once stonewalling (the fourth horseman) shows up, things are looking bleak. Stonewallers simply stop communicating, refusing to respond even in self-defense. Of course, all these "horsemen" drop in on couples once in a while. But when a partner habitually shuts down and withdraws, the final rapids of negativity (what Gottman calls the "Distance and Isolation Cascade") can quickly propel the marriage through whirlpools of hopelessness, isolation, and loneliness over the waterfall of divorce. With the arrival of the fourth horseman, one or both partners is thinking negative thoughts about his or her counterpart most of the time, and the couple's minds--as well as their bodies--are in a perpetual state of defensive red alert.

The stress of conflict eventually sends blood pressure, heart rate, and adrenaline into the red zone--a phenomenon Gottman calls flooding. "The body of someone who feels flooded," he writes, "is a confused jumble of signals. It may be hard to breathe . . . . Muscles tense up and stay tensed. The heart beats fast, and it may seem to beat harder." Emotionally, the flooded person may feel a range of emotions, from fear to anger to confusion.

The bottom line is that flooding is physically uncomfortable, and stonewalling becomes an attempt to escape that discomfort. When flooding becomes chronic, stonewalling can become chronic, too. Eighty-five percent of the time the stonewaller (among heterosexual couples) is the man. The reason for this gender discrepancy is one of many physiological phenomena that Gottman sees as critical to understanding why marriages go sour, and what people can do to fix them.

Though flooding happens to both men and women, it affects men more quickly, more intensely, and for a longer period of time. "Men tend to have shorter fuses and longer-lasting explosions than women," says Gottman. Numerous observations in the laboratory have shown that it often takes mere criticism to set men off, whereas women require something at least on the level of contempt. The reasons for this are left to speculation. "Probably this difference in wiring had evolutionary survival benefits," Gottman conjectures. An added sensitivity to threats may have kept males alert and ready to repel attacks on their families, he suggests, while women calmed down more quickly so they could soothe the children.

Whatever its origin, this ancient biological difference creates havoc in contemporary male-female relationships, because men are also "more tuned in to the internal physiological environment than women," Gottman reports. (For example, men are better at tapping along with their heartbeat.) Men's bodily sensitivity translates into greater physical discomfort during conflict. In short, arguing hurts. The result: "Men are more likely to withdraw emotionally when their bodies are telling them they're upset." Meanwhile, "when men withdraw, women get upset, and they pursue [the issue]"--which gets men more upset.

Here is where physiology meets sociology. Men, says Gottman, need to rely on physiological cues to know how they're feeling. Women, in contrast, rely on social cues, such as what's happening in the conversation.

In addition, men are trained since early childhood not to build intimacy with others, while women "are given intense schooling on the subject" from an equally early age. Socially, the genders are almost totally segregated (in terms of their own choices of friends) from age seven until early adulthood. Indeed, it would seem that cross-gender relationships are set up to fail. "In fact," Gottman writes, "our upbringing couldn't be a worse training ground for a successful marriage."

Yet the challenge is far from insurmountable, as millions of marriages prove. In fact, Gottman's research reveals that "by and large, in happy marriages there are no gender differences in emotional expression!" In these marriages, men are just as likely to share intimate emotions as their partners (indeed they may be more likely to reveal personal information about themselves). However, in unhappy marriages, "all the gender differences we've been talking about emerge"--feeding a vicious cycle that, once established, is hard to break.

Married couples who routinely let the Four Horsemen ransack their living rooms face enormous physical and psychological consequences. Gottman's studies show that chronic flooding and negativity not only make such couples more likely to get sick, they also make it very difficult for couples to change how they relate. When your heart is beating rapidly and your veins are constricting in your arms and legs (another evolutionary stress response), it's hard to think fresh, clear thoughts about how you're communicating. Nor can the brain process new information very well. Instead, a flooded person relies on "over-learned responses"--old relationship habits that probably just fan the flames.

All this physiological data has enormous implications for relationship therapists as well as their clients. Gottman believes that "most of what you see currently in marital therapy--not all of it, but most of it--is completely misguided."

For example, he thinks it's an exercise in futility when "the therapist says 'Calm down, Bertha. Calm down, Max. Let's take a look at this and analyze it. Let's remember the way we were with our mothers.' Bertha and Max can do it in the office because he's doing it for them. But once they get home, and their heart rates get above 100 beats per minute, forget about it."

Teaching psychological skills such as interpreting nonverbal behavior also misses the mark. "We have evidence that husbands in unhappy marriages are terrible at reading their wives' nonverbal behavior. But they're great at reading other people's nonverbal behavior. In other words, they have the social skills, but they aren't using them." The problem isn't a lack of skill; it's the overwhelming feelings experienced in the cycle of negativity. Chronic flooding short-circuits a couple's basic listening and empathy skills, and it undermines the one thing that can turn back the Four Horsemen: the repair attempt.

Heading Off Disaster

Repair attempts are a kind of "meta-communication"--a way of talking about how you're communicating with each other. "Can we please stay on the subject?" "That was a rude thing to say." "We're not talking about your father!" "I don't think you're listening to me." Such statements, even when delivered in grouchy or complaining tone, are efforts to interrupt the cycle of criticism, contempt, defensiveness, and stonewalling and to bring the conversation back on track.

"In stable relationships," explains Gottman, "the other person will respond favorably: 'Alright, alright. Finish.' The agreement isn't made very nicely. But it does stop the person. They listen, they accept the repair attempt, and they actually change" the way they're relating.

Repair attempts are "really critical," says Gottman, because "everybody screws up. Everybody gets irritated, defensive contemptuous. People insult one another," especially their spouses. Repair attempts are a way of saying "we've got to fix this before it slides any deeper into the morass." Even people in bad marriages make repair attempts; the problem is, they get ignored.

Training people to receive repair attempts favorably--even in the middle of a heated argument--is one of the new frontiers in relationship therapy. According to Gottman, "Even when things are going badly, you've got to focus not on the negativity but on the repair attempt. That's what couples do in happy marriages." He's convinced that such skills can be taught: One colleague has even devised a set of flash cards with a variety of repair attempts on them, ranging from "I know I've been a terrible jerk, but can we take this from the top?" to "I'm really too upset to listen right now." Even in mid-tempest, couples can use the cards to practice giving, and receiving, messages about how they're communicating.

Breaking the Four Horsemen cycle is critical, says Gottman, because "the more time [couples] spend in that negative perceptual state, the more likely they are to start making long-lasting attributions about this marriage as being negative." Such couples begin rewriting the story of how they met, fell in love, made commitments. Warm memories about how "we were so crazy about each other" get replaced with "I was crazy to marry him/her." And once the story of the marriage has been infected with negativity, the motivation to work on its repair declines. Divorce becomes much more likely (and predictable--consider that 94 percent accuracy rate in the oral history study).

Of course, not all relationships can, or should, be saved. Some couples are trapped in violent relationships, which "are in a class by themselves." Others may suffer a fundamental difference in their preferred style--validating, volatile, or conflict-avoidant--that leaves them stuck in chronic flooding. With hard work, some of these marriages can be saved; trying to save others, however, may do more harm than good.

In the end, the hope for repairing even a broken marriage is to be found, as usual, in the courage and effort people are willing to invest in their own growth and change. "The hardest thing to do," says Gottman, "is to get back to the fundamentals that really make you happy." Couples who fail to do this allow the Four Horsemen to carry them far from the fundamentals of affection, humor, appreciation, and respect. Couples who succeed cultivate these qualities like gardeners. They also cultivate an affirming story of their lives together, understanding that that is the soil from which everything else grows.

The work may be a continuous challenge, but the harvest, as my long-married friends Bill and Karen would say, is an enormous blessing: the joy in being truly known and loved, and in knowing how to love.

Four Keys to a Happy Relationship

Despite all his sophisticated analysis of how relationships work (and don't work), researcher John Gottman's advice to the love-lorn and fight-torn is really quite simple.

◆**Learn to Calm Down**. This will cut down on the flooding response that makes further communication so difficult. The most brilliant and philosophically subtle therapy in the world will have no impact on a couple not grounded in their own bodies to hear it, he says Once couples are calm enough, suggests Gottman, they can work on three other basic keys to improving their relationship

◆**Learn to Speak and Listen Non-defensively**. This is tough, Gottman admits, but defensiveness is a very dangerous response, and it needs to be interrupted. One of the most powerful things you can do--in addition to working toward the ideal of listening with empathy and speaking without blame--is to reintroduce praise and admiration into your relationship. A little appreciation goes a long way toward changing the chemistry between people.

◆**Validate Your Partner.** Validation involves putting yourself in your partner's shoes and imagining his or her emotional state. Let your partner know that you understand how he or she feels, and why, even if you don't agree. You can also show validation by acknowledging your partner's point of view, accepting appropriate responsibility, and apologizing when you are clearly wrong. If this still seems too much of a stretch, at least let your partner know that you are trying to understand, even if you're finding it hard.

◆**Practice, Practice, Practice.** Gottman calls this "over-learning," doing something so many times that it becomes second nature. The goal is to be able to calm yourself down, communicate nondefensively, and validate your partner automatically--even in the heat of an argument. ☐

--Alan AtKisson is a consultant and writer on sustainable development living in New York City. He is the author of Believing Cassandra, *published by Chelsea Green, 1999. This article appeared in the* New Age Journal *, November 1994.*

❑ Note: On Communication Styles

Most people tend to react to stress with one or more of four communication styles:

◆PLACATING. The placater is ingratiating, eager to please, apologetic, and a "yes" man or woman. The placater says things like "whatever you want" or "never mind about me, it's okay." It's a case of peace at any price. The price, for the placater, is worthlessness. Because the placater has difficulty expressing anger and holds so many feelings inside, he or

she tends toward depression and, as studies show, may be prone to illness. Placaters need to know it is okay to express anger.

◆BLAMING. The blamer is a fault finder who criticizes relentlessly and speaks in generalizations: "You never do anything right." "You're just like your mother/father." Inside, the blamer feels unworthy or unlovable, angry at the anticipation he or she will not be getting what is wanted. Given a problem, the best defense is a good offense. The blamer is unable to deal with or express pain or fear. Blamers need to be able to speak on their own behalf without indicting others in the process.

◆COMPUTING. The computer is super-reasonable, calm and collected, never admits mistakes, and expects people to conform and perform. The computer says things like, "Upset? I'm not upset. Why do you say I'm upset?" Afraid of emotion, he or she prefers facts and statistics. "I don't reveal my emotions and I'm not interested in anyone else's." Computers need someone to ask how they feel about specific things.

◆DISTRACTING. The distracter resorts to irrelevancies under stress, avoids direct eye contact and direct answers. Quick to change the subject, he or she will say, "What problem? Let's have Sam and Bridget over." Confronting the problem might lead to a fight, which could be dangerous. Distracters need to know that they are safe, not helpless, that problems can be solved and conflicts resolved.

Each style is a unique response to pain, anger, or fear, which keeps us from understanding each other. Knowing that, the next time you find yourself resorting to blame, you can conclude there is something painful or scary bothering you and try to figure out what it is. If it's your partner who is blaming, you can conclude he or she is possibly not intending to be aggressive or mean but probably afraid of some development. What's needed is to find a way to make it safe to talk about the worry; find out what is bothering him or her. (Editor's note: The intimacy exercises in module 10 may be a perfect way to initiate the process.)

-- Lori Gordon, Ph.D. Reprinted with permission from Psychology Today *Magazine. Copyright © 1993 Sussex Publishers, Inc.*

DEFINING TERMS

Ego Defenses

Flooding

Meta-Communications

WHAT DO YOU THINK

1. How is it that two people can fight and both believe they are right? List as many reasons as you can.

2. Why are people often touchy about receiving criticism?

3. If you were falsely accused of something by your partner, how would you react?

4. List some methods you could use to minimize a listener's negative reaction, if you have something to say that might sound critical.

5. Do you think it's sometimes better to "let sleeping dogs lie" than bring up something negative? When and when not?

6. What communications styles do you tend to fall into? How could you improve your communications

VIDEO VIEWER:

Rent "Terms of Endearment." Why is the communication so poor between each of the characters?   What differences in communications styles do you see?

☺ MEDIA WATCHER:

How do TV characters communicate about their problems? How realistic is it compared to your experience? Give examples.

<table>
</table>

Module Fourteen

Power and Conflict

Power is the dirty little word of relationships. No one likes to talk about it, but it is always present, as it is in all human interaction. People who talk about power are often seen as manipulative, power-hungry or at least unromantic in the extreme, but an understanding of power is critical in understanding relationsh ips, just as it is in other human interactions. People who feel powerless in areas of their lives tend to feel insecure, unhappy, and stressed, whereas those who have some control feel happier and confident. If the power balance between two partners in an intimate relationship is uneven, the less powerful one may feel unloved, depressed, and resentful, while the one with more power may feel critical, unsympathetic, and tied down by the one with less power.

Power is generally defined as the ability to get one's way, even in the face of opposition. It is the capacity to affect the behavior of others, from the expert who influences by his knowledge, the business person by her money, the baby by crying, the bully by violence or the model who influences by his or her looks. Power is firmly imbedded in the various aspects of relationships from dating all the way through marriage and/or divorce.

Chapter Preview:

Power

Conflict

Managing Conflict

Abuse
  Violence
  Child Abuse and Neglect
  Sexual Abuse
  Psychological Abuse
  Passive Aggression

Article: "When Parents Don't Agree"

Article: "Domestic Violence"

Experts have identified several different types of power: reward power--the ability to give or withhold benefits that the other person may desire, such as sex, affection, or money; coercion--the power to affect another by intimidation, anger and/or the threat of violence; authority--the acceptance of the legitimacy of the person's wishes, based on their position or role, such as parent or husband or wife; referent power--which exists when a person is well liked by another and the person wishes to please them, or be like them; and expertise--the power that accrues when one has a special knowledge in a particular area, as when one person knows how to fix the car, handle the checkbook, or make dinner.

Two specific sources of power are particularly important in personal relationships:

money and attractiveness. A number of studies have shown that the more attractive partner generally has more power in a relationship. Other studies have found the person who makes the most money is more likely to get their way in decision making.

Both these sources of power depend on their ability to be exercised, however. There is a third source of power: The principle of the least interest--sociologists have found that the person who is least interested in the continuation of the relationship has the power to dictate its conditions. Quite commonly, this power is determined by each partner's attractiveness and the availability of other options.

Power plays don't always work. They are most often successful when they are hidden, usually under the guise of rational discussions. Although rational discussion is important, it may not solve a problem if power issues are under the surface. Most people prefer to try to convince their partners to do what they want. If that fails, however, the use of power is usually the next step. When power issues become obvious, they can provoke resistance. Pressure can backfire. When power issues come to the forefront, the result can be conflict, the focus of the next section.

Conflict

Conflict in the area of marriage and intimate relationships is usually thought of as quarrels or arguments. In actuality, conflict includes a broad spectrum of behaviors from silent stand-offs to psychological tactics, all the way to emotional confrontations and physical attacks. Conflict is defined as any situation where the needs or wants of an individual or group run counter to the needs or wants of another. Open confrontation is not necessary for conflict to occur. Quite often families contain reservoirs of hidden conflict that are only noticeable through the occasional sarcastic remark, snub, or frown. These hidden conflicts are likely to break out into the open eventually.

Open conflict occurs when both people attempt to exercise their power. If one person declines or fears to use their power, the result is submission. If both decline to use their power, the result would be an attempt at compromise.

The situations that produce conflict in marriages are similar to ones that occur in other types of human relationships. A difference is that intimate relationships and marriages involve a greater degree of vulnerability. The closeness people feel as well as the substantial investment of feelings, hopes and dreams lead them to be much more easily hurt by a partner's or family member's actions.

Conflicts may erupt in many areas, most often in the arenas of sex, money, housework and child-rearing. Conflicts occur because partners' beliefs, values, or expectations differ in that arena.

Whatever the source of the conflict, the key problem is how to prevent the conflict from harming the relationship. For that reason, managing conflict is critical to the success of most marriages.

Managing Conflict

There are several strategies for making sure that conflict does not get out of hand:

♦ Bring things up frequently -- when conflicts are ignored, they tend to fester and build up. The sooner they are dealt with, the less the pressure and resentment. People should not be afraid to bring up things they think might be bothering a partner. Many couples use techniques like scheduling weekly meetings to make sure problems aren't ignored.

♦ Use communication skills -- How things are said is often more important than saying them. The previous chapter has hints at how to talk about sensitive issues.

♦ Handle anger -- Although some anger is inevitable in any intimate relationship, inability to manage anger causes conflicts to escalate and marriages to fail. Each partner must take responsibility to manage their own anger. A three step approach can be helpful:

[1] acknowledge your anger--people often deny they are angry, but sarcasm, derogatory remarks and tension are symptoms of anger that tend to provoke the other person.

[2] defuse the anger--most people find the direct expression of anger to be an attack. Take the other person off the hook: avoid blaming, pointing and putting them on the spot. Instead, let them know you don't want to be angry.

[3] ask for help--this puts the issue back into the realm of cooperation instead of conflict. Mace [1976] suggests something like, "I'm angry because of something you did; I don't like to be angry with you because I love you; Please help me to deal with the anger so I can be more loving . . ." This approach can not only eliminate the anger but invite a rational discussion which may solve the problem.

Abuse

Perhaps nothing in family life today provokes stronger reactions than abuse. Criminologists have long known that we are more likely to be assaulted or even murdered by a family member than a stranger. Recently, some experts have estimated that as many as one-fourth of all girls and one-tenth of all boys have been sexually assaulted, usually by a family member. Many other children have suffered from a passive form of abuse-- neglect. Whether the perpetrator is a husband, wife, father, mother, brother or sister or a more distant relative, the victim is harmed not only by the injury itself, but by the betrayal of trust. Adult victims of abuse report loss of confidence and self-esteem, increased depression and illness. Child victims may obtain psychological scars that carry on throughout their lives. A large number of convicted killers and child molesters were themselves abused in one way or another as children.

There are four main forms of abuse: physical violence, sexual abuse, psychological abuse, and neglect.

Violence

As well as being a place of comfort and nurturance, the home is a place of violence and conflict. For many years, crime statistics have shown as great or greater danger of homicide from relatives than from strangers. More police deaths in the line of duty come from domestic disputes than any other cause. Although domestic violence is more prevalent in lower socio-economic groups, abuse may be found among families of every social, economic or racial grouping. Domestic violence can be classified into two types, depending on its victims: child abuse and spousal abuse.

Factors contributing to the incidence of domestic violence include: stress, financial problems, spousal incompatibility and alcohol or drug abuse. Perhaps the most important factor is the family background of one or more partner. Individuals socialized in violent families are more likely to become both victims and perpetrators of domestic violence. Growing up in such situations leads people to believe that it is OK to act violently or permit violence.

National studies have shown that physical and verbal aggression against spouses is common from both women and men. But it is the males who by far form the more serious problem. Both moderate and serious injuries are much more frequently caused by men. This is primarily because of men's larger size and greater strength. Men, too, are taught how to fight, and when angry tend to hit with closed fists rather than open hands. A large proportion of homicides by females is probably due to self-defense, where women use a weapon to ward off a physical attack.

Abusers often may seem to be quite normal in other aspects of their lives. Underneath, however, they typically have poor self-images, and tend to rank high in aggressive tendencies. They tend to blame others for their problems, and have difficulty controlling themselves. Often they are very dependent on their spouses and are excessively jealous. Alcohol or drug abuse are also common among abusive personalities.

Victims of abuse may also tend to have low self-esteem or be dependent. They may have been brought up to believe it is important to please others or take care of them or simply that it is always possible to work things out. They may be confused by the sometimes loving, sometimes violent behavior of their lovers. Because of confusion or their passive or conciliatory beliefs, they are able to be exploited by abusers. Victims need to told that there is no excuse for violent behavior, and no reason to risk injury to maintain a relationship.

Child Abuse and Neglect

What is known as child abuse takes two forms: attack and neglect. Parents who physically attack and hurt their children are not necessarily emotionally ill as was once thought, but they do exhibit more psychological problems than other parents. Abusive acts can be triggered by children's difficult behavior, which parents may not expect or understand. In

this sense, parents' lack of knowledge about parenting can be seen as an important contributing factor. Abusive parents' often have negative self-images which they project onto their children. A child's normal but irritating behavior is then seen is manipulative or defiant. Stress and alcohol or drug abuse are also frequently involved in abuse.

Reasons for parents' neglect are similar. Often the neglect is rationalized as a form of punishment for a child's real or imagined misdeeds. Alcoholic or drugged-out parents may be unable to attend to child's needs, as well. Even normal parents may not be enough attuned to a child's real needs, or may be working too hard to attend to them, and if other family problems intrude, damage can be done to children's self-esteem.

The effects of child abuse can be devastating both physically and emotionally. Battered children may suffer fractures, lacerations, internal injuries, brain damage or even death. They also are likely to exhibit behavior disturbances, aggression and lower social skills. They are more likely to perform poorly in school, and in later life may exhibit problems including increased drug and alcohol abuse. Neglect, too, has surprisingly powerful effects. Neglected children become deeply convinced that they are unlovable, and are subject to a variety of mental disorders, especially depression.

Sexual Abuse

Sexual abuse is an eerily common, and often extremely harmful, form of abuse. Best estimates are that about 3% of boys and 15% of girls have been molested during their lives, but some researchers believe the amounts may be nearly double those figures. Despite stereotypes, 80-90% of molestations are not by strangers, but by relatives or friends of the family.   Nearly all molesters are male. Depending on the circumstances, the effects of sexual abuse can be severe.   Addiction, alcoholism, depression, anxiety, and eating and sexual disorders are more likely to occur to molested children.

The most well-researched type of incest (sexual relations between relatives) is between fathers and daughters. In many cases, but by no means all, the husband-wife sexual relationship is unsatisfactory, so the husband turns to the daughter. Usually premeditated by the father, the relationship begins with hugging, cuddling, and kissing which both may enjoy. The contact may then expand into wrestling, sexual caresses and even intercourse, usually without force being employed.   The daughter may feel intense guilt, but usually is afraid to call authorities. The relationship often continues until the daughter leaves home or gets a boyfriend.

Step-fathers are actually more likely to commit incest than birth fathers--by a factor of five. This is probably due to a lower incest taboo. Abuse can also occur between older and younger siblings, although some sexual play between closely spaced siblings is normal and rarely harmful.

Psychological Abuse

Not all abuse or conflict is physical. Nevertheless, despite the absence of visible scars it can have a powerful effect, through words, indirect actions and even non-action. Psychological abuse uses all these methods to attack and harm its victims.

Psychological abuse is verbal. It attacks personality, lowers confidence and self-esteem, and makes it easier to dominate. Victims give up. They are easily persuaded that they are unworthy. They readily believe that what they think, feel, want, and do is wrong. They are usually unaware of the power aspects of the psychological abuse they are experiencing. People who are psychologically abused usually believe that the partner's insults and criticisms are true. They do not trust their judgment in disputes and are afraid to express their opinions.   They feel depressed, guilty, worthless, and responsible for whatever failures or disappointments their partner experiences. They are afraid of their partner. They never know what will set off another attack.   Psychological abusers attack their partner's friends and relatives as well. They prevent or destroy potential relationships with others, so that the victim will be deprived of outside support and experiences that could bolster self-esteem. Psychological aggression, according to Straus and Smith, "interferes with dealing with actual issues, creates additional problems, and often sets in motion an escalating cycle of events that ends in physical violence" (1990, p. 254). This is an important, often overlooked fact. People who verbally abuse are angry people, who are likely at some point to cross the line into physical violence. Crisis counselors report that a common cycle is for the abuser to criticize and verbally abuse the other in an increasing fashion until finally coming to blows. At that point, the tension is released and the abuser feels sorry. The victim feels hopeful that the abuser has learned his or her lesson, but soon the verbal abuse begins again and escalates to the edge of violence. Lovers should consider that anyone who is verbally abusive has the potential to become physically violent.

Passive Aggression

Passive aggression is an indirect form of winning or getting even that, like psychological aggression, often goes unrecognized. It is behavior that seems to be well-intended, but that actually hurts another person. A husband may accidentally-on-purpose ruin the laundry or buy the wrong store items, or a wife may burn the dinner or throw out important letters or favorite possessions, because they are unhappy with their tasks or with some other factor in their marriage.

Of course, all of these things really can happen accidentally, and it is important to avoid becoming paranoid. If a person suspects the other of this kind of tactic, it is helpful to probe for unexpressed dissatisfactions. Usually this kind of behavior occurs only when resentments have built to a high point or if the partner is deeply emotionally disturbed.

According to Miller et al. (1988), some of the more subtle, psychological ways to maintain control, win, or put down include: refusing to discuss certain topics, always changing the subject or monopolizing the conversation; leaving out important information in a discussion so that the other does not understand and feels confused (or stupid); mumbling or talking too softly so that one's partner cannot hear and feels frustrated and tense. All of these tactics are examples of attempts to control another person.

One contrary note is important to be sounded. Because passive aggression is an indirect form of power, it is sometimes used by victims of verbal or other types of abuse. Afraid to directly confront their abusive partners, victims may resort to passive aggression to salvage their esteem and discharge their frustration. While this is certainly understandable, passive aggression is not ultimately likely to succeed. It further prevents free and open communication (already a dim hope), which is essential for really resolving conflicts. □

References

Crosby, J.F. 1991. *Illusion and disillusion.* Belmont, CA: Wadsworth.

Dahl, Robert. 1957. "The concept of power." *Behavioral Science.* 2:201-15.

French, J.R. & Bernard Raven. 1959. "The bases of social power." in D. Cartwright (ed.) *Studies in social power.* Ann Arbor, MI: University of Michigan Press.

Jones, C.L. et al. 1995. *The futures of the family.* Englewood Cliffs, NJ: Prentice- Hall.

Mace, David. 1982. *Love and anger in marriage.* Grand Rapids, MI: Zondervan.

Miller, J.A. et al. 1988. *Passive Agression.* New York: Random House.

Shehan, C.L. & K.C. Kammeyer. 1997. *Marriages and families: Reflections of a gendered society.* Boston: Allyn & Bacon.

Strauss, M.L. and R.J. Gelles. 1990. *Physical violence in american families.* New Brunswick, NJ: Transaction Books.

Strauss, Murray. 1994. *Beating the devil out of them.* New York: Free Press.

❏ When Parents Don't Agree

Nancy Marriott

"Honey, I'm home!" So goes the familiar refrain of the 50s sitcom, heralding the return of the patriarch after a long day's absence. Cheery wife and eager kids rush to embrace Dad, and all is well in nuclear family land.

But in real life, this wasn't quite how things went. More likely, once Dad got through the door and settled down with slippers and pipe, Mom would hit him with a list of the day's transgressions, those of the kids cowering in their rooms where they awaited the fulfillment of Mom's threats: "Just wait 'til your father gets home! He'll . . . . . .!" (Fill in the blank, depending on how desperate Mom was that day!)

If life in the nuclear family wasn't so cheery and nice, at least it was simple. Parents knew their roles, and when it came to discipline, showed their kids an impenetrable united front. Kids knew their place as well, and accepted their punishment dutifully. Parents rarely questioned each other's dictums, and if they did, it took place behind tightly closed doors. To disagree or fight in front of the children was a sure sign of shame and failure as parents. Such was the model most of us grew up with, and, whether it worked or not, many of us still hold it up as a standard when we attempt to discipline our own children today.

But for modern families, the hierarchical, united front approach no longer works. More often than not, today's parents are both out winning the bread, and when at home, find themselves together in their parenting efforts. Even if Mom stays home, she no longer relies solely on Dad-power to keep the kids in line. Modern life is too complicated to delay a child's comeuppance, and today's moms either ignore the errant behavior or administer justice single-handedly at the scene of the crime.

Typically, first-time parents are confronted with a scenario like this: Awakened by a piercing 3 AM yowl, Sandra leaps from her warm bed to rush to the crib of her 2-year-old son. John, her husband, tries to stop her. "Let him scream, for once!" he admonishes. "You're just spoiling him by attending to his every whimper! For God's sake, I can never get any rest around here!" Sandra feels unsupported and tries to explain: "I can't sleep when he's crying, so I might as well see what he needs. Maybe he had a nightmare and is in need of some comforting. Why can't you be more understanding and help out once in awhile?"

So begins a dialogue that over time devolves into a nasty fight, leaving both parents ineffective and feeling guilty for not being in agreement. But the truth is that disagreements are natural when two people with differing backgrounds, beliefs, and expectations are engaged in parenting their children. It's normal, and there are ways to do it constructively. But first we have to give up the old model of a united front that doesn't leave room for differences, but rather assigns roles. Then we can begin to build effective strategies for handling those differences.

Can parents disagree and still be good parents? I think they can, but it takes an approach and some new tools that Ozzie and Harriet would never have dreamed of using.

Get Honest

A first step for parents who butt heads often is to assess just exactly what it is they are fighting about. Is it really your children's behavior that has you so bent out of shape, or is it a struggle for power and control in your relationship with your spouse that spills over into the discipline arena? Fighting can get dirty when personal issues are collapsed with child discipline issues, and we need to recognize when this is happening to avoid it.

Joe worked hard to make good money at his job, and liked to stash a good portion away into the family savings account. So when wife Ruth went on a shopping spree, he often reprimanded her for being wasteful. Ruth resented this tightening of the reins and, frustrated that she couldn't resolve it with her husband, "got back" at her husband when he attempted to discipline their 11-year-old son. "I've already given you your allowance and so the answer is NO," was his abrupt response to Tim's frequent request for extra money. Just as frequently, Ruth jumped in to defend Tim with an attack on her husband: "You are so tight! You never give him enough! What's wrong with you that you have to be so stingy?"

How do you know when it's a personal power struggle and not a more healthy expression of your differences over the kids? Signs to watch for are sarcasm, put-downs, defensive feelings like the need to be right, feelings of powerlessness, domination, and revenge fantasies. These are all signs that you are engaged in "dirty fighting" and have most likely collapsed personal issues with your concern over the children's behavior. At this point, you both need to put down the ax and quit making your children's lives the battleground for settling your own personal scores. A more suitable arena for this kind of activity would be in the office of a trained therapist who could help you focus on issues in your relationship.

A New Model

Once you've clearly separated your personal power issues from your issues with your children, you're ready for an entirely new approach to parenting and discipline. The new model is teamwork, and it relies on the art of mutual empowerment. In this approach, parents support and empower each other to be effective. Children understand that parents are united in discipline efforts, without having the perception that there is an impenetrable wall. Instead, kids are presented with two adults who act as individuals working together to support each other more like a net than a wall.

Following are some constructive ways to deal with conflicts so that when differences arise, parents aren't caught off guard by personal issues.

First, take some time in private together to find out where you can agree and how you can support each other. This calls for an open and honest discussion, with both putting their individual values on the table and then communicating what rules should follow to enforce those values. It's important to respect each other and not get caught up in arguments about who's right and who's wrong. Remember, you are equal partners of a team, and your goal is to call the plays before you're on the field.

Decide which values and rules you have the strongest feelings about, and which your spouse feels strongest about. Explore why you feel this way. Is it because you were raised with these values, or because you deem them vital to your family's health? (Often rules and values which are entrenched because "that's the way my parents raised me" need replacement by rules more specific to your current family situation.)

Then, agree to divide up disciplinary responses according to what each spouse feels strongest about. A give-and-take strategy might look like this: Kids eating junk food is non-negotiable, but kids watching TV before bedtime might be negotiable.

The next step would be for you both to agree that the parent who has the strongest feelings will deal with the child on that issue, and the other will take a back seat. For example, he agrees to let her lay down the law about junk food, while she agrees to let him handle the TV before bedtime requests. Neither of you intervene when the other is handling a situation in a way you don't like, but have agreed to abide by.

For example, when the 3-year-old cries at night, Sandra might say to Josh:" I wish I could feel okay about letting Sam cry and go back to sleep like you do. But I can't listen to him cry, so I'm going to get up. I don't expect you to get up too, because this is something I feel strongly about." Josh can pledge to support her by not criticizing her approach.

While this give-and-take method of mutual support and empowerment works well when you've had time to make decisions and agreements, it can also work when divisive discipline issues pop up without warning. Keeping good teamwork rules of respect, ask your partner that you be the authority in an area by explaining to him or her that you feel very strongly about the situation. Since you have an agreement to let the parent who feels strongest handle the situation, refer to this, and your partner will probably yield.

Or, request to handle a situation when you may want to demonstrate a different way of getting results. For instance, Fred and Melanie often fought over how to discipline their children. He used punishment and rewards to get good behavior, while she was trying to shift and use logical consequences.   Instead of objecting when her husband launched into a critical tirade at the kids, she requested that she be allowed to manage the situation and demonstrate her alternative technique. In this way, they avoided being at loggerheads and worked more closely as a team. A later discussion gave them time to evaluate what had worked and what had not.

Divide and Conquer

Parents can easily have their teamwork undone when children manipulate parents by using the strategy of divide and conquer to get their way.

When 8-year-old Julie tried to dig in the garden alongside her mother, Linda, she was told, "Don't dig here because I'm planting some new flowers." Julie begged, but to no avail. She went into the house and asked Mark, "Dad, can I dig in the dirt?" Mark, immersed in the paper, responds without looking up. "Sure," he says absentmindedly. Julie bee-lined it to one end of the garden where she dug a huge hole before Linda yanked her away. "You're mean," she shouted at her mother. "Daddy said I could dig here!"

While Dad was an innocent bystander in this situation, often, children will take advantage of one parent's tendency to say yes when the other has already said no. In the new model of teamwork, parents agree that if one has said no in a situation, it's not acceptable for a child to go to the other for a different response. In communicating this to children, Linda might tell Julie: "Daddy and I know that you went behind my back in order to do what you wanted to do, and we don't like that. Dad might add: "The next time, when your mother says no, don't ask me for something you already know she doesn't want you to do." Both parents could then display support by requiring Julie to put the dirt back in the hole she dug.

Another way children pit parent against parent is to complain angrily about one to the other. "Mommy is mean! She makes me eat stuff when I'm not hungry, and told me I couldn't leave the table until I finished!" The temptation is to be the nice guy and yield to the child's wishes, later telling your spouse you felt the order was too harsh. Then the issue falls between you and your spouse, and the spotlight is deflected from whatever your child did in the first place that prompted such an order. Guess who wins!

A more effective approach might be to respond by listening to the complaint and suggesting your child tell your spouse what the problem is. Encourage her to work out the dispute by saying, "It's between you and your mother, not you and me. I know you can talk it over and find a solution." Alerting your spouse about what you've suggested can further support a more positive outcome.

When the Unavoidable Happens

No matter how accommodating your spouse may be, or dedicated to mutual empowerment and support, it's unrealistic to think there won't be situations in which you will find yourself dueling fiercely over what's right for your children. Below are some ground rules for fighting fair when this occurs:

1. Avoid sarcasm, blaming or putting down your partner. Likewise, lecturing and trying to convince him or her to do it your way in front of the children will only get you more opposition.

2. Don't involve the children or speak disparagingly about them in the midst of the disagreement ("You're turning our son into a wimp!"). When you do this, you make the child feel responsible for his parents "mistakes." Statistics show that children of divorced parents often blame themselves for the separation, which is understandable considering the kinds of statements parents often make in front of their children when they fight.

3. Call for a parental time out when you recognize that you are hooked by your partner's words or behavior. Leave the room together and have a short, private discussion on how best to handle your disagreement. One solution might be that you yield temporarily to your spouse and

get agreement for a future team plan to deal with the situation should it arise again..

4. Do some damage control after an unavoidable battle by reassuring children that they are loved and not in anyway responsible for parent's fights.

5. Go easy on yourself! Remember that your children will learn from your modeling how to resolve conflicts and be better parents themselves one day for having watched you fight fair!□

–Used by permission.

❑ Domestic Violence

Bruce Deyarmond

Bruce Deyarmond is the Director of Chemical Dependency Services, Bridge Counseling Center in Las Vegas, Nevada.

You've seen or heard the story: the anger, the screaming, a man striking, a woman sobbing. A situation supposedly based on love has turned to hatred, violence. The sad truth is that more people are assaulted and even killed at the hands of someone they love, than by strangers.

What is this social interaction we call domestic violence? It appears to have many forms, is ever present globally and is the secret misunderstood behavior between people who know each other. Culminating with the O.J. trial, domestic violence has been consistently portrayed over the last generation as a major problem, yet the behavior persists. If you didn't know history you might make the assumption that this is a relatively new phenomenon, a product of modern society that is perpetuated by the breakdown the traditional family, and in fact this reason is often given.

The truth is that friends, lovers, husbands, wives, fathers, mothers, aunts, uncles, grandparents and any other people, related or not, who live in close proximity or with each other have used this behavior as a means of control since man was able to walk upright.

Since the 1960s when our society began to emphasize the rights of the individual a shift began to take place. This new awareness brought domestic violence out of the secretive confines of our homes and victims at last had a chance to expose their abuse to the public view.

In looking at this issue, the first question one is bound to ask is, "Why doesn't she just leave?" But when we jump to this obvious question we only further traumatize the victims. The question should always be, "Why is he doing it?" Let's not focus primarily on the victim, but on the abuser where the weight of the responsibility belongs.

Men have been socialized (globally) that they are the dominant forces in the household almost without exception. The authority figures that are called to intercede when domestic violence erupts are predominately male; this can perpetuate the gender inequality surrounding domestic violence. The victims of domestic violence are caught in a double bind, which too often leads to their silence, or worse, feeling that the violence is their fault. When this happens the abuser is validated and the victim is shamed.

In my practice as a substance abuse counselor, I am frequently confronted with the issue of the victim not recognizing that she is the victim! All too often these women are willing to take the blame for their unfortunate circumstances. A 27-year-old female, with repeated sexual abuse as a child, shared in-group that she had been raped. When asked how she felt about the rapist she was surprisingly ambivalent, she stated he was a nice guy and she saw no problem with his behavior. The group then asked her how she felt about

being raped. "It's really no big deal, I've been raped before." In her constant role as a victim it was probably the only way she knew how to cope with the repeated abuse she had endured her whole life.

Another frequent response is given by many of my patients: "It was my fault, if I hadn't complained so much he would never have hit me," or "If I wouldn't have been drinking I wouldn't said those things to him, he had every right to hit me." These women are convinced that they are at fault, they have been socialized to believe that it's OK for men to strike out at their partners. This false information only serves to keep victims stuck in the abuse and willing to falsely accept responsibility for the abuser's behavior.

It is evident that education of all parties is the answer to reducing the problem of domestic violence. There has been a shift in the attitude of some state governments and police to see the victims for who they are. Victims all too often have refused to cooperate with law enforcement due to past histories of mistrust and the fear of being further abused when those arrested return home. It is through this new education that abusers are being arrested on a mandatory basis even without the cooperation of the victims.

But enough about the victims, what about the batterers? Evidence is accumulating that many batterers fit a profile:

◆Batterers may be highly romantic, even charismatic. Batterers often highly value the relationship, which may have many good points, except for the violence. This may account for why both the batterers and victims are willing to stay.

◆Violent men may have difficulty processing certain kinds of social information, misinterpreting cues to believe the worst possible interpretation of their partners' behavior.

◆Batterers are very dependent on their partners. They may constantly want their wives attention, interpreting inattention or attention to another as rejection. Jealousy and fear seem to be strongly related to violence.

◆Violent people are poor communicators. They may be articulate, but they lack a fundamental communication insight: the ability to listen, and tailor one's approach to their audience. They are poor at negotiating and compromise. Batterers are quickly frustrated and swiftly resort to threats and violence.

◆There is a cycle of violence, often starting with verbal abuse, building into physical violence. After the violence is spent, batterers may feel remorse. They may apologize and promise to change. And they may seem to change for a while. But eventually, tensions build and the cycle repeats.

If you recognize yourself or your partner in this profile, get counseling. It is possible to change this behavior, but it does take work. However, if the behavior is severe, the first concern is to get out, to get out of danger.

There will be no quick fix to this problem; it will change slowly and with great effort. Any resocialization process is a long-term proposal, but on a family level when we are able to teach our children values that promote communication, trust, and gender equality, and when these values are reinforced by our society, we will facilitate changes necessary to reduce and hopefully eliminate domestic violence.□

–Used with permission.

DEFINING TERMS

Power

Conflict

Accomodation

Neglect

Passive Aggression

WHAT DO YOU THINK?

1. Why is power a "dirty word" in relationships? Would it be better if it were brought out more into the open? Why or why not?

2. What types of power do you use in your family and/or relationships? What kind do family members/partners use on you?

3. What are constructive ways parents can manage their conflicts over child-rearing?

4. If a partner hits and hurts you, but then is sincerely sorry, should you forgive him or her? Why or why not? What could you do to see it doesn't happen again?

5. Could verbal abuse ever be a justification for physical violence? Why or why not?

6. Is physical punishment (for kids) the same as abuse? Why or why not? If not, where should one draw the line?

⊕ VIDEO VIEWER:

Rent "Once Were Warriors" or "Men Don't Tell." What perpetuates the cycle of violence? Give examples.

☹ MEDIA WATCHER:

What programs have you seen that deal with child abuse or domestic violence? What have you learned from them?

Part Six
Changes

Module Fifteen

Crisis and Change

---

*C*hange is a part of all human life. However, as sociologist Max Weber observed over a hundred years ago, the vast majority of human actions are dictated mainly by habit. The family, as has been noted in Module Two, is an institution, and institutions are parts of society characterized by repetitive social interactions. When the social interactions of a society stop being repetitive--that is, start to change--as when sexuality becomes accepted outside marriage, the institution [of marriage] is naturally disrupted. Similarly, in individual families, changes in the roles, membership, behavior or attitudes of one or more family members tend to change the habitual patterns of other members and disrupt the family's stability to a certain degree.

There are a number of different kinds of changes that can occur within the family, each of which has a different degree and kind of impact on the family unit. The following are some types of changes that can occur:

♦ *A*ccession -- the addition of a family member. In Module Eleven, we have seen how the birth of a child changes the husband-wife dynamic.   Later births often disrupt the

---

Chapter Preview:

Types of Changes

Crisis

Coping with Change and Crisis

Article: "How Kids Grieve"

Article: "Surviving Infidelity"

---

relationships between parents and older children.

♦ Growing up/Aging -- As children pass through different stages of development, their needs change, their behavior changes, their roles, responsibilities, and expectations change. All these can change or disrupt the lives of both parents and siblings. Similarly, the transition by parents from young adulthood to middle-age can affect each other and their children

♦ Economic changes -- Changes in the family's standard of living can have a profound impact on the family. The type of home, the budget for school, meals and clothing, vacations, are all affected by economic changes.

A father changing jobs, a mother returning to work, changes in business conditions, inflation or recession have both economic and social impacts on the family, by changing the amount of a parents presence in the family and their role, as well as their economic effects.

♦ Role changes -- Role changes have, in their own right, significant impact on the family. These can occur when family members take on a new job or a significant avocation, such as a sport, religion or community project, or returns to school, each of which demands from the person important financial, time or energy commitments. These things also effect how the family member sees him or herself, the family, or is seen by the family. Changes in any of these require adjustments by everyone involved.

Crisis

Significant changes which are serious enough to threaten the stability or even the survival of a family unit are called crises. A crisis is a drastic change in the course of events, a turning point that affects the trend of future events. Hill [1949] lists several types of crisis: accession crisis--unwanted pregnancies, the return of a deserting spouse; dismemberment--serious illness, separation or death of a family member; and demoralization--loss of functioning of one or more family members through unemployment, alcoholism, infidelity, severe depression.

Any one of these may trigger a crisis, or a number of smaller changes may combine to create a crisis. Another significant source is when conflicts escalate into a crisis. Once a crisis occurs, a period of instability occurs with severe strain on family members and their physical and emotional resources. A number of outcomes are possible ranging from complete disintegration of the family to a reorganization on a higher level than previously, or anything between. Much depends on the family's ability to marshal resources from within as well as

outside the family, and its ability to withstand stress. Also extremely helpful is the family's ability to experiment with new arrangements and roles.

Coping with Change and Crisis

Once change or crisis occurs, the question becomes how to adapt to it and resolve the problems it involves. Frequently, the initial response by individuals or families is to keep feelings to one's self, to try to "think positively," relieve tensions by eating, drinking, or smoking, or distracting one's self. What all these strategies have in common is avoidance. Avoidance can buy time to allow family members to adjust, and can minimize conflicts, but in the long term can not be sustained. Sooner or later, problems must be confronted. There are a number of ways to aid in meeting problems constructively.

♦ Utilize support networks -- this includes informal networks of friends, family and neighbors, as well as support from formal sources like professionals and government agencies. Depending on the problem, types of support can include such things as emotional support, financial help, baby-sitting, advice, and feedback. In the 1990s, "support groups" have become a popular method for exchanging information and support between people sharing similar problems. The importance of this step can not be exaggerated, because family resources, whether financial, physical, or emotional can be rapidly exhausted.

♦ Plan and communicate -- Studies show that people who plan feel more in control of their lives, and are better able to take advantage of opportunities. Even if plans must be changed, abandoned or modified a number of times in the course of a crisis, it is better than simply suffering through it. Communication is important to keep other family members informed, and to enlist their support for potential solutions.

♦ Reduce stress -- Most people find it difficult to perform well under a continued state of emotional arousal. This state of decreased functioning is known as stress. Stress reduction is extremely helpful in weathering crises, and in finding optimal solutions. Stress reduction techniques include "reframing" (a way of thinking about problems to see them as opportunities), meditation, relaxation tapes (available in many bookstores), massage, and daily exercise.

References

Boss, P. 1988. *Family stress management.* Newbury Park, CA: Sage Press.

Burr, W.R. & S.R. Klein. 1994. *Reexamining family stress.* Thousand Oaks, CA: Sage Press.

Hill, R. 1949. *Families under stress.* New York: Harper & Row.

Weber, Max. 1946. From *Max Weber: Essays in sociology.* (ed. by Hans Gerth & C.W. Mills) New York: Oxford University Press.

❏ How Kids Grieve

Jennifer Cadoff

Two years ago my brother-in-law died unexpectedly of a pulmonary embolism. He was just 40, and he left behind two young children and his wife, my husband's sister. Our family was dazed with shock and grief, barely able to function. How could we explain to our three-year-old daughter what had happened, when just days before she had been tumbling around our living room with her cousins and Uncle Emil?

I must have stumbled through some sort of explanation, although I can't recall the words I used. I do remember thinking that I was doing it all wrong. Everything I said seemed false or incomplete or too frightening for a toddler.

I now know I wasn't alone in feeling this way. Death, according to several experts, has replaced sex as the topic parents have the hardest time discussing with their children.

"How do we tell the kids?"

"The main thing is to keep it simple, and the younger the child, the simpler your explanation should be," says John Schowalter, M.D., professor of pediatrics and psychiatry at the Yale Child Study Center, in New Haven, Connecticut.

"It's important to use the correct vocabulary," adds Helen Fitzgerald, coordinator of The Grief Program at the Mount Vernon Center for Community Mental Health, in Alexandria, Virginia. "Avoid 'she expired' or 'we lost him.' Use the real words: 'dead,' 'funeral,' 'cancer,' 'heart attack,' or 'AIDS.' " You might say, for example, "Grandma had a very bad heart attack and died."

Encourage their questions

After telling your child the facts, as briefly and honestly as possible, it's best to turn the floor over to her. Ask whether there is anything she wants to know. Don't be concerned if she does not respond right away. "As is true with sex and other emotionally charged areas, the discussion often works best if you give your child time to think and then to ask questions. Make it clear that she's free to come back to you later," says Schowalter.

Although parents tend to think that they should "be strong" when they deliver the bad news so as not to frighten or upset their child experts agree that crying in front of your child is both normal and healthy.

"We should allow ourselves to be human. This is not easy to do. We can tell our children that we hurt a great deal when someone dies. Even if we can't find the right words, we can say that we aren't thinking as clearly as we would like because of our sadness," suggests Phyllis Silverman, Ph.D., an associate in social welfare in the Department of Psychiatry at Massachusetts General Hospital, in Boston, and principal investigator in an ongoing study of child bereavement . "Younger children may not be able to understand the full range of feelings and emotions that adults or older children have. With an older child, it may be possible to share some of the feelings you have and to invite her into a dialogue. Together, then, both parent and child can develop a better understanding of what's happening."

John W. James, who founded the Grief Recovery Institute in Los Angeles in 1981 after a son died, wholeheartedly agrees.

"The most helpful thing adults can do for children is to be emotionally honest about their own feelings," he says. It's not always easy to be emotionally honest, however, because most of us have been coached since childhood to keep a stiff upper lip and to go to our rooms to cry. "A child who sees this immediately thinks there must be something wrong with crying," James continues. "If, on the other hand, we could just stand in the kitchen and cry, our children could come up and ask, 'What's wrong?' We could then say, 'Grandpa just died and I'm very sad.' Then you have the beginnings of an emotionally honest conversation about grief."

"Mommy, what's 'dead'?"

After stumbling through telling my daughter that Uncle Emil had died, I learned that children's simplest questions can be the hardest to answer. Rebecca's was "Mommy, what's 'dead'?" I hesitantly said something about not breathing and hearts not beating, feeling, once again, hopelessly inadequate for this terrible task.

"I think that's all you need to say," Silverman affirms. " 'Dead' is when all functions stop; you don't breathe, you can't see."

Grief counselor Helen Fitzgerald describes a simple yet powerful game she used with one group of five- to twelve-year-olds. "I started by saying, 'I'm alive, I can stomp my feet. The kids got into this immediately, saying things like, 'I'm alive, I can cross my eyes,' and even some gross and silly things like, 'I m alive, I can pick my nose.' Then, after we'd gone around the room, I said, 'When all of that is gone, that is what "dead" is, at least as we know it here on this earth.' It got really quiet for a few minutes. They weren't upset; they were just letting it sink in."

"Is she in heaven?"

Whether or not religious beliefs enter into the discussion with your child is entirely up to you.

"Parents should simply tell their children what they believe," says Elizabeth Weller, M.D., director of child and adolescent psychiatry at Ohio State University, in Columbus. "You shouldn't tell children about life after death if you don't believe in it yourself. It's also fine to simply say, 'Some people believe this and some people believe that, but I don't really know what happens.'"

That's the approach Phyllis Silverman took with her own child. "When my son was five, he asked what happens after people die," she recalls. "I told him that I didn't really know, that some people believe nothing happens, the body returns to nature and nourishes the soil and we live on in people's memories. Some people believe we go to heaven, and they see heaven in a very concrete way. And others simply believe that in some way the spirit lives on. My son thought for a while, then said, 'I think I believe that somehow your soul lives on.' And that was the end of it. That was all he needed to hear."

Fitzgerald, who has a new book out called *The Grieving Child* (Fireside), adds one caveat: "I think we have to be careful about such comments as 'God loved her so much he took her' as if God goes around zapping people and they're gone." Schowalter agrees: "It can be confusing. If you've been told that Grandpa has gone to heaven and that heaven is a wonderful place, then why are all of these people crying?" Of course, Grandpa is still missed in this life, and it may help to explain that to your child.

When can children understand death?

Children ask questions; parents try to answer. But just how old does a child have to be for the reality of death to truly sink in?

John Schowalter says, "People argue about this, but it's probably somewhere around age ten that death is understood to be irreversible." Of course, there are no hard-and-fast rules.

"There are some five-year olds who will not have a hard time grasping death in its true sense, that death is a one-way trip, that you go and never come back," says Weller. Adds Silverman, "I do think kids understand much earlier than we realize, especially if they've had an experience with an actual death. This doesn't mean that ten minutes later they won't ask, 'When's Papa coming back?' but I think that's a kind of reality testing."

How much it hurts

How deeply a child will be affected by a death depends on several factors other than age. Losing a grandmother who lives down the street, a close school friend, or a cousin who plays with the child every weekend is likely to be felt deeply.

On the other hand, if the child has not had a significant relationship with the person who died, she may not feel the loss intensely, notes John James.

Older children, however, may have a strong reaction to the death of a relative they weren't close to. They may feel sadness that the chance to know that person, and to have that person know them, is gone.

Children's secret fears

A few months after the death of her great-grandmother, and about a year after her Uncle Emil died my daughter, Rebecca, dropped a bombshell. "Is it almost time for Daddy to die?" she asked quite matter-of-factly as I drove her to nursery school one sunny spring day.

"What? Good grief, of course not!" I sputtered.

Had I said the right thing? How could I promise my child that our family would be spared, when tragedy had struck so close to home?

"You might have said, 'Daddy is very healthy, and he and I will do everything we can to stay that way. We are probably going to live a long time, until you are all grown up,' " says Helen Fitzgerald. "You could say it's rare that someone as young as Uncle Emil dies."

Weller suggests pointing out that "not all daddies die" and mentioning some friends whose families are intact. She adds that it's very common for children to worry that someone close to them, of the same sex and age as the deceased, will also die.

There are several other fears that these experts say are common after a death has occurred. A child may worry that somehow she made the person die. "You have to give a lot of reassurance that thoughts and words don't kill," says Fitzgerald. If a child has thought about getting rid of a pesky cousin, or told her grandfather in a fit of anger that she wished he were dead, and that person dies soon afterward, the child may hold herself responsible.

Death, darkness, and sleep also seem to be universally linked. "Darkness is a time when children fear someone's going to come get them, and anthropomorphically speaking, death does come and get you," says Schowalter.

Since death might be thought of as the ultimate punishment, the idea of death as retribution for bad actions or thoughts is very common," adds Schowalter. A child may then ask what the dead person did wrong or whether he was bad. The child may worry that he's going to die too, since all kids know they've done some pretty bad things in their time.

Older children worry about their own deaths, Weller comments. She recommends saying something like, "It is true that someday everybody will die. But usually death is due to the aging process or a serious illness, and you are still very young and healthy."

Helping children handle complicated feelings

How can we know if a child is harboring one or another of these fears?

Sometimes it's obvious. "Often if a child does not master the process of understanding this complicated issue, he will bring the subject up over and over again," says Weller. "The parents might think, 'Oh my god, is this child obsessed?'" But he is just trying to make sense of what happened."

Other children will suddenly start playing funeral, hospital, or car crash. "This doesn't mean they are cruel or that they are having fun with a subject that causes the rest of us pain," says Weller. "Play is the work of childhood.

Through it all, they try to understand and master what we teach them."

Talking is often a good way for children to sort through issues they don't understand, although some children just aren't comfortable talking about feelings. "The easiest way to help your child to talk is for you to go first," suggests John James. You might start by saying, "I really feel bad that I never told Grandpa how much fun I had when we went to that basketball game together," and then ask, "Is there anything you wish you had said or hadn't said to him?" Having your child write a letter to his grandfather and then read it either at the grave or to a photograph of him can help lay this type of nagging regret to rest.

Helen Fitzgerald suggests getting younger children to draw "something they wish they'd done differently. If something's making a child feel bad and she can't get it out, it becomes a deep, dark secret."

Books can help too. One that Fitzgerald uses in her kids' bereavement groups is The Tenth Good Thing About Barney (Aladdin Books), about a child who counts the reasons he loved his dead cat. "I read that a lot," she says, "and then I ask the children to think of ten things about the person who died, but I do tell them that the things don't all have to be good. Not all memories are happy. It's a relief for children to know that it's okay to remember the not so great stuff too." (For more on reading, see "Books About Death.")

What about the funeral?

Funerals are an important way of paying respect and saying good-bye to someone when he dies, what experts term a "conclusionary ritual." But how can a parent know whether this ceremony will be good for a child or too frightening and upsetting?"

"There's a wide diversity of opinion about this," says John Schowalter. "In studies I've done, I've found that children under nine or ten tended to be quite disturbed about funerals but only if they were forced to go. It is my feeling that the decision should be left to them. If your child doesn't want to go, she should not be made to feel that she is abandoning anyone or doing something wrong."

If your child does want to go, she needs to know what she's getting into. You need to tell her, briefly, what's going to happen, whether there will be a casket present, for example, and whether it will be open or closed. Be sure to tell her that people will be crying--even Mom and Dad--because they're sad. Then answer any questions, keeping it simple, advises Fitzgerald. Also let your child know that she can leave the service at any time if she needs to.

Taking your child to the burial is even more problematic, according to Schowalter: "For the child who is not really sure that dead people are going to stay dead, and again, this tends to mean younger than age ten or so, seeing someone put in the ground in a box and covered with dirt is a lot to handle."

Cremation can seem awfully frightening, although Fitzgerald comments that the children she has counseled have no particular trouble with the concept, as long as it's presented sensitively and simply, with additional details provided only as asked for. If a young child is attending only a memorial service, you may not need to broach the topic at all. Older children, and those who are exposed to the planning of a cremation, tend to be interested in how it's done ("in a large kiln, lined with fireproof bricks so that intense heat causes the body to become ashes"); what the ashes look like afterward ("light-gray flour, about the size of a five-pound bag"); and what will be done with them.

If a child decides against going to the funeral, then later regrets her decision, reassure her that at the time, she made the best decision. "You might then arrange a special ceremony," suggests Fitzgerald. This could be something as simple as a poem read at church, or flowers and a letter taken to the grave.

Sometimes a simple ceremony of the child's own devising can be particularly fitting. Fitzgerald mentions one that the children in her group came up with: "Yesterday each of them wrote a message on a silver helium balloon to the person who had died. We picked a spot in the parking lot, under a tree, and planned a very simple ceremony. We all held the string, counted to three, and, as we let the balloon go, said together 'We sure hope this gets to you!' We watched the balloon until we could no longer see it. "Of course," she says, "we had talked about how the balloon couldn't really get to the people we wrote to, but also how doing stuff like this makes us feel better anyway. And it did." □

-- From Parents *magazine, April 1993. Copyright ©* 1993. *Gruner + Jahr Publishing. Reprinted from* Parents *magazine by permission.*

☐ Surviving Infidelity

Fred Freeman

Sometimes it seems we live our whole lives by TV. And after a decade that started with Clarence Thomas and Anita Hill, then proceeded to Joey Buttafuoco and Amy Fisher, then O.J. and Nicole, and finished with the most famous adultery of the century, the President and Monica, we have seen how we use our media events to process our views of personal and sexual issues. Each event gives us a context to raise issues and explore our responses. So what did the world's most famous adultery cause us to discover?

Our views

According to a TIME/CNN poll of Americans' sexual attitudes conducted in the summer of 1998, during the Monica Lewinski scandal but not directly related to it, 86% of respondents believe that adultery when committed by men is "morally wrong." A statistically indistinguishable 85% of Americans also feel that adultery is morally wrong for women. No double standard there. The significant increase in these numbers since TIME conducted a similar survey in 1977 (in the promiscuous Boogie Nights era only 76% of Americans thought infidelity was morally wrong) should calm those who feared the White House scandals weakened the nation's virtue.

What exactly is infidelity? As President Clinton illustrated, people have varying ideas. I first found this out some years ago when I surveyed (by anonymous questionnaire) my patients about infidelity and found that women outscored their male counterparts. My theory that females were striking a blow for women's liberation by cheating bit the dust when I found that women commonly included kissing, while

men abided by a stricter definition. According to the TIME/CNN poll, 95% of Americans agree that "having sex with a prostitute" counts. On the other end of the survey's scale is "casually flirting with someone else," considered adulterous by a minority of 35%. Somewhere in the middle are "having a sexually explicit conversation with someone on the phone" (69% define that as cheating), "having a sexually explicit conversation on the Internet" (67%) and "holding hands with someone else" (44%). Interestingly, an American Medical Association poll of medical students published in 1999 showed 2/3 didn't consider oral intercourse as "sex."

Most recent polls show about 25% of couples report infidelity. The TIME poll corroborated this by finding a similar number who "believed infidelity was unavoidable in marriage." Presumably, these are the same people who themselves could not avoid "the unavoidable."

Whatever the state of their own relationships, most Americans have some personal experience with infidelity. According to the TIME/CNN poll, 69% say they know at least one husband who has strayed; 60% say they know at least one wife who has been unfaithful. These numbers may well be low. An Internet "Click-Poll" on the same web page where this survey was posted found that 89% of respondents knew someone who had cheated. While Internet polls are not random-sampled, and therefore not scientific, this one may be more accurate than the TIME poll. People are less likely to be honest if they have to face their questioner with a positive answer on a sensitive topic, then to click honestly on a completely anonymous Internet poll. If this is true, a fudge-factor must be introduced to self-reports, which could push the rate of infidelity as high as 40%.

Types of Infidelity

So we know that infidelity is not rare. What else do we know about it? One leading expert is Dr.Frank Pittman, a psychiatrist who has seen "thousands" of adultery cases and written two books, and several magazine articles on the subject. He describes four categories of adulteries.

1. "Accidental infidelities" -- unintended incidents that occur often after drinking, running around with buddies or traveling. Most of these cases are men. Often, these cases drastically change the adulterer's view of themselves and/or their marriage.

2. "Romantic infidelity" -- Pittman claims these are the most destructive. They happen not because of meeting a "wonderful person" but because the person is going through some kind of crisis. They pick someone to fall in love with as a kind of escape, like taking a powerful drug. Unfortunately, like an addictive drug, they are costly to maintain, causing great emotional ups and downs and ultimately wrecking peoples lives. Many suicides and homicides come out of this type of infidelity.

3. "Philandering" -- more common among men than women, philanderers really like the power over the opposite sex as much or more as the sex itself. Each affair is a proof of one's self-esteem, and must be constantly replicated lest one think that he has "lost it." This may be the kind of behavior with which President Clinton has been accused.

4. "Marital arrangements" -- where one or both partners creates an on-going affair to be able to continue a marriage that is not satisfying, but hard to get out of. This seeming relic from bygone days still exists, sometimes because of children in marriages, other times because one or both simply fear divorce. Often, the other partner in the affair believes the marriage will end, only to be disappointed.

What to do about an affair

Several questions frequently come up. The biggest is always, "Should I tell?" The answer is not always simple. Many experts feel the rule of thumb is that if it is in the far past, don't.

Many adulterers feel tremendous guilt, and upon ending the affair, hope for absolution. That rarely happens. Though most marriages do survive, there is a tremendous loss of trust and rarely complete forgiveness. Sometimes, even a partner may feel the need for revenge by an affair of her own. Generally, a better use of guilt is to motivate an absolutely firmer resolve never to stray again. On the other hand, if the affair is continuing, it is often a better policy to be honest. This is because for many people the lying is as bad as the adultery. Each is a profound breach of trust. Pittman points out that adulterous marriages can only begin to be repaired when the secret is out in the open. But don't expect it to be easy.

The second biggest question is whether to forgive. The answer depends of course on the type of person the adulterer is, and the kind of adultery. We are rightfully concerned about forgiving a philanderer who may be encouraged to try it again. But the accidental affair, even the romantic affair, is something that can be overcome by examining the causes and devising solutions together. Another question to ask is how good is the marriage, otherwise. Wives and husbands often do forgive each other because of the good in the marriage and the love that both partners share.

For those who have never gone through that experience, the biggest question, of course, is how to avoid it. Probably the best approach is intensive communication. Creating an atmosphere of total openness and honesty about outside attractions helps bring about a context where agreement about rules of conduct can be discussed. Ultimatums rarely work, and tend to create coverups. For many couples, the lies are at least as devastating to trust as the actual infidelity and sometimes more. For that reason openness and honesty usually work better. By frank discussion, both partners create a sense of empathy that lowers the risk of betrayal, and they can commit to rules they know are agreed with by the other. Another hint is simply to avoid situations where temptation can arise. Accidents do happen, but as any good boy scout knows they rarely occur to those who are prepared. Discussing which situations are troublesome before they occur is probably the path of wisdom.□

—Used by permission.

DEFINING TERMS

Accession

Demoralization

Dismemberment

Philandering

WHAT DO YOU THINK?

1. What are some of the changes your family has gone through? How did you each respond?

2. What kind of stresses and changes are hardest for you to manage and why? What kinds are easier?

3. Do you feel it's appropriate to try to shield children from death and separation? Why or why not?

5. When is an infidelity forgivable in your book? Why? When not?

4. What helps you cope with grief and loss? What helps you cope with stress?

6. "Reframing" is defined as putting a different perspective on a problem that is otherwise not solvable. Take a problem from your past and try to "reframe" it.

 **VIDEO VIEWER:**

Watch "A Soldier's Daughter Never Cries." How do the characters adapt to growing older, moving, the death of the father?

☺ **MEDIA WATCHER:**

What types of crisis and change have you viewed lately on TV? How have the participants tried to cope?

Module Sixteen

Divorce

*T*he United States has one of the higher divorce rates in the world, but it is certainly not the only country in that condition. Extremely high divorce rates have been reported in Scandinavia, the former Soviet Union and in modernizing Moslem countries like Egypt, where one reporter noted that in some circles, a person with ten marriages and divorces is not all that uncommon. In nearly every country, divorce has been increasing. Just as the United States has been in leader in technology, production and popular culture, it may well be showing the world what is in store in the realms of marriage and divorce.

Although it is difficult to pin down the divorce rate precisely (we won't know the exact rate until the generation measured dies), most estimates are that around 50% of all marriages will end in divorce. The rate of divorce seems to have nearly tripled over the last thirty years. Many conflicting explanations have been offered to explain the rise, including more permissive attitudes about divorce, women's increasing participation in the workforce, liberalized divorce laws, and higher expectations of marital partners. Our society is obviously too complex to determine any definitive answers, and it may well be that all of these explanations have some part to play.

*W*e do know that demographic factors influence the divorce rate, and although they do not pinpoint which couples will divorce, they do indicate the probabilities of divorce for different groups. Probably the most important factor is age at marriage. Couples with one partner under age 18 are more than twice as likely to divorce as those over 24. Religion is also an important factor. Jews and Catholics are the least likely to divorce (despite highly different degrees of disapproval of divorce). Liberal Protestant denominations like Presbyterians and Episcopalians are next lowest, and conservative denominations like Baptists and Pentacostals are higher, with people reporting no religion the highest. These rates tend to disprove the notion that morals and social disapproval reduce divorce rather the differing divorce rates among these groups are due to socio-economic status and social cohesion among the members.

Chapter Preview:

Demographics of Divorce

Divorce and Adjustment

Remarriage

Article: "The Crisis of the Absent Fathers"

Note: Why Children Need Fathers

Article: "When Children of Divorce Become Parents"

Socioeconomic factors themselves are the next most important in explaining divorce. The higher the education of couples the less likely they are to divorce. Men with higher than average income are less likely to divorce than the average, but high-income women are more likely to divorce. It is unclear if this is because divorced women have to work harder or if women with more money feel freer to divorce. Some other factors: black Americans are more likely to divorce than white Americans, who are more likely to divorce than Asian Americans; and Southerners and Westerners are more likely to divorce than Easterners or Mid-Westerners. Childless couples are more likely to split up than those with children, and those whose parents were divorced are also more susceptible to divorce.

Demographic factors, while important, do not offer much insight into why particular couples split up. Various studies have come up with different results, but several factors consistently score high. For both husbands and wives, the leading cause of breakups are communication problems, incompatibility or too different backgrounds, and sexual problems. Infidelity and alcoholism are also major causes.

Divorce rarely happens suddenly. A number of experts have described a process of alienation or disaffection between the partners that gradually erodes positive feelings within the marriage and replaces them with negative ones. Frustrations with inabilities to solve problems build, and each partner begins to focus more and more on the negative traits of the other rather than the positive ones that brought them together. The process of alienation is extremely difficult to reverse. What Thomas Scheff calls interminable arguments (arguments which are unresolvable because they are built on layers and layers of previously unresolved arguments) contribute to a sense of hopelessness. Eventually each

partner begins to withdraw their emotional investment from the marriage.

Amazingly, the majority of couples who divorce make no attempt to seek professional help to save their marriages. While marital counseling often fails, it does succeed in the majority of cases. Communications training is also extremely helpful in reducing the likelihood of divorce. Individual counseling may also be necessary when one partner's personal problems are a major source of conflict.

Divorce and adjustments

Divorce is often an extremely traumatic experience. The loss of a partner, the loss of hopes and dreams, facing the stigma of failure in marriage, all can trigger intense emotional turmoil. Divorces are most traumatic when they are sudden, involve children, and when lawyers are involved. Probably the best advice that can be given is to go slowly and try to work out things together.

Divorce is also traumatic if one person wants the divorce and the other does not. Other factors that affect divorced people are social attitudes. Most people feel a divorce to be some kind of personal failure. This is particularly true if the divorced person comes from a background where divorce is disapproved, or when few friends or family members have previously divorced.

Probably the most important factor in helping people get through the adjustment period is the existence or development of some kind of social support system, whether it is made up of friends, family members or members of some kind of support group. Friendship and companionship are essential for healing emotional scars incurred during divorce.

Children may also be affected strongly by divorce. Depending on the age of the children, the quality of the marriage, and the total amount of communication between parents and children, and between the divorcing parents, divorce may be relatively smooth for children, or intensely traumatic. In the short-term, most children do experience divorce as a major negative event. Many go through a period of mourning or grief. Other common reactions are sadness, heightened sense of insecurity, and self-blame. Later these feelings may turn to anger and resentment to one or both parents. On the other hand, if the marriage is extremely conflict-ridden, children may experience relief at its termination.

In the longer term, researchers are divided as to the negative effects. Several studies that have shown that after the first year there is little difference between children of divorced and still-married parents. However, another study found deep problems in divorced children ten years later, although the findings were not complete in that they did not compare the divorced children with a control group.

Remarriage

Despite the high divorce rate, marriage remains quite popular, as evidenced by the high number of remarriages. Since divorce is so common, and because the majority of divorced people remarry, remarriage is now a common phenomenon. The probability of divorce of these new marriages is actually slightly higher than even first marriages, but since surveys show few differences in satisfaction between first and second marriages, the reason is probably a simple decrease in the psychological barriers against divorce within each partner. Third marriages, however, are much more likely to succeed. One probable reason is simply that fearing yet another failure, they are more likely to stick things out.

Remarriages tend to contain a number of complications that do not occur in first marriages:

✦ learning to get along with stepchildren, and stepchildren getting along with each other.
✦ dealing with ex-spouses, including possible jealousies of the previous partner, expectations and fears based on the previous marriage, which can cause disappointment or over-sensitivity
✦ financial problems due to child support issues
✦ lack of clearly defined roles in step-relationships which can cause conflict.

Given the obstacles facing them, it might seem surprising that anyone in remarriages would be able to stay together at all. Nevertheless, the determination to succeed and the gaining of wisdom from experience are two factors which often help remarriages to survive.□

References

Coleman, M.H. & L.H. Ganong. 1991. "Remarriage and step-family research in the 1980's" in A. Booth. *Contemporary Families: Looking forward, looking back.* Minneapolis: National Council on Family Relations.

Kitson, G.C. & L.A. Morgan,. 1991. "Multiple consequences of divorce." in A. Booth. Op Cit.

Scheff, Thomas. 1986. *Sociology of Emotions.* Unpublished manuscript.

Wells, J.G. 1991. *Choices in marriage and family.* Alta Loma, CA: Collegiate Press.

White, L.K. 1991. "Remarriage and stepfamily research in the 1980's." in A. Booth. Op Cit.

❑ The Crisis of the Absent Fathers

Richard Louv

Richard Louv is a columnist for the San Diego Union-Tribune, *and is author of* The Web of Life *(Conari Press).*

In a counselor's office at a Wisconsin high school, boys and girls discuss their largely absent fathers. One girl says that her father has barely said a word to her for two years. Another says that after her parents' divorce, her father "had the right to see me every weekend and stopped it, without explaining why." She has not seen her father in ten years.

"My dad's nobody to me," says one boy. "I've never once sat down and eaten dinner with him. But we've got pictures of me and my dad; we were real close when I was young."

According to the school counselor, the students' stories are typical not just of troubled kids but also of over achievers, the brittle students so eager to please. Asked to describe their vision of a "good" father, the teens are blunt:

"You can't stay out partying till five in the morning. If you're a father, you've got to be there to tuck your kid in and tell him bedtime stories at eight-thirty at night."

"The father of my kids is going to do stuff with them. He's not going to run away."

"If things don't work out between us, I don't care if he leaves me, as long as he doesn't leave the kids."

Is the United States in danger of becoming a fatherless society, shorn of its male parents not by war or disease but by choice? A look at the statistics of family life suggests that the answer may be yes.

How often fathers see--or don't see--their kids

Increasingly, fatherhood has become a volunteer commitment. In 1990 more than one in four of all births was to an unmarried woman, a fivefold increase in 30 years, according to the Census Bureau. Today nearly a quarter of the children born in this country live in female-headed households. More than half of all children in the United States can expect to live in such households before they turn 18.

Being raised by a single mother does not automatically deprive a child of a father, but 40 percent of kids who live in female-headed households haven't seen their fathers in at least a year. Of the remaining 60 percent, only a fifth sleep even one night a month in their father's home. Even fewer see their father at least once a week, according to a study by Frank F. Furstenberg Jr. and Kathleen Mullan Harris, both of the University of Pennsylvania.

Men between the ages of 20 and 49 spend an average of only seven years living in a house with young children, a decline of nearly 50 percent in three decades. What accounts for the high drop-out rate from fatherhood among U.S. men?

In many of my interviews around the country, fathers spoke in vague terms about their impact on their kids. They understood that fathering was important, but they often had a difficult time pinning down just what is important about it; they often struggled for words.

Our culture isn't much help. It suffers a kind of paternal amnesia, a masculine stumble. It seems to have forgotten the importance of fathering and to have divorced manhood from fatherhood. Too many men and women view fatherhood as a confusion, a burden, a list of chores and vague expectations. Fatherlessness itself is not the main problem; there are plenty of fathers. The problem is the loss of father love.

In its deeper dimensions, father love is nurturing, community building, and spiritually powerful. But at its most fundamental level, father love is expressed through a man's daily involvement with his family. As mothers have moved into the work force, the   logistics of raising children have become increasingly difficult. Clearly, fathers who share the work, pain, and love equally are needed more than ever.

Why does research focus on the mother-child bond?

The media, social scientists, psychologists, and pediatricians, however, have given little attention to the necessary role that fathers must play in their children's lives. For instance, most past research on child care and development has focused on infant-mother attachment. Among psychologists, the generally accepted theory is that children with a secure attachment to their mothers, especially during infancy, are more likely to feel confident and have good relationships with teachers and peers. But until recently; the father's role as a nurturer was viewed by many researchers as secondary to the mother's.

Similarly, most research on infant health has focused on the behavior of the expectant mother. But what is the impact of the expectant father? The father's support of the mother may play a larger role in an infant's health than factors such as maternal income and educational attainment. For example, the mortality rate of infants born to college-educated but unmarried women is higher than for infants born to married high school dropouts.

Most single mothers work full-time, earn no more than $18,000 a year, and receive little child support. Half of children being raised by single mothers live in poverty, compared with 8 percent of those from two-parent families. But the cost of raising children without fathers is more than economic.

A rise in academic and behavior problems

Children from divorced families (who usually live with their mothers), on average, score lower on reading and math tests. Children living with a single mother are twice as likely as children living with two parents to drop out of high school. Other long-range studies have shown that elementary school children from divorced families are absent more; are more anxious, hostile, and withdrawn; and are less popular with their peers than their classmates from intact families are. Almost twice as many high-achievers come from two-parent homes as come from one-parent homes, according to a study conducted by the National Association of Elementary School Principals.

Children from single-parent homes are more than twice as likely as children from two-parent families to suffer emotional and behavioral problems, according to a National Center for Health Statistics study. Moreover, the most reliable predictor of juvenile crime is not income or race but family structure. Seventy percent of imprisoned U.S. minors have spent at least part of their lives without fathers.

It is true that many of these outcomes would be different if society offered more financial and emotional support to single mothers. But an equally important goal, one that is more important in the long run, is the improvement of the quality of fathering.

The vast majority of current fatherhood programs are directed toward poor parents, a reflection of society's prejudice that fathering is problematic mainly for the poor. This, of course, is not true. Some of the most interesting fatherhood programs, however, are now serving primarily poor teenage fathers. Charles Augustus Ballard president of the National Institute for Responsible Fatherhood and Family Development, a Cleveland group that works with teenage fathers, once asked a group of 15 boys how many were fathers. Only two raised their hands. When he asked how many had babies, 14 hands went up. "They just don't think like fathers," Ballard says. "They don't connect pregnancy with marriage or husbanding or fatherhood." At least 65 percent of his clients never had meaningful relationships with their fathers. Ballard is currently organizing similar programs in 17 other U.S. cities.

Many young fathers, however, are eager to help their children. The institute has offered vocational services, counseling, and prenatal and parenthood classes to nearly 2,000 teenage fathers and prospective fathers. In the 11 years since the program was started, more than eight in ten participants have reported daily contact with their children; 74 percent say that they have contributed to their children's financial support. Progress is possible.

What is needed across the country is an ongoing effort to support and nurture good fatherhood, not only for low-income and teen parents but for fathers at all economic and age levels. Schools, churches, YMCAs, and businesses should offer more fatherhood courses. Some hospitals, for example, now offer classes to promote the bond between father and infant. Paul Lewis, creator of a fatherhood curriculum known as Dads University, says, "I tell men, 'Do it for your kids.' Most men, including noncustodial fathers, want to do what's right for their kids but need help learning what the right thing is."

Needed: tougher laws on responsibility

Beyond education programs, however, other policy changes are needed. Marriage must be encouraged; divorce laws must be reformed; and mediation to help divorcing parents resolve their child-rearing differences should be widely available. Today, dissolving a business contract is much more difficult to do in the United States than dissolving a marriage. No other contract may be breached as easily. Our laws should discourage separation by creating a braking mechanism, a waiting period of nine months before a divorce becomes final.

The Progressive Policy Institute, an offshoot of the Democratic Leadership Council, proposes that a "children first" principle should govern all divorces involving children. The judge's main task would be to piece together the best possible agreement to meet the needs of the children and their physical guardian.

Another theory gaining currency espouses eliminating Aid to Families With Dependent Children (AFDC), the nation's largest welfare program (created 58 years ago to support widowed women and their children), and replacing it with a system to support families that include fathers. Current AFDC rules prevent a woman from receiving full benefits if the father is at home and has an employment record or works more than 100 hours a month.

Child-support laws and collection techniques must be radically reformed. To help assure that fathers pay their child support, the Social Security number of both parents should appear on a child's birth certificate.

From the time of each child's birth, absent parents should be expected to contribute a portion of their income to that child's support. Payments should be collected by employers (just as Social Security taxes are today) and sent to the federal government, which would then send the money directly to the custodial parent.

Failure to pay would be comparable to tax evasion.

Society tends to view change as something that happens either at a personal level or through national legislation. But James Levine, director of The Families and Work Institute's Fatherhood Project, a research and consulting group on fatherhood, sees a vast area for change between these two extremes. Levine maintains that unless the institutions that have a direct impact on families' lives--businesses, hospitals, churches, synagogues, social-service agencies, and schools--are transformed, neither personal change nor national legislation will accomplish much.

Levine points out a cultural resistance to fatherhood within business institutions as an example. "No matter how many hours he puts in at work, a father who is worried about his children is unlikely to be fully productive," he says. We do not tend to think of fathers as worried working parents. Before such assumptions can be challenged, they must be the topic of open, and probably organized, conversation within company walls.

Even those institutions whose mission it is to care for and help children must examine their own attitudes toward fathers. Levine, for example, has found some of the strongest resistance to paternal involvement among women who work with and for children. "When we discussed their resistance to fathers, they would say, 'Yes, we know we should get fathers more involved,' but they were making little effort to do that," Levine says.

"Their ambivalence is emblematic of the attitude among many helping institutions-- hospitals, mental-health organizations, schools," he continues. "My point is not to blame women. We must give voice to these feelings as the first step toward making men and women equal partners in caring for their children."

Each family also must identify and challenge its own cultural prejudices about fatherhood. For example, when a man does take family leave or decides to be a part- or full-time dad, he may encounter subtle or not so subtle messages from relatives, such as, "Aren't you working? Don't you have a job yet?" The father may also send out mixed messages. He may say that he wants to do more at home but may also find the pressure to be the breadwinner a useful excuse to dodge his own responsibilities.

The truth, however politically untidy, is that men will not move back into the family until our culture reconnects masculinity and fatherhood, until men come to see fathering, not just paternity, as the fullest expression of manhood. Married, single, or divorced, a man is enriched by fatherhood, and a child's life is better for it. The good news, the great good news, is that an enormous payoff awaits society and individual men and their families as men move deeper into the dimensions of fatherhood. That movement has already begun. □

□Note: Why Children Need Fathers

Despite a paucity of studies on fatherhood, considerable evidence does exist attesting to the influence of nurturing fathers on their children.

Children with involved fathers are more nurturing themselves and are much more likely to raise pets than other kids are, according to Yale Child Study Center psychiatrist Kyle Pruett, M.D. "I believe that these kids will find it easier to nurture their own children, notes Pruett.

A 2-year study shows that paternal involvement was the single strongest parent-related factor in the development of empathy. "The father's influence was quite astonishing," says psychologist Richard Koestner, Ph.D., of Montreal's McGill

University. Fathers who spend time alone with their children more than twice a week giving baths, meals, and basic care reared the most compassionate adults.

Boys with strong, warm, nurturing fathers are more socially competent, more persistent at solving problems, and more self-directed, according to Norma Radin, M.S.W., Ph.D., a social-work professor at the University of Michigan, in Ann Arbor. –Richard Louv□

–Reprinted with permission.

□ When Children of Divorce Become Parents

Claire Berman

Ruth Lewisohn's parents divorced when she was two years old. Before her fourth birthday, Ruth saw her mother remarry, and before her fifth, a half-brother was born. "As I experienced it," says Ruth, "I lost both parents simultaneously: my father to his grief, my mother to a new marriage and new family. I grew up feeling isolated, like a visitor in my own home. "

Now a 36-year-old accountant, wife, and mother of two girls, ages 7 and 4, Ruth has her own home and, she tells me, is dedicated to keeping it secure: "I will not do to my kids what was done to me. The goal of my life is to make this family work."

This strong commitment to family stability is echoed by countless other men and women who grew up with parental divorce. Psychologist Judith Wallerstein, Ph.D., whose landmark study of men, women, and children a decade after divorce is reported in her book *Second Chances* (Ticknor & Fields), says, "I'm finding that adult children of divorce tend to

raise the issue early on, even prior to having children, and I find this fascinating. They're holding on to this core identity, 'I am a child of divorce' and to the strong wish to have children and provide a happier childhood than they themselves experienced."

As all parents discover when they go about the business of raising children, it takes work. For children of divorce, however, being a parent tends to be even more complicated. Because of their parents' divorce, many have negative perceptions of marriage and family even as they eagerly desire to succeed at both.

If there is a guiding principle behind these parents' own nurturing styles, it is the one embodied in Ruth Lewisohn's declaration: "I will not do to my children what was done to me." How this gets played out can vary tremendously, depending on the individual's personality and experience with divorce. Nevertheless, for men and women who grew up with divorced parents, some issues do stand out.

Learning to trust

Even as adult children of divorce are eager to create a successful family, they are often struggling to let their spouse in as full partner in that process. Trust and the sharing of feelings and emotions can be threatening, so children of divorce hold back.

When their own children arrive, these parents find it easier to maintain control by making unilateral decisions. "When your own parents betray you, who do you trust?" asks Cora Sanders, 34, whose parents divorced when she was 13. "It's difficult for me to depend on anyone." Unfortunately, "anyone" includes Cora's husband, Frank, who complains that he feels like an on-looker in the lives of his children, Delsie, seven, and Frank Jr., five. "I often get the feeling that Cora is running the whole show, to the point of shielding the children from me," says Frank. "And I wish she'd let me in."

In distancing the children from their father, Cora works against the very goal that she most hopes to achieve: a unified, happy family. Trust is a learned process. "I am not Cora's father," says Frank. "I'm in it for the long haul." But it is up to Cora to accept the fact that the two men are different, and to trust her husband as both a friend and a father to their children.

Just as parents of a child who has survived a serious accident or illness are likely to become overly vigilant, the child of divorce also runs the risk of becoming an overprotective parent. In this case, although it's the parent who is the survivor, the goal is the same: to safeguard her child from experiencing the traumatic event.

For many of these parents, the trauma to be prevented is the witnessing of frequent and furious fighting in the home. Many people who grew up with divorce learn to distance themselves emotionally or physically from disagreements because, as children, that's how they survived the turmoil of family life. When they become parents, they strive to keep their own children innocent of any family strife.

"My mother and father constantly screamed at each other about everything, even whether the scrambled eggs were too runny," recalls Susan Langer, who was sixteen when her parents separated for the final time.

How to avoid repeating the past

Studies consistently have found that divorce rates are higher for people who grew up with divorced parents than for those raised in intact households. According to professionals who study and work with families, however, a child of divorce need not be condemned to repeating the past. The following are suggestions for how to move forward. Coming to terms with the impact of divorce is not an easy task to accomplish on one's own, though; you may want to explore any or all of these issues with a trusted counselor.

Acknowledge, examine, and try to resolve the anger that you still feel over your parents' divorce and its aftermath. There are many good reasons for doing this, not the least of which is the potential that anger has to destroy other relationships.

Learn how to manage conflict

If you were taught to handle disagreements by walking away from them, learn to communicate what is bothering you. On the other hand, if the behavior you grew up with was confrontational (if there was yelling or abuse), strive to change the pattern by, for example, setting a specific time with your partner or your children when troubling matters can be raised, discussed, and resolved.

Strive to gain self-confidence. Many children of divorce carry into adulthood the feeling, "If I had been better, my parents would have stayed together." This lack of self-esteem affects all future relationships, including those with your partner and your child. Understanding that you did not cause the divorce, that a parent leaves a marriage because of unhappiness with a spouse--not with a child--can free you to create your own family, unfettered by the pull of the past.

Ask your parents to explain, adult to adult now, why the divorce took place. Don't lecture. Don't judge. Don't personalize. Try to understand the situation they were in and the pressures they grew up with in their own families of origin. Understanding your parents is an important step toward letting go of the pain of the past and moving, with greater confidence, toward the future.

"Mother would try to reassure me, 'The time to worry is when Daddy and I stop fighting.' She was shocked when my father, still raging, walked out. So was I."

Today Susan, 42, a lawyer, is married to Marc, an electrical contractor. They have two sons: Judson, nine, and six-year-old Max. "Marc and I never fight in front of the children," she says. "In fact, while we've faced some serious problems over the years, we hardly ever fight at all. It's hard for me to express anger.

"Once, one of our boys was around when things became really tense, and he said, 'Did I do something wrong?' I said, 'No, this is between Daddy and me, and you should forget about it.' As a child, I was quick to take the blame for everything, I'd think, 'If I'd been a little better in school, then Dad might not be yelling.'

"It's also upsetting to me when my children get angry," Susan adds. "I go absolutely nuts when that happens, and I try to stop them from fighting. I do worry that the boys will have some problems later on with expressing anger, but I don't know what to do about it."

People who, like Susan, grapple with this problem would be wise to find some middle ground between the constant conflict that they experienced as children and their current aversion to all disagreement. They ought to do this for their children's sake and for their own. Parents who never fight in front of the children paint an unreal portrait of the marital relationship, one that has ups but no downs.

In addition, they deprive their children of a model of how to have a healthy argument and then make up. "It may be that what these parents actually fear is not that they will repeat their parents' hostility in their own family but that one day they will explode with unresolved anger about the breakup of their original family," says therapist Ann Kliman, of the Center for Preventive Psychiatry in White Plains, New York.

Making up for past mistakes

Hilary Evans, 41 was 6 when her parents split up and 8 when they remarried (within days of each other); their new spouses also had children. She says, "My parents constantly used me as a messenger: 'Tell your dad not to send his check late,' or 'Tell your mother that I want you to be with our family at Christmas.' At either end, I knew that the messages would not be well received. There was a lot of pressure on me to worry about the logistics of the family, to be the peacemaker, to be old before my time. In technical terms, Hilary was "parentalized," made to take on responsibilities that are inappropriate for a child. As a mother, Hilary is very clear about one thing: "I never want my children to have that kind of responsibility. I want my kids to feel free to be kids."

One way she tries to achieve this is by encouraging her sons Nicholas, eight, and Alexis, seven and daughter Sage, five, to be assertive.

"I want my kids to feel secure enough in this family to speak their minds," she says. So far so good, as long as the children's "assertions" involve fairly manageable requests (to visit the zoo instead of the playground)." There's a fine line between permissiveness and overindulgence, I know," says Hilary, laughing. "I think I've managed to stay on the safe side of the divider."

Mimi Stewart, on the other hand, has crossed over to the other side. "Everything I do in my life is for my children," confesses this 37-year-old woman, whose parents divorced when she was 9 and who still feels hurt by the subsequent struggle of her single-parent family to survive.

"One scene from my childhood is etched on my soul: skipping home from school to find our furniture on the lawn. We'd been evicted. My children are never going to want for anything."

Kliman is concerned about parental indulgence that is taken too far. "Permissiveness is particularly a problem for parents who are children of divorce," she says, "because through their children, they try to make up for their own childhood experience of loss and because they want their children to love them. This comes from a parent's need. Parents who are children of divorce are needy; there's no question about it."

For adult children of divorce, the risk of over indulgence, either giving their children too much leeway or showering them with material goods, is matched by the danger of their becoming over-involved in the lives of their children. All of us grow up with visions of the ways that families are supposed to be: vacations at the shore; sit-down dinners each Sunday at six. But life doesn't always happen that way. The child of a broken home grows up feeling even more keenly the absence of unifying family rituals. And when this child of divorce later has children of her own, the importance of "doing things together" becomes paramount.

Such a parent may be very concerned about being there for her child, being the one to take the youngster to school, being available to the child on weekends, and that can be good. A problem arises when the child's needs begin to override the need of either parent for time alone and, perhaps more important, for husband-and-wife time. "It's good for kids to know that sometimes Mommy and Daddy want to be alone," says Joyce Slochower, Ph.D., associate professor of psychology at Hunter College and a psychotherapist in private practice, both in New York City.

Over-involvement also becomes a problem if the parent "marshmallows" (doing anything and everything for the child, attempting to cushion any possible fall), according to Silvio Silvestri, Ph.D., founder of the Center for Adult Children of Divorce, in South Lake Tahoe, California. The child may then get the idea that there is something wrong with him or that danger lurks around the comer.

The distant parent

There is a flip side to this phenomenon that occurs when the parent finds himself unable to give to his children what he didn't get as a child, notably, the love and attention of the noncustodial parent, generally the father. Following the breakup of a marriage, almost 90 percent of children continue to make their home with their mother. As time goes by, studies have shown, many see less and less of their fathers, and some lose contact entirely.

For some of these boys, Judith Wallerstein observes, the carry-over into adulthood is that becoming a parent precipitates a depression. Why? "Because it raises so many memories. It brings up the depression they've tried to avoid, which is the terrible sense of 'I was abandoned; therefore I wasn't lovable. I wasn't worth staying around for.' So what this son, this child of divorce, feels is, 'If I am to my child what I never had, then it activates in me the terrible sadness of what I missed.' "

John Lindstrom, a 43-year-old musician, was little more than a year old when his mother and father separated. Thirteen years went by before he saw his father again. Then, every three or four years, there would be a letter from him. Today John is married and has two daughters, ages eight and eleven.

"I don't know how to be a husband and father," John confesses with obvious pain. "I have trouble living up to what seems to be expected of me. I don't know what games to play. I don't have any traditions to follow. At Christmas, for example, I'd just as soon go off and watch the Bowl games. But I have to push myself for my kids' sake, and it's a constant struggle."

"When your own childhood has been basically shut off by parental divorce," Silvio Silvestri explains, "it's hard to get into the childhood of your sons and daughters; you can't empathize, play, or put yourself in the child's shoes."

It's hard, but it's not impossible. Arthur Comman, a 31-year-old army sergeant, has been married for seven years and is the father of two children: Jason, 4 years old, and Alexandra, 16 months. Like John, Arthur didn't get to spend much of his boyhood with his father . . . and still doesn't see much of him, a situation that continues to rankle. ("You'd think that he'd be interested in knowing his grandchildren," Arthur says.)

"My father was in the air force," Arthur explains, "so he wasn't home a lot anyway. I always knew that I'd someday join the army, but I never pictured myself having a wife and kids. It just didn't seem important." Today Arthur's family is the pride of his life. "Jason was 9 pounds, 5 ounces, and 21 inches long at birth," he boasts. "When we left the hospital, I went straight to the barracks to show him off. He's four, but people take him for six.

"When I was a kid, I was very shy. I feel that's because my father would come by for a couple of hours, and then he'd be gone for a week or two, or several years. That's what caused me to close up. So with my own children, I talk to them. I read to them. We go to the wildlife refuge and find new parks and playgrounds.

"When Alexandra was two months old," Arthur continues, "I was sent to Saudi Arabia during the Gulf War. I wrote to my wife. I wrote to Jason. I wrote to Alexandra. I made postcards and drew pictures on them with colored pencils and markers. I got quite a few chuckles from the guys who handled the mail. I tried to make sure that my family knew I was thinking of them and that I would be back."

"When I was growing up, I would forget for long periods of time that I even had a father," Arthur says. "Now that I'm a father, the thing I can see that works in a relationship is just being there when you're needed. My family knows I am there."

Putting the past in its place

As Arthur has learned, adults who grow up in divorced families are not necessarily fated to replay the mistakes made during their childhood. They can change the patterns:

◆Ask yourself some questions, suggests Joyce Slochower. What am I worried about repeating with my own family? In what ways might I be mixing up my child with myself as a child? Do my spouse and I find time to be alone together? Am I satisfied with the amount of time that I spend with my family? If you decide that a problem exists, then you can begin to make changes.

◆ Redefine the father role. Silvio Silvestri's work with adult children of divorce has focused largely on fathers, many of whom have a hard time showing a tender, vulnerable side. Take heart, though, because change can be brought about in several ways.

For example, a man can remodel his definition of "father" by finding role models in other, well-adjusted fathers (and observing them interact with their children), reading books and magazines on child rearing, or nurturing himself, giving himself some of the attention that he did not get as a child. "This is a pretty difficult task," admits Silvestri. But it can be done.

◆Keep moving forward. The past does not have to dictate the present. Studies affirm the therapeutic benefits for those who grew up with divorce of committing to marriage and building families of their own. Becoming a parent gives the child of divorce a second chance at a family. It is an opportunity to succeed, and to heal.□

–from Parents *magazine, July 1992. Copyright ©
1992, Gruner + Jahr USA Publishing. Reprinted by
permission.*

DEFINING TERMS

Custody

Joint Custody

Child Support

WHAT DO YOU THINK?

1. Why are the children of divorced couples more likely to undergo divorce?

2. Should couples stay together because of the children? Why or why not?

3. Most divorced people end up remarrying, but a majority redivorce. What do you think people learn from going through divorce? What should they learn?

4. What effects do absent fathers have on their children?

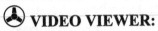 **VIDEO VIEWER:**

Watch "Kramer vs Kramer." What were the problems that came up during the couple's divorce? Why were they so difficult?

☺ **MEDIA WATCHER:**

What do TV dramas, soaps, and news programs tell us about the consequences of divorce?

APPENDIX

HOW TO WRITE A REACTION PAPER

The purpose of a reaction paper is to apply the information or theory of an article in order to gain some insight into some aspect of your life. A good way to do so follows below:

1. A summary of the article. This lets the instructor know you have read and understood the material and sets the stage for your paper.

2. The key: This is the part of the article to which you wish to respond. Explain what it is and why you chose it.

3. The narrative: Relate this to a personal experience of your own or someone you know. Tell the actual experience, not just your opinion about it. Give enough detail so the reader understands.

4. Evaluation: What insights does this article add to your experience? How well did it explain what happened? Are there things from your experience that could add to the author's theory or explanation? Relate any other relevant sources to the article.
